Indigenous Women's Voices

Indigenous Women's Voices

20 Years on from Linda Tuhiwai Smith's *Decolonizing Methodologies*

Edited by
tebrakunna country and Emma Lee & Jennifer Evans

BLOOMSBURY ACADEMIC
LONDON • NEW YORK • OXFORD • NEW DELHI • SYDNEY

BLOOMSBURY ACADEMIC
Bloomsbury Publishing Plc
50 Bedford Square, London, WC1B 3DP, UK
1385 Broadway, New York, NY 10018, USA
29 Earlsfort Terrace, Dublin 2, Ireland

BLOOMSBURY, BLOOMSBURY ACADEMIC and the Diana logo are trademarks of
Bloomsbury Publishing Plc

First published in Great Britain 2022
Reprinted in 2022
This edition published by Bloomsbury Academic 2022

Index by Mei Yen Chua swallowbooks.com.au

Cover image © *Inner Flame* by Billi Lime, @billilime,
Melbourne-based artist, billilime.com.au

A catalogue record for this book is available from the British Library.

Library of Congress Control Number: 2021940824

ISBN: HB: 978-1-7869-9841-5
      PB: 978-1-3503-7431-7
      ePDF: 978-1-7869-9840-8
      eBook: 978-1-7869-9838-5

Typeset by RefineCatch Limited, Bungay, Suffolk

To find out more about our authors and books visit www.bloomsbury.com
and sign up for our newsletters.

We dedicate this volume to Indigenous and First Nations women everywhere and their contributions to making life fairer and a more equitable world for our children and communities.

Contents

Part 4 De/colonizing Minds

Part 5 Seeing Ourselves

About the Editors

tebrakunna country and Emma Lee

Dr Emma Lee is from Tasmania, Australia, a *trawlwulwuy* woman whose *tebrakunna* country is a co-author for her scholarship. She has had 25 years in land and sea management, notably being one of the first crop of Indigenous Australian archaeologists. Emma's work as an Aboriginal and Torres Strait Islander Research Fellow at the Centre for Social Impact, Swinburne University of Technology, Victoria, Australia, has assisted in creating Indigenous rights in Tasmania. These impacts include establishing a market for cultural fisheries, gaining state constitutional recognition and devising a whole-of-government strategy that reimagines social justice as regional development for Aboriginal benefit. Emma is a recipient of numerous awards and prestigious fellowships for this work.

Jennifer Evans (Dharug)

Dr Jennifer Evans is a Queer Dharug woman living on, and with connections to, *palawa* country, *lutruwita* (Tasmania), Australia. Jennifer is a Blaq social and cultural geographer whose research and advocacy blends technology, country and queerness to create safe spaces for Indigenous methodological research. Dr Evans is passionate about community participation and empowerment in decision-making processes, a resilience borne from a lifetime of lived experiences, including being an architect to picking fruit to survive. She now works as an Aboriginal Research Fellow at the College of Health and Medicine, University of Tasmania, to support *palawa* students to reach their goals. She has won multiple community awards for her business and social impact.

About the Contributors

Lauren Booker (Garigal)

Lauren Booker (Garigal clan) lives and works on Gadigal land, and her ancestries connect her through her mother to the saltwater mouth of the Hawkesbury River and through her father to Nagasaki prefecture, Japan. Lauren is a researcher and PhD student at Jumbunna Institute for Indigenous Education and Research, University of Technology Sydney. She has worked across the libraries, archives and museums sector to support language and cultural revitalization projects, assisting communities in accessing their cultural material and records held in institutional collections. Lauren's work currently focuses on collecting institution ethics and transparency, and she is an advocate for repatriation, Indigenous Cultural and Intellectual Property Rights and Indigenous Data Sovereignty. Lauren is also a member of the Indigenous Archives Collective.

Angela Burt (*palawa*)

Angela Burt (MEd) is a *palawa* woman from *trouwunna*, Cape Barren Island, Tasmania. With a career in education spanning 20 years, Angela currently holds the position of Head of Programs at the Korin Gamadji Institute, the centre for Aboriginal and Torres Strait Islander youth leadership at the Richmond Football Club. Currently undertaking a PhD at Swinburne University of Technology, Angela's research privileges the voices of First Nation's women and positioning our knowledges as central to the decolonization of education policy.

Liz Cameron (Dharug)

Professor Liz Cameron holds the position of Chair of Indigenous Knowledge's at Deakin University and is affiliated with the Dharug Nation, north west of Sydney, NSW. Cameron has spent over 35 years specializing in Indigenous knowledges from art-based practices within a counselling framework to environment, social and emotional wellbeing under the banner of "Healthy Country, Healthy People," which incorporates identity, belonging and connectivity.

Lori Campbell (2-Spirit nēhiyaw āpihtākosisān)

Lori is 2-Spirit nēhiyaw āpihtākosisān and is a member of Montreal Lake First Nation, Treaty 6 territory. She is an intergenerational survivor of the Indian Residential School system and a child from the Sixties Scoop generation. Lori has made it her career advocating for social justice and working towards a more equitable society for all. Most recently, she was a federal candidate in the 2019 election. With over 14 years of progressive leadership in student services, academics, research and administration, Lori is an experienced leader in education with a proven track record, particularly in advancing processes of Indigenization, reconciliation and decolonization. Lori holds two undergraduate degrees (Indigenous Studies and Psychology), a master's degree in Adult Education and is working towards a PhD in Social Justice Education. She currently holds the position of Director, *Shatitsirótha'* Waterloo Indigenous Student Centre and is an Adjunct Lecturer in the Indigenous Studies academic program at St. Paul's University College, at the University of Waterloo.

Pauliina Feodoroff (skolt sámi)

Pauliina Feodoroff is a director of film and theatre and a writer, known for among others, *CO2lonialNATION* (Giron Sámi Teáhter, 2017) and *Non Profit* (film, 2007) for which she was awarded the SARV (The Finnish Critics' Association) Critical Incentives Prize in 2007. Feodoroff has fought for water and land rights as well as to preserve the reindeer husbandry in the old forests of Nellim in the east of Sápmi/Northern Finland. She has served as elected President of the Sami Council, a period during which she visited many remote Sámi communities in Russia where she addressed the issue of mining companies occupying the land. She also participated in a multiannual study of land occupation which resulted in the critically acclaimed publication, *Eastern Sámi Atlas* (Snowchange Cooperative, 2011).

Karen Fisher (Ngāti Maniapoto, Waikato-Tainui, Pākehā)

Karen Fisher (Ngāti Maniapoto, Waikato-Tainui, Pākehā) is an Associate Professor in the School of Environment, University of Auckland. She is a geographer, whose research is focused on society–environment interactions, environmental governance and the politics of resource use. Current research interests include exploring the creation and implementation of co-governance arrangements over the management of rivers in Aotearoa New Zealand as well as marine-based research focused on social and political dimensions of ecosystem-based management approaches.

Kelly Menzel (Ngadjuri)

Kelly is a proud Ngadjuri woman from mid-north South Australia with ancestral connections to Bundjalung Country in northern New South Wales. She is a nurse by trade. She has been in adult education for 20 years and is an Asst. Professor in First Nations Health. She has lived in and worked with First Nations communities all over the world. She has a Masters degree in women's studies and has completed a PhD in Indigenous Knowledges. Her research area of expertise is radically challenging race-based violence in institutions.

Donna Moodie (Gomeroi)

Donna Moodie is a Gomeroi woman born in Gunnedah, New South Wales. She is a Lecturer in Contextual Studies in Education in the Faculty of Humanities, Arts, Social Sciences and Education (HASSE) at the University of New England (UNE) Armidale, New South Wales. Donna's current research involves moving towards and celebrating raising Indigenous voices, deconstructing and decolonizing Western academic epistemologies, and honoring and being conscious of cultural relativity.

Nikki Moodie (Gomeroi)

Associate Professor Nikki Moodie is a Gomeroi woman, born in Gunnedah, New South Wales. After an early career in the public service, she moved into research focusing on social networks, Indigenous policy and the governance of Indigenous knowledges. Nikki is the Deputy Director and Program Director of the Atlantic Fellows for Social Equity, a 20-year philanthropic program focused on Indigenous-led social change, based at the University of Melbourne.

Kelly Ratana (Ngāti Tūwharetoa, Ngāti Rangiwewehi)

Kelly Ratana is a Māori researcher from Ngāti Tūwharetoa and Ngāti Rangiwewehi, whose lands and waters are located in the central North Island of Aotearoa (New Zealand). Kelly is committed to working with Māori communities to explore their research questions. She has a real passion for working at the interface of Māori and other knowledge systems to deliver outcomes on the ground for these communities.

Ehara taku toa i te toa takitahi, engari he toa takitini

Kelly is privileged to have lived and worked alongside many amazing communities from across the Pacific, and endeavours to honor those connections by ensuring that Indigenous knowledge leads enquiry and drives the research she is a part of.

Jacinta Vanderfeen (*trawlwulwuy*)

Jacinta Vanderfeen is a proud *trawlwulwuy* woman of *tebrakunna* country of *lutruwita* (Tasmania), with family ties to Mannalargenna through his daughter, Woretemoeteyenner, a matriarch to the Dalrymple Briggs descendants. Jacinta is an early career researcher at the University of Tasmania with a background in Behavioural Science and has a passion for social justice.

Distinguished Professor Maggie Walter (*palawa*)

Maggie Walter (PhD, FASSA) is *palawa* woman from *lutruwita*/Tasmania and is a Distinguished Professor of Sociology at the University of Tasmania. The center of Maggie's intellectual curiosity is Indigenous data, Indigenous quantitative methodologies and Indigenous data sovereignty. Recent books include *Indigenous Data Sovereignty and Social Policy* (co-edited with T. Kukutai, D. Rodriguez-Lonebear and S. Russo Carroll) (2020, Routledge).

Acknowledgments

Indigenous and First Nations women bear the brunt of unrelenting pressures of life and workplace racism, bullying and harassment. We internalize the emotional and physical hardship of balancing competing demands of unequal, two-world learning and we suffer the toll of being unpicked and fragmented across history by others.

For these various reasons, two scholars who originally wanted to contribute were unable to complete their essays. In the case of one, the risk of losing a career over contributing her research brought home how real and dangerous research work can be for Indigenous and First Nations women. It seems unbelievable in this day and age that women cannot write safely, yet this is a familiar refrain for each of us here in this volume.

To these sisters: while you were prevented by structural discrimination to make your voices heard, at the very least we know that your work matters and your narratives are worthy of having space. So, we devote this acknowledgement to you, and others, in recognition of your sorrows, while celebrating your power to increase cultural presence and effect, in spite of immense challenges.

Open access funding has been provided by Swinburne University of Technology, Australia.

Foreword

Professor Linda Tuhiwai Smith

It is a strange and wonderful thing to see your work develop a life of its own and influence research in ways unimaginable. Just over 20 years ago I had published *Decolonizing Methodologies: Research and Indigenous Peoples*; now it is a third edition in 2021. To galvanize and spur a field of research that spirals outward from the knowledge of Ngāti Awa and Ngāti Porou *iwi* I have grown from has become a reciprocity compact with other First Nations and Indigenous Peoples to be unashamedly proud in how we tell our stories.

This volume brings together 13 Indigenous women in four countries who write of how *Decolonizing Methodologies* has influenced their lives, work, research and writing. While these essays have been compiled to amplify a longevity of my research culminating within that special book, they do it through their own tenacious female voices of standing strong on cultural ground. To see the next generation of Indigenous women taking back our rights and talking up and back to the academy is to assert the intellectual and cultural principles behind *Decolonizing Methodologies*.

I welcome this volume and these powerful women whose essays have moved and delighted me with how *Decolonizing Methodologies* has guided, reaffirmed and supported their own critical thinking and advocacy to improve our lives away from colonizing structures. I congratulate these women on continuing to define what research means to them and how *Decolonizing Methodologies* has shaped new pathways for their unique and cherished voices to be heard. It is a great honor to be celebrated through their research and stories that tell of my influence. I, in turn, celebrate all Indigenous Peoples and communities who have shared with me their stories and knowledge that have been core to my life and work over the past two decades.

Indigenous women's voices: 20 years on from Linda Tuhiwai Smith's *Decolonizing Methodologies*

Jennifer Evans (Dharug) & *tebrakunna* country and Emma Lee

Introduction

Indigenous women across the globe are precious and rare: we comprise about 1.5 per cent of the world's population (Garnett et al 2018), yet the mark we leave is far greater than our numbers. We have nurtured, stewarded, loved and cared for our planet across thousands of generations in every place that our evolving humanity has been found. We are as integral to the world's health as the air we breathe. We are the grandmothers, mothers, daughters, sisters, aunties and nieces that sing and grow into being the lands, skies and seas, biodiversity and giving environments that sustain families, communities, societies and life through our deep knowledges and worldviews gained from "caring for everything" (Danjoo Koorliny Social Impact 2019, p. 60).

We work, live and love with our men as whole families and communities like any other, yet atypical to Western nuclear family ideals. Rather, we respect the rights and autonomies of women and men and prize our own knowledge domains, as they are "entwined ... not separate" (Gay'wu Group of Women 2019, p. xxi). Therefore, we are strong in using the term *women's business* to delineate our powers to make decisions that affect our cultural, spiritual, economic, territorial and family lives. *Women's business* to us is a celebration of the many forms of our female identities, including what we know also as *Queer women's business*, which gives us the cultural authority to exercise such powers.

Women's business is important (Purcell 2002). Women's business is critical to the way we think, write, see, move across and experience the world as Indigenous women with sovereign rights to govern our domains of influence (Bunda 2007).

Yet we have been cast as the "Others" (Said 1978) – the poorer, the lesser, the most in need of correction, discipline and welfare – by dominant and alien forces that colonize us, particularly within research and its practice. We do not see ourselves as the Other, as this volume reveals, instead we are central to the stories of deep time, world histories and shaping of our societies today.

It is critical to explain here the terminology our authors use to refer to their cultural and political affiliations. Our volume originates from Australia and thus the majority of essays are grounded within Indigenous Australian terminologies, including the use of "Black" in its many forms, such as "Black", "blak" and "Blaq". In Australia, "Black" carries deep cultural ties and reflects the long Australian histories of broad reference to the two main populations of "blackfella" and "whitefella" (Lambert-Pennington 2012). The terms used to describe our Indigeneity are various and include Indigenous, Black female, First Nations and Aboriginal and Torres Strait Islander. So too the cultural and political extensions of how we write ourselves – terms such as "Country" are spelled variously with a capital "C" or lowercase, while grammar reflects Indigenous-used language styles. Further, authors from Tasmania have a mix of spelling and affiliation that is specific to their histories and for safe affiliations.

We do not conflate or appropriate terminologies, nor try to introduce a characterization of Indigeneity as "Black", but rather we approach our volume as one of self-determining rights to locate language within the cultural frameworks and political identities that we find ourselves in. Therefore, we support each of our female authors to use the language that suits their localities and circumstances, identities and country: our own preference for "Black female" is indicative of our recognition that we should not be exclusive in our terms, particularly for those who are beginning to learn about their own Indigenous histories, families, broken connections and place. We understand that colonization is personal; it strips out the right of diversity of language, yet at the same time we value the political weight and history of terms such as "Black" that have given rise to our rights to exist as Indigenous Peoples, particularly in Australia. Thus, we respect the rights of every reader and scholar to use a terminology that belongs to them and to use it with genuine intent to decolonize the worlds we live in.

In carefully respecting our authors, we draw together thirteen international Black female voices from Canada, New Zealand, Australia and Finland as essay authors, plus two distinguished professors and Elders who foreword and close this volume. The authors are the torchbearers and next generation researchers and practitioners to implement and improve the ways in which we decolonize the world around us through leveraging Indigenous knowledges from a position of strength, solidarity and self-determination. This volume, in cherishing women's business and honoring the work of an inspirational Indigenous academic, Professor Linda Tuhiwai Smith, has been purposely restricted to curating essays only from Black female voices. We do this to recover from the loss, weakening and non-recognition of our governance forms – women's business – within, among others, the academy and publishing spheres (I. Watson 2005). As a separate and distinct characteristic of our personal lives that follows us professionally, women's business allows us to create a culturally safe space to stand together as Black female bodies who experience colonization and report back to wider society what those conditions and impacts look and feel like to us.

Honoring Linda Tuhiwai Smith and *Decolonizing Methodologies*

The struggle, however, is all too real in reporting and repairing these harms of Othering that haunt and traumatize our Black female bodies. One woman though, a Ngāti Awa and Ngāti Porou scholar from New Zealand, Professor Linda Tuhiwai Smith, has evened the playing field. In 1999 she gifted the world her seminal work *Decolonizing Methodologies: Research and Indigenous Peoples* (Zed Books). In responding to the theoretical and cultural calls emanating from each page of *Decolonizing Methodologies*, our volume is a tribute to her and recognizes that Linda's work has provided a deep, intellectual appeal across diverse research themes, political and social justice approaches, and community-driven action for positive change across two generations.

Linda's presence within Indigenous scholarship is "unparalleled" and "monumental" (Denzin & Lincoln 2008, pp. xiii, xiv). Twenty years ago, Linda claimed her position proudly as a both an Indigenous researcher and person, defining with clarity the experience and concept of decolonizing research: "Decolonizing research is not necessarily post-colonial research. Decolonization is a process that critically engages, at all levels, imperialism, colonialism, and postcolonality. Decolonizing research implements indigenous epistemologies and critical imperative practices that are shaped by indigenous research agendas" (Smith, cited in Denzin 2005, p. 953).

Linda reflects in her second edition, that, at the time "the term 'Indigenous' was also contentious and 'dirty' in some contexts" (Smith 2012, p. xi). Today, we see the profound influence of Linda's work as the field of decolonizing and Indigenous methodologies has "come of age" as a "critical, interpretative thought and enquiry beyond rage" (Denzin & Lincoln 2008, p. xii). The ripples of her work are felt deeply across time and space, speaking to the hearts of those in Indigenous research practice, both as beginners and respected scholars. Among these voices are testaments of the impact of Linda's work, from affirmations of Indigeneity in our research to confirmation that we already know how to do decolonizing work intuitively. Linda's work has provided us with the platform to push back against the colonial project and given us the sustenance to do the heavy lifting required to counter Western epistemologies using an array of non-theoretical and theoretical frameworks.

Social shifts and research impacts

With over 22,000 Google citations (Google Scholar 2020) and 20 academic reviews of the first and second editions of *Decolonizing Methodologies* (see Crothers 2014; Hall 2000; Jørgensen 2010; Malsbary 2008; Ortley 2005; Tuck 2013; Wilson 2001), it has been a slow rise to prominence in the non-Indigenous academy. Initially, the first edition was valued as "brief and readable, sufficient to get students into the issues ... [a] valuable supplemental text" (Hall 2000, p. 568). Similarly, Wilson (2001, p. 217) provided an "ethnocentric" review, interested more in the perspective of a non-Indigenous researcher, but realized the focus of the book was on "developing a research agenda for 'insider' research with Indigenous communities". A few years on, Ortley (2005, p. 285) described Linda's work as a "convenient template for viewing the impact Western-minded research has had", while giving recognition for the "epistemological shift required to improve research practices with Indigenous communities". Ortley (2005, p. 287) also concluded that "[t]he success of Smith's thesis must be measured in how well she is able to convince her readers that the Imperial-minded methods behind Western research must be re-examined for their fairness and sensitivity for gaining a perspective of Indigenous culture". These early reviews grossly underestimated the power and force that Linda's work would bring over time.

Nine years after the release of the first edition we hear the contrastingly passionate voice of a woman working in decolonizing spaces, Malsbary (2008 para. 7), who reflects on *Decolonizing Methodologies* as "a wonderful achievement ... Her [Smith 1999] scholarship – polished, refreshing and emotionally prescient – is important and healing". A new, emic narrative around the meaning and influence of Linda's work emerges. These sentiments are followed by Eve

Tuck (2013), an Unangax scholar, on the release of Linda's second edition. Here, the first-person impact that *Decolonizing Methodologies* had on Eve's scholarly development speaks for many of us when she writes "I was captivated by the layered wisdom ... [and it] has profoundly influenced my generation of critical researchers. It has given us an anti-colonial lexicon of research, and an ethics of making *space and showing face*" (Tuck 2013, p. 365). At this point, we are hearing from the heart and mind of another Indigenous female voice, who is both enacting and responding to Linda's call to create and own decolonizing methodologies with a heartfelt closing message: "Dr. Smith, I ask you to receive our appreciation for you and your work, for now and for every generation" (Tuck 2013, p. 371).

Eve's gratitude is reflected in the multiple scholars who similarly pay their respects to Linda's work in their introductions and opening chapters, claiming her as a significant influence on their work (see Allen 2012; Denzin, Lincoln & Smith 2008; Denzin & Salvo 2020; S. Wilson 2008). There is also an "increasing number of articles, special issues of journals, monographs, collections, and academic events organized toward the ideals articulated by Smith" (Allen 2012, p. xxi). We too follow in this vein and openly acknowledge our volume could not be possible without Linda and her work.

Although Linda reflected soon after the release of the first edition, that "the best reviews that I have had have been directly to me ... by Indigenous communities" (Smith, cited in Battiste, Bell & Findlay 2002, p. 173), many of her academic reviews were generated by non-Indigenous scholars. For example, Jørgensen (2010, p. 3207), a self-identified, European, middle-class woman, proposed a work-around in Indigenous-specific theory as a means for "conceptualising the situatedness of knowledge without reducing it to the identity of the knowledge producer". Crothers (2014, p. 880), meanwhile, tries to reduce and flatten Linda's influence by boxing the Black gaze as "too close a focus on these applied settings means that there is not an opening up to possibilities of Indigenous academic contributions to cosmopolitan knowledges". What is missed here is the fundamental notion of what it means to be an Indigenous scholar – the power of Linda's work is that she speaks to us as worthwhile, legitimate and necessary and for our stories to be told by us, for ourselves and with our wellbeing in mind.

Linda gave us a space to call our own and to question those seeking entry without qualification, especially those who thrust "identity epistemology as the border between the West and Indigenous peoples [and] is made decisive for the distinction between more and less legitimate knowledge" (Jørgensen 2010,

p. 325). From this place, Black women can stand firm and state that "[t]he self-ascribed western reviewers can only debate *Decolonizing Methodologies* with a circumscribed voice" (Jørgensen 2010, p. 326). "Outsiders" who wish to engage with Indigenous research and its methodologies are squirming in the discomfort from a lack of legitimacy and restricted potential for what is seen as "producing legitimate knowledge in the debate of 'marginalised perspectives'" (Jørgensen 2010, p. 326).

While we will disengage in defense of toxic identity politics and deficit discourses from those that seek to harm us through colonizing privilege, this debate around the legitimacy of the "insider" to produce critical knowledge continues to be rich terrain for our exploration and response. This is the gift of Linda that keeps giving: an anchor to grasp, a canvas for us to articulate our situatedness, our Indigeneity, and our right to develop and carve out new scholarly spaces and methodologies. This is our action of decolonization – we are not a "marginalized perspective", but a site of empowerment. We do not have to placate or appease non-Indigenous worlds; rather we care for our domains and Black female bodies through employing a decolonizing methodology that is geared towards women's business.

Local to global and back again

Linda's work has inspired Indigenous scholars in many unexpected ways across multiple cultural and continental contexts. In *Decolonizing Methodologies* Linda situated herself "from the vantage point of the colonized" (Smith 2012, p. 1) both at a local and global level. As Linda "'talked back to' and 'talked up to' research" (Smith 2012, p. i), her invitation to Indigenous scholars to seek new ways to conceptualize and conduct our research, while keeping our communities safe, creates local outcomes that build global bodies of Indigenous scholarly knowledges. Her work has contributed to the development of research practices, theory, ethical processes and, ultimately, positive outcomes for our communities over the last two decades.

There are many scholars who attribute the fundamental influence that *Decolonizing Methodologies* has had on the conception and development of their theoretical work. The depth and reach of Linda's influence includes, for example, Indigenous standpoint theory (see Foley 2003; Moreton-Robinson 2013; Tur, Blanch & Wilson 2010); whiteness studies (see Kynard 2015; Moreton-Robinson 2004; Saito 2005); trauma theory (see Pihama et al 2014); Kaupapa Māori (see Barnes 2000; Bishop 2005; Smith 1999; Smith 2012; Smith 2015a); decolonizing work, critical race theory and Indigenous methodologies (see Archibald et al 2019; Denzin et al 2008). Likewise, Linda's footprint is felt in the development of Indigenous research paradigms from post-colonial/counter-colonial/anti-colonial, Indigenous knowledges approach, Indigenism, trans-Indigenous methodologies, Indigenous storywork and ceremony as methodologies (see Allen 2012; Archibald et al 2019; Chilisa & Tsheko 2014; Doyle et al 2017; Grieves 2009; Kunnie & Goduka 2006; Nicholls 2009; Rigney 2006; S. Wilson 2008).

This pulse and creativity of her work is multi-facetted, practical, theoretical and inspirational, and has spearheaded these paradigms into real Indigenous methodologies. Linda has invited us to create decolonizing methodologies distinct to Western methods by "bringing to the centre and privileging Indigenous values, attitudes and practices" (Smith 1999, p. 125). Our communities can breathe, can exercise what we know works and sits well with us as permission to do so while operationalizing and theorizing our Indigenous research practices. Since "Indigenous methodologies tend to approach cultural protocols, values and behaviours as an integral part of methodology" (Smith 1999, p. 15), we have created holistic approaches that allow us to underpin our practices with strength, enabling us to do our work and share our research globally.

Decolonizing Methodologies has been a key global influence on many scholars. In Australia, Linda's work has provided enduring foundations in many areas such as racism and identity (see Bodkin-Andrews & Carlson 2016; Carlson 2016; Clark, Augoustinos & Malin 2016); data and Indigenous research practice and statistics (Walter 2005; Walter & Andersen 2013); Indigenous methodologies (Bawaka Country et al 2013, 2014, 2016; Blair 2019; Doyle et al 2017; *tebrakunna country* & Lee 2019); Indigenous philosophies (Stronach & Adair 2012); story research practice (Blair 2019); yarning (Bessarab & Ng'andu 2010); Indigenous pedagogy (Yunkaporta 2009); and decolonizing university curricula (McLaughlin & Whatman 2011). This is only a snapshot. Likewise, the list of scholars who have been influenced by Linda's works elsewhere is extensive. A minutiae would include Kaupapa Māori research in New Zealand (see Barnes 2000; Bishop 2005; Smith 1999; Smith, cited in Mertens, Cram & Chilisa 2013); whiteness, race and decolonization in America (see Brown 2018; Kynard 2015; Saito 2015; Writer 2008); and Indigenous knowledges, the politics of representation and decolonizing practices in Canada (see Baskin 2016; Daniel 2005; Kincheloe & Steinberg 2008; Kubota 2019).

Today, the ongoing development of Indigenous research and decolonizing practices remains a "risky business" (Smith 1999, p. 198), particularly the voices of the silent majority still being under-represented in the literature (Denzin & Salvo 2020). However, Linda's work continues to receive homages, dedications and claims as a major literary influence in the broader Indigenous scholarly literature. *Decolonizing Methodologies* is named as key literature that is "bringing [a] wider lens to the meaning of indigeneity" and is still inspiring voices of a new generation in their work in Indigenous research (Mertens et al 2013, p. 12). Perhaps one of the most dangerous lenses is that pertaining to sexuality, gender, and queering intersections within Indigenous research. Indigenous scholars have begun to question traditional gender boundaries as they relate to cultural practice and identity within anti-colonial contexts as an extension of Linda's work (see Barker 2017; Chisholm 2018; Clark 2015; Finley 2011). This is a new frontier and application of theory that is needed not just for Black female (and male) bodies, but across the entirety of the decolonizing fields of research for benefit to wider communities. The use of *Decolonizing Methodologies* to carve out Indigenous-led solutions to mainstream issues is untested ground across the academy.

New voice for Indigenous researchers and practitioners

Academic kinship connections are being forged between those that are responding to Linda's work, and each other, as we share our experiences of the power struggle to find our voice and be heard. With Linda's foundational text, scholars can see and hear themselves as they explore the "materiality, orality, spatiality, and temporality that continues to animate the study and practice of distinct Native literary traditions" (Washuta & Warburton 2019). As Linda's body of work grows, so too does her influence and ability to osmose and translate her core concepts of freedom in practice and centering localized theory that avoids "universal characteristics that are independent of history, context and agency" (Smith 1999, p. 229). Yunkaporta (2019) demonstrates this freedom through his "sand talk", a way of engaging with life through yarning (Bessarab & Ng'andu 2010) and unfettered from Western academic norms, referring to Linda among those writers who "helped me with my thinking" (Yunkaporta 2019, p. 280).

Decolonizing Methodologies is neither the first nor last word on new forms of Indigenous-led academy practice from Linda, as the depth of her ongoing research demonstrates her commitment to expand the canon she has helped found. Latter works include: *Twenty-Five Indigenous Research Projects* (Smith 2004); *Building a Research Agenda for Indigenous Epistemologies and Education*

(Smith 2005a); *Researching in the Margins* (Smith 2006); *On Tricky Ground: Researching the Native in the Age of Uncertainty* (Smith 2005b); *The Native and the Neoliberal Down Under: Neoliberalism and "Endangered Authenticities"* (Smith 2007); *Handbook of Critical and Indigenous Methodologies* (Denzin et al 2008); *Social Justice, Transformation and Indigenous Methodologies* (Smith 2014); *Decolonizing Knowledge: Toward a Critical Indigenous Research Justice Praxis* (Smith 2015b); *Indigenous Knowledge, Methodology and Mayhem* (Smith et al 2016); and *Indigenous and Decolonizing Studies in Education* (Smith et al 2019). It is likely that broad-ranging scholars, even touching the margins of these research spheres, have been influenced in/directly and un/knowingly by Linda's. Our authors too remark on both the happenstance and purposeful occasions in meeting Linda's work for the first time, often acknowledging the legitimizing effect of having practiced her theory without knowing, and then arriving at, her corpus.

There will be more of us to follow and those who will unbridle themselves from a "Western cultural conceptual rubric" (Kovach 2009, p. 31) and explore new ways to employ decolonizing and Indigenous methodologies in practice. These are the audiences Linda "wanted to reach" and "write for" (Smith, cited in Battiste et al 2002, p. 173). These are the Indigenous communities that Linda wanted to "do something more than just deconstruct Western ideas about research ... you cannot deconstruct everything into a blank space. We need a way to proceed" (Smith, cited in Battiste et al 2002, p. 173). Linda's message is clear: to "research for ourselves, and talk back to the Western research academy" (Smith, cited in Battiste et al 2002, p. 175). At the time Linda wrote the first edition of *Decolonizing Methodologies*, she noted that "I point to Africa and a lot of the writing around decolonisation was about the change of power in Africa. There is an absence of voice around the Pacific and around our experiences" (Smith, cited in Battiste et al 2002, p. 175). Since then, the void of the Pacific is rapidly transforming into a hub that radiates cultural and intellectual growth within global academies.

This volume

As Linda's work is taken up by more non-Indigenous researchers, the arguments and narratives have deepened. There are those wishing to create a space to participate and gleam Indigenous understandings, while being hopeful of putting aside their colonizer privileges. Then there are others who insist on theorizing with Western epistemologies as a justification, finding cracks to squeeze through so they can eke out a space in Black places to participate. Then there is us: those who have a knowing right and place within the Indigenous research domain or those who write women's business together (Gay'wu Group of Women 2019), not only in our realms of influence, but also in the places where we are diminished and reduced to attenuate our lives and learning.

We use Linda's theories to expand out the concepts and application of women's business as a vital component of research and practice in addressing deep societal problems of uneven economies, environments and rights. We write as Indigenous female voices who take pride in our scholarship, practices and cultures that will overcome our displacement and dispossession in all parts of society. This volume, then, is a place of refuge for us to explore the potent agency we have as Black women outside of the constant noise and "distraction" of defining and justifying our existence and proving our humanness (Morrison, cited in Seamster & Ray 2018, p. 333). It is a space that would not exist if not for the influence of *Decolonizing Methodologies*.

Our volume is not a hagiography of Professor Linda Tuhiwai Smith nor are we replicating her work. Our authors write as a testimony to the legacy of *Decolonizing Methodologies* and celebrate the spaces for women to position Indigenous perspectives without fear. Linda's central message is that we can do our own work in our own ways. Thus, some essays are deeply reflective of Linda's direct influence, while others only make fleeting mention to the actual text of *Decolonizing Methodologies*. Many of the essays show that women were on this journey of decolonizing work before becoming intimately acquainted with Linda's body of research. Thus, we acknowledge Linda's influence in different ways to confirm our processes, enlighten our methodologies and bind our work to our communities.

In honoring the message and the messiness that is decolonizing work, our authors have made a compact to be honest in our journeys – we do not pretend to be experts in any field, let alone decolonizing work and Indigenous methodologies, and instead draw down on the tensions and strengths in reckoning our own positions first. These essays, then, are borne of love. Love for our own flawed, healed and whole identities, cultures and experiences makes us strong advocates and powerful women in an academy that has never wanted us, let alone as speaking Black female beings.

Yet we have forged a path and we come together as women across the globe doing extraordinary work in keeping our cultures alive with dignity and respect.

We do this in our research, the arts, education, in our jobs as scientists, teachers, change-makers and managers, and in our lives as women who navigate two-world complexities with our families, friends and communities. Often in our advocacy work we fail in gaining our freedoms as Indigenous women and for our communities, yet we pick ourselves up and push on – there is no "endpoint" in work required to decolonize and heal traumas, so we continue until we cannot.

This is reflected in the central themes of our essays – discovering and celebrating Linda's corpus in *Decolonizing Methodologies*, recognizing the hard work that goes into maintaining ourselves as Black female bodies and Indigenous women within colonized settings, and the ferocious learning we do in aid of the rights and better worlds we create. We say ferocious because each of these essays is deeply reflective and unflinching in interrogating ourselves and our excluded place in the world, but nevertheless we find the ways to come out on top. Our colonization does not preclude our clear and instructive scholarship, nor does it define us. We are writing women's business from a position of cultural and critical strengths because we have Linda's blueprint to guide us.

Our essays in honor of Professor Linda Tuhiwai Smith

Here, thirteen women in four countries offer their critical thinking that honors and recognizes the influence that Linda's work has in our lives, as we share experiences of decolonizing work and strengthening Indigenous methodologies through research impact. In addition, we have a reflection chapter from Distinguished Professor Maggie Walter, who reviews our work within a contemporary setting. She highlights how essential this volume is as a contribution to a global awakening to the necessary business of decolonizing work. In creating our base camp, we have attempted here to arrange the essays according to the themes of *Decolonizing Methodologies* that resonate in our research and practice. From the essays, we have found five themes that demonstrate how Linda's processes of research action are as relevant today as they were when first introduced 20 years ago.

In our first Part, "Country and Connection", we respond to Linda's call for research that is located in our "territories of life" (Pimbert & Borrini-Feyerabend 2019), the places of creation, environment, Country and ancestral beings from which our identities as Indigenous women spring from and connect us to our spiritual and cultural worlds. Therefore, Karen Fisher opens our volume with a masterclass on situated and embodied knowledges. In exploring more-than-human relations between people and place, she plaits family stories with her work as a conservation scientist to reveal the gaps in global environmental governance and management that ignores and misunderstands Country. Using rivers as a site of connection, Karen invites us to think beyond nature and engage with her ancestral rights to care for Country on her community's terms.

In our second essay, Jennifer Evans creates a heightened effect with the deployment of Indigenous methodologies to frame queerness on Country. Through questioning if queer theory can apply to agency of Country, she initiates decolonizing modes for queer connections and relations with Country, by setting precursory boundaries by which men may weave baskets with respectful intent. Proposing a novel methodology, Jennifer uses critical and political theories in the form of "clubs" to cast onto Country to explore queer propositions and challenge colonizer accounts of gendered cultural practice.

Our second Part, "Violence and Safety", is dedicated to the core task of decolonizing the Imperial projects that Linda warned of and that will continue to destabilize and terrorize our communities through acts of research and practice violence. Thus, in a long overdue examination, the third essay sees Jacinta Vanderfeen analyze Indigenous-specific forms of violence through the lens of Jeremy Bentham's panopticon. In teasing out the characteristics of a Black panopticon that sees us disciplining ourselves within a colonizing framework, she draws an arc between the violence and pathways for safety in the very communities that experience its negative effects.

The special fourth essay is written by a collective of women, including mother and daughter academics who are a vanguard of women's business. Their essay reveals the experience and disciplining of violence in the academy and reaffirms Indigenous methodologies as a place of cultural and theoretical safety in decolonizing research, teaching and learning. Donna Moodie, Kelly Menzel, Liz Cameron and Nikki Moodie deliver a timely and necessary reminder that the colonizing acts of violence on women within the academy are never far away and that Black female voices will not be muted or denied justice in developing the safety that promotes our wellbeing.

Our third Part, "Wisdom and Knowledge", introduces us to a key message within *Decolonizing Methodologies* to set new agendas that center our knowledges and ways of knowing as core to the research project. In the fifth essay, Kelly Ratana critically uses the language of Te Āo Māori to explore how Elders have shaped her life, work and connections to place. She sees her work as a bridge between two-worlds and their knowledge systems, a connector between science and culture to herald new ways of integrating Indigenous methodologies into the academy.

Angela Burt meanwhile, in the sixth essay, draws on the generational strength of familial women in education to critically reclaim a maternal ancestor's life-story as an anthropological subject of a 1939 Harvard University expedition. She shrewdly applies *Decolonizing Methodologies* to Black female writing in response to the Harvard expeditioners and highlights Black agency and gaze over scientific collection processes, surprising us with whose narrative, in the end, will become more powerful over time.

Our fourth Part, "De/colonizing Minds", opens with Lori Campbell's exhilarating essay on the purpose and distortion of Indigenization of higher education. *Decolonizing Methodologies* has a dedicated chapter on the supposed superiority of Western knowledge systems and its institutions that continue to harm us through control and discipline as the Other. The seventh essay, then, is a stark appraisal and antidote in recognizing how colonizing structures are still implemented in higher education against Indigenous Peoples and expands out to avoiding the pitfalls of becoming another colonized mind. The freedom to think outside of Othering is a liberating experience, when we have Linda's and Lori's decolonizing tools working in tandem.

What does it feel and look like to have a colonized mind? The eighth essay is *tebrakunna* country and Emma Lee's contribution and delves into the personal journey of how research has brought to the fore an awareness of possessing a colonized mind. To engage with the theory of *Decolonizing Methodologies is* firstly to understand how each of us has been subjected to colonizing structures and, for Emma, it has been learning to write in the first person, Black female voice that has shifted her scholarship into richer terrain.

We close our volume with the fifth Part, "Seeing Ourselves". Linda's work stresses the definition of insider research as a space that collectively belongs to us for Indigenous-led research and practice – we are best placed to know ourselves and our remedies for decolonizing our lives, histories and cultures. Yet we cannot avoid seeing and knowing ourselves as the Other within public spaces. The hold of the Imperial project is almost cast-iron in the arts and collecting institutions and our ninth essay from Lauren Booker concludes that they are ripe spaces for seismic change. Lauren shows us another way: Indigenous artists and collection workers are leading and shifting the dialog around national, and contested, narratives of belonging.

In our final essay, Pauliina Feodoroff bears witness to the impacts of dispossession, exile and bullets upon Black female bodies within her own family and community. Her essay unfolds as a journey that mimics the process of colonization – signposts are absent to grasp the encounter. It is not the responsibility of any Black female to nullify the disorientating effects that others may experience in reading our stories. If you stop for a moment to take in Pauliina's essay, inescapable proofs arise of what colonization is and does through research and practice. What she does is flip the desensitizing effect of being overwhelmed by the injury and trauma to millions of Indigenous Peoples to nurture the individual connection to her story and really see ourselves. What does it mean to be us, as Indigenous women, in the face of loss and longing, recovery and repair? What is the purpose of our decolonizing work and restoring our governance, our ways of knowing and sense of self? While Pauliina struggles with the answers, and regardless of whether they are there or to be found in our decolonizing journeys, she has given us a certainty that we survive and thrive as strong and powerful women.

In curating these essays, we cherish Professor Linda Tuhiwai Smith as a female warrior and founding Elder of Indigenous research. In our celebration of her lifetime corpus, and especially *Decolonizing Methodologies*, we wanted to show Linda that her decades of unstinting service to us has succeeded. In this volume, here is the next generation of Indigenous academics and practitioners that have been deeply influenced by the power and truth of her work. We are humbled and privileged by her thoughtful, careful and uncompromising theories of Indigenous research and methodologies, decolonizing practices and centering the strongest and most beautiful of voices – ours.

Part One

Country and Connection

1

Decolonizing rivers in Aotearoa New Zealand

Karen Fisher (Ngāti Maniapoto, Waikato-Tainui, Pākehā)

Introduction

I live on the fish caught by Māui using a magic fish-hook made from his grandmother's jawbone. The exploits of Māui, a mischievous demi-god, have been told and re-told in Aotearoa New Zealand (and elsewhere among Polynesian societies) for generations through storytelling, proverbs and sayings, carvings and artworks (including film). In this particular tale, Māui went fishing with his brothers, against their wishes, with a fish-hook made from the jawbone of his *kuia* (grandmother), Muriranga-whenua. Using his own blood as bait, and whilst chanting a *karakia* (prayer, incantation), Māui pulled a fish out of the sea. This fish, Te-Ika-a-Māui, was, in fact, land that is now known as the North Island of Aotearoa New Zealand. The geographic features that characterize the North Island (mountains, valleys and hills), were formed by Māui's brothers as they wounded and killed the fish and trampled over its surface.

In an alternative telling, the North (and South) Island of New Zealand is the exposed part of a largely submerged continent named Zealandia, which was once part of the supercontinent, Gondwana. The rifting 82–85 million years ago that caused the Tasman Sea to open also caused Zealandia to break away from Gondwana; 10 million years ago, the land mass recognizable as New Zealand started to form (Williams 2017). New Zealand's shape is due to the convergence of the Australian and Pacific plates, which move in relation to each other, creating two zones of subduction (with the Pacific Plate being subducted below the Australian Plate underneath the North Island, and the Australian Plate being subducted below the Pacific Plate underneath the South Island). Tectonic forces, along with changes in sea level (submergence and emergence), geological and geomorphological processes (uplift, volcanism, sedimentation, erosion and deposition) have shaped the physical characteristics of the country (Ballance 2009; Williams 2017). These processes continue into the present day, with New Zealand one of the most mobile and dynamic places on Earth (Ballance 2009).

These different accounts of the formation of Aotearoa New Zealand[1] reflect different ontological traditions that continue to co-exist and influence how socio-natural relations are performed, practiced and constituted. For Māori, the polytheist Indigenous population of Aotearoa New Zealand, demi-gods such as Māui along with other gods, animals, humans, human-animal hybrids, supernatural humans, supernatural creatures, spirit(s) (*wairua*) and *mauri* (life essence) constitute an assemblage of humans and non-humans that make up the world within which Māori live. The interconnectedness of the human–non-human–spiritual within Te Ao Māori, or a Māori world view, emphasizes relationality, exchanges, interactions and reciprocity between humans and nonhumans, spirits, the supernatural, and eschews a linear conception of time (Salmond 2014; Tipa 2009; Tipa, Harmsworth, Williams & Kitson 2016). Places and spaces are constituted through practices, performances, rituals and utterances that extend beyond the present into the past and future. This ontology conflicts with conceptualizations of the environment and the place of humans within it derived from a Western modern ontology, which has dominated our ways of knowing, being and governing (Blaser 2013; Chandler & Reid 2018).

In contrast to the relational Indigenous ontology reflective of a Māori worldview, the modernist world is characterized by a nature/culture divide wherein there is one universal reality accessible through scientific knowledge. Whereas Māori relational ontologies emphasize the interweaving of human and more-than-human beings, biophysical, social, and spiritual, Western modernist ontological assumptions separate land/water, freshwater/saltwater, nature/culture, and scientific/spiritual and apply universalist (and universalizing) techniques and measures to know (and enact) the world (Blaser 2013; Chandler & Reid 2018). Indigenous knowledge is, thus, practical and performative and has the capacity to take the non-human seriously (Chandler & Reid 2018). Differences in perspective are explained through differences in culture, which is organized hierarchically with Enlightenment thinking at the peak. This way of thinking about the world (and culture) spread along with colonial (imperial)

---

[1] I echo Mahuika (2009) and acknowledge the differences among different *iwi* or tribal groups in terms of detail regarding the stories of Māui and other gods, which reflect the situatedness of *whakapapa* (genealogy) and the *mana* (authority, prestige of each *iwi* and *hapū* (sub-tribe)) in relation to these accounts.

expansion across the globe, including to Aotearoa New Zealand. Notions of progress, as a corollary to modernity, emphasized linear (teleological) conceptions of time and movement towards a better (modern) future (Blaser 2013, 2014; Chandler & Reid 2018; de La Cadena 2010; Latour 1993; Waikato Regional Council 2014).

In settler societies such as Aotearoa New Zealand, the modernist ontological assumptions underpinning colonization influenced conceptualizations of the environment – and the place of people in it – and the institutional arrangements created to manage it. Colonization enabled the rapid and large-scale transformation of environments in relatively short timeframes, which profoundly affected landscapes, waterways and marine environments through clearing of indigenous forest, draining wetlands, conversion of land for agricultural production (and intensification), fisheries exploitation, industrial development, human settlements and so forth (Memon & Kirk 2012; Parsons & Nalau 2016). The entrenchment of localized systems of settler-colonial power, both historically and in the present day, marginalized Indigenous knowledges and practices in favor of Western conceptions of the world (Bacon 2019; Veracini 2017, 2018). Indigenous knowledges and ways of knowing as well as Indigenous space, thus, have been colonized (Smith 1999). Smith (1999, p. 51) attests to the power of colonization to remake landscapes according to Western ideals whereby "the landscape, the arrangement of nature, could be altered by 'Man': swamps could be drained, waterways diverted, inshore areas filled, not simply for physical survival, but for further exploitation of the environment or making it 'more pleasing' aesthetically". Increasingly, however, Indigenous groups around the world, including Māori, are asserting their rights to protect their relationships to nature and to take an active role in the governance and management of environmental resources (Berry, Jackson, Saito & Forline 2018; Jackson 2018).

In this essay, I give attention to Indigenous ways of knowing and being to consider the possibilities for attending to human and more-than-human relationships and connections in more compassionate terms. I focus in particular on Aotearoa New Zealand and the possibilities afforded by Te Ao Māori, which emphasizes relationality and reciprocity, to repair the damage done to the environment and to repair the damage done to people (especially Indigenous people) in terms of how they interact with the environment. As an academic researcher, I am motivated by Indigenous and more-than-human geographies, studies of the Anthropocene and feminist ethics of care, to find ways to acknowledge multiple ways of knowing (de Leeuw & Hunt 2018) to enable just and sustainable futures, as well as by those seeking to decolonize research, institutions, disciplines, and selves. As a Māori (Indigenous) woman, I am motivated by my own experiences and coming to know the world and my place in it, where my first lessons about the formation of Aotearoa were based on a carving of Te Ika-a-Māui (the fish of Māui) that hung on the wall in my family home.

In exploring notions of decolonization and repair, I focus on rivers as sites of ontological inconsistency that increasingly challenge modernist assumptions of "rivers" because of legal and governance changes that have created opportunities to incorporate *mātauranga* (knowledge, wisdom), cultural values, and *kaitiakitanga* practices premised on Te Ao Māori (Salmond 2012). I am particularly interested in the agency of *taniwha* (supernatural creatures that live in rivers) to disrupt dominant scientific (and legal) conceptions of river management and share my experiences of coming to know the *taniwha*, Waiwaia, and how this has influenced my thinking around rivers. My intention in this essay is to offer glimpses into processes to divest bureaucratic, cultural and linguistic formations of colonial power (Smith 1999).

River ontologies: different ways of knowing rivers

Western approaches to knowing rivers have drawn heavily on science (in myriad forms), which has strongly influenced what counts as knowledge and what a river is. In privileging colonial systems of classification and representation, Western interests remain dominant (Smith 1999); however, the possibility for repair (of peoples and knowledges) finds hope within Western science itself. Indeed, research about rivers reveals a range of perspectives and epistemologies that emphasize relationality, complexity and connectivity and suggest that how rivers are defined is not as straightforward as it may initially seem (Law & Lien 2013).

For instance, fluvial geomorphologists such as Fryirs and Brierley (2013, p. 1) emphasize the importance of viewing rivers within their landscapes and catchments and describe rivers as "largely products of their valleys, which, in turn, are created by a range of geologic and climatic controls". They connect fluvial geomorphology to other physical processes that "create, maintain, enhance or destroy habitats" as well as chemical and ecological processes that influence the form and functions of and within rivers (Fryirs & Brierley 2013, p. 2). Concerns over the physical degradation of rivers has motivated scholars to investigate restoration and rehabilitation to repair damage done largely due to anthropogenic influences (Ashmore 2015; Friberg et al 2016; Lave et al 2014; Wohl, Lane & Wilcox 2015). Such scholarship has focused on ways to improve hydrologic, geomorphic and ecological processes within degraded environments, while also raising questions about what constitutes a "restored" state and revealing the variability in meaning about what a healthy river is and what ought to be measure (Blue 2018; Blue & Brierley 2016). Thus, rivers are "known" through sediment supply and delivery, Macroinvertebrate Community Index, morphological condition, turbidity, water clarity, and multiple other measures and values (including, in Aotearoa New Zealand, swimmability) (Fryirs & Brierley 2013; McCormick, Fisher, & Brierley 2015; Tadaki & Sinner 2014).

Among scientists, there is also a growing recognition of the importance of acknowledging the multiple factors and facets that constitute socio-biophysical landscapes and a repositioning of humans within landscapes as more than a boundary condition or perturbation. In this way, rivers are seen as co-produced systems co-constituted by social and natural processes (Ashmore 2015; Mould, Fryirs & Howitt 2018). Researchers have also identified the relationships between geomorphology and culture as important for co-producing landscape and advocate combining landscape analysis and a focus on forms, processes and evolution, with human spatio-temporal relationships connected to space and home, and sociocultural interactions (Mould et al 2018; Wilcock, Brierley, & Howitt 2013), including an acknowledgement of intercultural communication, particularly with regard to Indigenous Peoples and Indigenous knowledges (Wilcock et al 2013). Such ways of seeing rivers in holistic terms are promising because they emphasize relationality, situatedness and complexity, which provides opportunities to dislodge dominant (modern) ontological framings and to accommodate epistemological and ontological differences, including Māori ways of knowing, doing and being (Fox et al 2017; Paterson-Shallard, Fisher, Parsons & Makey 2020; Wilcock et al 2013).

Ki uta ki tai – from the mountains to the sea – is a Māori concept that emphasizes the interconnectedness and complexity of natural and social systems (Tipa et al 2016). This way of thinking is emblematic of the ontological assumptions underpinning Te Ao Māori in which the environment is understood as an indivisible and holistic system. Te Ao Māori is characterized by a relational ontology that connects humans to other humans and nonhumans across time and space. Within Te Ao Māori, *mātauranga* is an encompassing term used to refer to Māori ways of viewing and perceiving the world through traditional culture and knowledge originating from ancestors (Harmsworth, Awatere & Robb 2016; Salmond 2014). Te Ao Māori and *mātauranga* Māori comprise a range of concepts, values, knowledges, ethics and principles founded on traditional knowledge, philosophy, religion and beliefs. The customary practices that emerge from Te Ao Māori and *mātauranga* reflect cultural, physical, spiritual and metaphysical values. *Mātauranga* is enacted through a range of means including *whakapapa*, *tikanga* (customs and protocols), *kaitiakitanga* (guardianship), *karakia* (prayer and incantations), *mōteatea* (chants), *pūrākau* (stories and narratives), *pepeha* (tribal sayings) and *whakataukī* (proverbs).

For Māori, rivers, mountains, oceans and all other beings and entities carry their own distinct *mauri* and spiritual integrity (*wairua*) (Harmsworth et al 2016; Ruru 2018). The natural world is entwined with identity and *whakapapa* such that individuals locate themselves in relation to biophysical features and family/ancestral histories; all are inextricably bound to their environment (*taiao*) through *whakapapa* and as direct descendants from Papatūānuku (Earth Mother) and Ranginui (Sky Father) (Harmsworth et al 2016; Ruru 2013; Salmond 2014; Te Aho 2010, 2019; Tipa 2009). This is exemplified in an individual's *pepeha* or verbalization of *whakapapa*, where the explanation of who you are is positioned geographically, temporally and in the context of ancestors (Te Aho 2019). Based on one's *whakapapa*, the identification of a mountain, an ocean, a river, a *waka* (canoe), a *marae*[2] or an ancestor provides a means of placing and locating a person into a far bigger web of relations. Within this conceptualization, the interrelationships between individuals and collectives (human, ecological and metaphysical communities) is emphasized; identity is, thus, framed geographically, genealogically and politically (Smith 1999).

For Māori, rivers are a lively assemblage of physical, social and metaphysical properties, knowledges and relations that connects people, places, waters and beings (including the supernatural) across time and space. Rather than a singular "worlding" (Blaser 2013) of "River" as a universal and stable category knowable through scientific measurement, Indigenous ways of knowing emphasize rivers as relational and inseparable from identity, ways of knowing and being, history, and the indivisibility of rivers as a physical and metaphysical entity. Rivers are, thus, multiple, and are brought into being, or rendered invisible, through sets of socionatural practices (Mol 2002); accommodating different conceptualizations of what a river is and how "actors constitute realities in power-charged fields" (Blaser 2013, p. 548) has not yet been resolved.

---

[2] Courtyard or open area in front of the meeting house where formal greetings and discussions take place. Often also used to include the complex of buildings around the *marae*.

Managing rivers in Aotearoa New Zealand

The Treaty of Waitangi, signed in 1840 by representatives of the British Crown and more than 500 Māori *rangatira* (high ranking, chiefly), established a collaborative partnership between Māori and the Crown, and conferred obligations and responsibilities on the Crown and its agents towards Māori (Brierley et al 2019; Salmond 2014). The Treaty has been the subject of intense debate and scrutiny since 1840 not least because there were two versions in two different languages – the Treaty of Waitangi (in English) and Te Tiriti o Waitangi (in Māori) – that were not direct translations of each other (Brierley et al 2019; Jones 2016; Mutu 2018; Williams 2011). While now regarded as the founding document of New Zealand and part of the fabric of New Zealand (Williams 2011), this was not always the case. In 1877, James Prendergast, the then Chief Justice of New Zealand, dismissed the Treaty as a "simple nullity" (*Wi Parata v Bishop of Wellington*). While there were attempts made by legislators to reflect the Treaty in law, at other times, governments "evaded or flagrantly breached the terms of the Treaty" (Williams 2011, p. 3) leading to failures by the Crown to uphold their obligations (Mutu 2018).

The Treaty facilitated the formal colonization of Aotearoa and provided the Crown and settler government with authority to assert settler-colonial ideology and systems of representation and classification that worked to ensure the dominance of Western ideas (Smith 1999). Freshwater management approaches in Aotearoa New Zealand since colonization, as in other settler societies, have tended to reflect a Eurocentric conception of human–environment relationships in which humans are separate to nature, and were influenced heavily by modern ontological and scientific understandings and knowledge (Salmond 2014; Salmond, Tadaki & Gregory 2014). Such ways of knowing, shaped by settler-colonial discourses and political economic structures, meant river management often relied on the use of technocratic means to solve freshwater "problems". Thus, rivers were channelized, diverted and modified to reduce flood risk, wetlands were drained to reduce health risks to settler societies and to support productivist enterprises, and land- and waterscapes were radically transformed and 'improved' in the name of progress (Parsons & Nalau 2016). Freshwater management provides evidence of how, according to Smith (1999), Western ideas came to dominate practice, and Indigenous views of history were dismissed as "primitive", "incorrect" and counter to settler-colonial ideology and aspirations. Moreover, the institutionalization of European property regimes, and the loss of Māori land through confiscation, land sale, and appropriation via myriad legal and policy mechanisms negatively affected the relationships between Māori and their rivers (Burton & Cocklin 1996).

From the perspective of Pākehā settlers, the unruliness, unpredictability and undesirability of water (as floodwaters, as wetlands and as a constraint on agricultural transformation) shaped the institutional framework governing water management in Aotearoa (Davis & Threlfall 2006). Initially, the system of water rights brought by migrants to Aotearoa resembled English common law riparian water rights whereby riverbeds were vested in the Crown to the tidal limit and, thereafter, rights of access and use were held by landowners on either side (to the center-line).

A similar approach was taken to groundwater whereby those who owned land also "owned" water (specifically, rights to exclusive access and use) beneath their land (Burton & Cocklin 1996; Memon & Skelton 2007).[3] Changes in 1903 saw rights regarding navigable rivers vested in the Crown; riparian rights for non-navigable rivers remained for landowners until the passing of the Water and Soil Conservation Act (NZ) in 1967, which extinguished riparian rights and vested all rights to (surface and ground-) water in the Crown (Memon & Skelton 2007). Absent from these considerations of rights regimes over water, which centered on Eurocentric understandings of property and ownership, was the recognition of Māori *tikanga* and principles that governed their relationships to and with water. For Māori, for whom social organization centered on *whanau* and *hapū* and which emphasized the collective over individuals, (private) ownership regimes that privileged individualistic rights (to use, exclude and access "resources") were completely foreign. Māori ways of knowing and being in relation to rivers became obscured through the operationalization of sets of rules and practices within entrenched systems of colonial power, which ensured the dominance of Western interests and knowledge (Bacon 2019; Smith 1999).

Notably, in terms of dominant international discourse on water management, especially in the 1990s and early 2000s (which advocated holistic and integrated catchment or watershed approaches) (see, for example, Calder 2005; Falkenmark 2004; Rahaman & Varis 2005), Aotearoa New Zealand has a relatively long history of catchment-based approaches to freshwater management with the establishment of river boards dating back to 1868 (Davis & Threlfall 2006). Until 1991 and the passing of the Resource Management Act (RMA) (NZ), the

---

[3] See also Coal-Mines Act Amendment Act 1903 (NZ).

management of rivers and catchments was focused largely on flooding and erosion control (and, in some instances, the development of hydroelectricity dams), with less attention given to the complex and entangled land-water assemblages and virtually no consideration of the cultural or spiritual dimensions of rivers and water.

Prior to its enactment in 1991 (and despite the focus on catchments for managing rivers and water), the management of land, water and soil, among other environmental features, was administered by different bodies and different government departments according to different statutory purposes and mandates (Warnock & Baker-Galloway 2015). Fragmented institutional arrangements reflected a utilitarian and anthropocentric way of seeing the natural environment as providing "resources" to be exploited for the benefit of humans (and those things important to humans) from a largely Eurocentric and science/engineering perspective. Indeed, engineers dominated water management: they possessed the technical skills and expertise to control rivers and drain wetlands (Parsons, Nalau, Fisher & Brown 2019).

Prior to the RMA, the ability for Māori to assert their rights, interests or agency in relation to rivers was circumscribed by legal and administrative processes that effectively excluded Māori participation. Instead, at the time the RMA was adopted, there were numerous Māori claims to the Waitangi Tribunal (and the general courts in Aotearoa New Zealand) seeking redress (or remedy) for the damage done to the environment and to the wellbeing of Māori people (Burton & Cocklin 1996). In practice, the extent to which Māori/*iwi* interests and Te Ao Māori are given credence in river management under the RMA has been fairly limited. Despite specific references to the principles of the Treaty and principles such as *kaitiakitanga*, the risk for Māori is that the Treaty (and, to a lesser extent, *kaitiakitanga*) may be reduced to one of several factors to be balanced against others in implementing the RMA.

For Māori, the Treaty underpins their dealings with the Crown (Mutu 2018); however, failure by the Crown to uphold their duties and obligations to the Treaty and ongoing resistance by Māori led to the establishment of the Waitangi Tribunal in 1975 to investigate Treaty breaches (Wheen & Hayward 2012). The Waitangi Tribunal is a permanent commission of inquiry responsible for inquiring into and reporting on claims made by Māori, then presenting their findings and making recommendations to the Crown (Jones 2016; Mutu 2018, 2019; Wheen & Hayward 2012).

Beyond the RMA, settlements made as part of claims against the Crown for breaches to the Treaty of Waitangi and subsequent legislation in respect of rivers provide a means by which to endorse Māori values and knowledge while also strengthening the position of Māori in river governance and management (Ruru 2018). In this way, the hegemony of a modern ontology that privileges science and Western understandings has been challenged by the enactment of legislation that makes room for the rights of interests of Māori to be recognized and provided for. For example, in 2018, the Whanganui River was granted legal personhood status with all the rights, powers, duties and liabilities of a legal passing, while other legislation in relation to rivers has recognized the importance of rivers as an ancestor, and the importance of supernatural creatures and reciprocal relations of care as central to Māori identity.

Taniwha as agents of repair

Indigenous ways of being extend ontopolitical ethics to include more-than-human others (Chandler & Reid 2018), including spiritual and metaphysical beings. In the context of caring for (or managing rivers), such an approach emphasizes the liveliness of rivers beyond mere geomorphic, biological and hydrological features. As with other rivers in New Zealand, the Waipā has experienced serious environmental decline as a result of land use changes and intensification of agricultural activity.

The Waipā River is located in the central North Island of Aotearoa New Zealand, being the major tributary of the Waikato River (the longest river in New Zealand). The Waipā catchment covers 306,569 ha and the river flows through land that was once native bush, wetlands and peat bogs. Approximately 78 per cent of the catchment area is in pasture, 21 per cent is native vegetation, scrub and other land uses, and 1 per cent is production forestry. The catchment comprises 4,825 km of mapped stream and river channels as well as 14 peat lakes, which are valued for their genetic diversity, scientific interest, recreational opportunities, and cultural and spiritual values. The catchment comprises erosion-prone soils and areas of instability that deliver high loads of sediment to tributary streams and the main channel. The habitat quality of streams in the catchment is below average within the Waikato region, while ecological health is around the regional average. Habitat quality and ecological health in streams ranges from poor to excellent across the zone, depending in part upon the upstream land use and activities next to the stream (Hill 2011; NIWA 2014; Waikato Regional Council 2014). Under the RMA, Waikato Regional Council is responsible for managing the Waipā River and for ensuring no further degradation occurs. In performing this role, the Council adopts an integrated catchment approach and implements policies and plans that regulate access and use, discharge pollution control, riparian management and aquatic biodiversity.

The relationships between the Waipā River and Ngāti Maniapoto, whose ancestral affiliations with and responsibilities for the river are deeply intertwined and connected, have been undermined as a consequence of colonization. Ngāti Maniapoto are the *iwi* with *mana* in relation to the Waipā based on a longstanding relationship premised on *kaitiakitanga* and *whakapapa*, which pre-dates European settlement in the early nineteenth century. In contrast to Western ways of knowing rivers, Ngāti Maniapoto recognize the Waipā River, including its material and metaphysical constituents, as an indivisible entity. The Waipā River became the subject of a claim to the Waitangi Tribunal following on from a settlement between the Crown and Waikato-Tainui in respect of the Waikato River in 2010. The Waikato-Tainui settlement acknowledged the ongoing degradation of the Waikato River (and tributaries) and the need to protect and enhance the river. Since the Waipā River is the largest tributary of the Waikato River, the co-governance and co-management arrangements for both rivers are closely aligned (Paterson-Shallard et al 2020).

On 27 September 2010, Ngāti Maniapoto and the Crown signed a deed of settlement in relation to co-governance and co-management of the Waipā River, which recognizes the importance of the Waipā River as a *taonga* to Ngāti Maniapoto; the obligation and desire to restore, maintain and protect all of the waters that flow into or fall within the Maniapoto *rohe* (territory); and, the *mana* of Maniapoto in respect of the Upper Waipā River. For Maniapoto, thinking about, and caring for (managing) the Waipā necessarily includes attending to Waiwaia, a *taniwha* and *kaitiaki* of the Waipā River and the Ngāti Maniapoto people. *Taniwha* are supernatural creatures that inhabit rivers, lakes or caves, and are the metaphysical and metaphorical embodiment of the relations between Māori and their rivers. To Maniapoto, Waiwaia is held to be the essence and wellbeing of the Waipā. The story of Waiwaia was told to me as follows:

> Waiwaia began life as a totara tree (*Podocarpus totara*) on the summit of Rangitoto. The totara tree was made *tapū* (sacred) by a Tohunga (spiritual leader) who used to sit at its base and recite *karakia*. One day, a child was playing in amongst the branches, which angered the tree. Because of this, the land opened up and swallowed the whole tree. The tree then came back out through the Waipā as the *taniwha* Waiwaia. Waiwaia travels the Waipā and the Waikato

Rivers, and has many resting stops along the Waipā; although Waiwaia may travel beyond the waters of the Waipā, he always returns to the Waipā.[4]

In 2012, the Ngā Wai o Maniapoto (Waipa River) Act 2012 (NZ) came into effect. The cultural significance of the Waipā is identified in the legislation as being at the heart of Maniapoto spiritual and physical wellbeing and tribal identity and culture. It clearly states that, to Maniapoto, the essence and wellbeing of the Waipā is Waiwaia. In naming the river, physical and metaphysical elements, including *mauri*, are detailed. In articulating the obligation Maniapoto feel towards the Waipā for present and future generations, *tikanga, kaitiakitanga* and *mana* are made explicit: Maniapoto are charged with the care and protection of *the mana tuku iho o Waiwaia* (the ancestral authority and prestige handed down from generation to generation in respect of Waiwaia). Waiwaia has been put to work in legal and bureaucratic processes. The legal work performed by Waiwaia is further enabled through the Waiwaia Accord (established at the same time as the deed of settlement), which establishes formal relationships between Ngāti Maniapoto and a raft of government departments as well as the Prime Minister. Waiwaia actively affects how Ngāti Maniapoto personally encounter the Waipā, and how Ngāti Maniapoto environmental managers and *kaitiaki* relate to the Waipā (for example, in restoration efforts, planning, management and regulating access to the River and its resources).

The cultural significance of the Waipā River to Ngāti Maniapoto, and the centrality of the Waipā to Maniapoto spiritual and physical wellbeing, and tribal identity and culture, is also explicitly recognized in the Ngā Wai o Maniapoto (Waipa River) Act 2012. Throughout the legislation, including the principles of interpretation, there are clear attempts to accommodate Te Ao Māori values and knowledges. Māori concepts form the foundation for co-governance and co-management with specific guidance given to the interpretation of the key concepts *mana, rangatiratanga* (chieftainship, right to exercise authority), *kawanatanga* (government, rule, dominion), *kaitiakitanga* as they relate to Ngāti Maniapoto and the Waipā. Moreover, principles relating to processes and procedures for working together to ensure efficient and practical outcomes emphasize partnership (under the Treaty of Waitangi), integration (across a number of levels and a range of agencies) and integrity (a shared commitment to act to protect the integrity of the deed) as fundamental to the co-governance and co-management framework.

---

[4] This story of Waiwaia appeared in a booklet with illustrations completed by children from a Kōhanga Reo (Māori language pre-school) in Otorohanga.

Between 2009 and 2016, I attended numerous *hui* (meetings) and *wananga* (forum) focused on the Waipā River in my capacity as someone who identifies as a member of Ngāti Maniapoto, and as someone with an academic interest in environmental governance and, later, as someone who worked for and with Ngāti Maniapoto. These meetings were mostly in relation to the settlement agreement to establish the co-governance and co-management arrangements, as well as in relation to the development of planning documents and to prioritize river restoration. Waiwaia was present at each of these gatherings. First, through *whakapapa*: while the meetings were open to all Ngāti Maniapoto, most of those attending were from families who have been located along the Waipā for generations.

For Māori, articulation of identity positions individuals in relation to land, water, mountains, the *waka* that brought ancestors across the Pacific to Aotearoa, to ancestors, to extended family and immediate family. In this way, Waiwaia and the Waipā are embodied in those Maniapoto who affiliate to Ngā wai o Waipā (the waters of the Waipā). Second, through *kōrero* (to speak, talk). At the meetings, people spoke of their personal encounters with Waiwaia; in many of these accounts, Waiwaia appeared in the river as a log. There were stories of people being saved by Waiwaia, as well as people "being taught lessons" in response to behavior deemed by Waiwaia to be displeasing or inappropriate. Third, through *tikanga* and *kaitiakitanga*. *Tikanga* refers to custom and practices; these can be mundane or highly ritualized. *Kaitiakitanga* is most commonly translated as guardianship or stewardship; a *kaitiaki* is an individual who acts as a guardian. Such practices (and accounts of *kaitiakitanga* and *tikanga*) connect Maniapoto directly to the Waipā and to Waiwaia. Fourth, through co-governance and co-management arrangements enabled through Treaty settlement. This is how I have encountered Waiwaia.

This encounter profoundly influenced my thinking about governance and management of rivers in Aotearoa New Zealand, strategies to enable the decolonization of rivers (and other dimensions of life in Aotearoa New Zealand and in other settler-colonial contexts more broadly), relational ontologies, and the interconnectedness of humans and more-than-human others.

By centering a *taniwha* into all considerations of the Waipā River, and the relationship between Waiwaia, the Waipā and Ngāti Maniapoto, the river became more than a physical object or entity to be carved up into discrete resource units to be managed. Concerns over how any proposed activity or action might affect Waiwaia (positively or negatively) require a more holistic approach than implied within an integrated catchment management approach (as adopted by the Waikato Regional Council).

My encounter with Waiwaia also reminded me of the "other" ways of knowing I had benefited from (such as *pūrākau* about Maui and my family's carving), but which I had come to take for granted (though never dismissed). While I was initially interested in the Waipā co-governance and co-management arrangements because of my academic training, I was enticed by Waiwaia to learn more about the myriad spaces that *taniwha* (as an example of a powerful more-than-human being and a *kaitiaki*) now inhabit. I have taken Waiwaia with me (as a colleague) to teach cohorts of students about Te Ao Māori and different ways of knowing, and to explore ontological and legal pluralism at conferences and seminars in Aotearoa New Zealand, Australia, and the United Kingdom. I have focused on Waiwaia as an agent of repair, who disrupts Western ways of knowing rivers and re-focuses questions about river health and water quality away from metrics and calculative practices designed within positivist and reductionist framings. In working with Waiwaia it is clear to me that Western science alone cannot answer the question of how to manage for a *taniwha* or, more importantly, how to manage a river.

Conclusion

Indigenous knowledge and practices have been threatened by colonization and assertions of colonial ideology that sought to oppress and control Indigenous Peoples, including Māori (Smith 1999). Nevertheless, Indigenous Peoples from around the world continue to resist and to (re)assert their rights at local, national and global scales. The emergence of Indigenous practices that disrupt hegemonic political formations can, therefore, be seen as evidence of the destabilization of dominant (Western) knowledge systems (Blaser 2013, 2014; de La Cadena 2010).

The story of Te-Ika-a Māui is representative of stories that connect humans with non-humans and that transcend the physical to include the supernatural and spiritual. In comparison to scientific accounts of the world and the forces acting on its materiality, this kind of story reorients relationships between humans and nonhumans and allows different values to be recognized and acknowledged. By asserting these stories and emphasizing their significance, bureaucratic, cultural and linguistic formations of colonial power are disrupted and possibilities for doing things differently emerge (Smith 1999). Māori ways of knowing and being, thus, have the potential to enhance the management and care of rivers in Aotearoa New Zealand by emphasizing relationality and reciprocity between all things across time and space and for its focus on rivers as more-than-material and more-than-human.

For Ngāti Maniapoto, Ngā Wai o Maniapoto (Waipā River) Act (NZ) and the deed of settlement signed as part of a Treaty settlement go some way to repair the damage done to their *mana*, as a consequence of colonization, by recognizing and asserting their rights and interests in relation to the Waipā. This ultimately enables the repair of the relationship between Ngāti Maniapoto and the Waipā River as well as environmental repair as a result of restoration efforts. By legally recognizing the importance of a *taniwha* as central to the relationship between Ngāti Maniapoto and the Waipā River, and in acknowledging the role of *taniwha* as a *kaitiaki*, river management and restoration practices must account for *mātauranga* and Te Ao Māori. This requires the Crown and its agents (including Waikato Regional Council) to find ways to work with Ngāti Maniapoto and has the potential to transform river management from a technical exercise that deals primarily with physical and material elements of rivers to consider approaches that support and enhance the non-tangible, cultural, social and metaphysical dimensions as well.

Finding ways to ensure a *taniwha* (such as Waiwaia) can thrive requires more than limiting nutrients, planting riparian margins, reducing sediment loads or regulating use. It is not simply a matter of what is done, it is also how it is done; managing (or caring for) the Waipā requires the application of *mātauranga* by *kaitiaki* – accumulated over generations – through *tikanga* and other practices deemed appropriate and necessary by Ngāti Maniapoto. At a personal level (myself included), encounters with more-than-humans (be they metaphysical, spiritual or nonhuman entities and beings) can be transformational and generate deeper-felt connections and collective caring towards rivers than a list of values or set of indicators that attempt to measure and define a river. The benefits of decolonizing river management in Aotearoa New Zealand, thus, outweigh maintaining settler-colonial institutions for both rivers and people (Māori and non-Māori alike).

2

Can men weave baskets in Queer country?

Jennifer Evans (Dharug)

Introduction: decolonizing *nokegerrer* and queering *lutruwita* country

In *lutruwita* country (Tasmania, Australia), *loonner* (women) are of the sea (Cameron 2016; Cockerill 2018; *tebrakunna* country & Lee 2017) and moon (Ryan 1996), and *panner* (men) are of the sun (Ryan 1996). The practice of *nokegerrer* (basket making) is considered women's business and symbolizes the traditional carrying of seascape resources and continuation of *pakana* culture (Gough 2009; TMAG 2009). The uniqueness of *loonner nokegerrer* has made *terri* (baskets) desirable objects. However, there is a new wave of colonization in *lutruwita* country, where arts and curatorial movements are co-opting *palawa*[1] culture to buttress their prestige and privileged status. Tensions exist between traditional gendered *loonner* cultural revival and the legitimacy of non-gendered sharing and learning of *nokegerrer* practices. This new wave of colonization can be viewed as what Professor Linda Tuhiwai Smith refers to as the material consequences of colonization, where Western conceptions of gender, space and time are used to determine "what counts for real" (Smith 1999, p. 44).

Absent in the discourse of both revival streams is the concept of agency of *melythina* (country) and its role in gendered cultural practices. Country has its own agency and power, commanding ontological relations with place temporalities (Evans 2019; Graham 2009; Lee 2017; West 2000). *nokegerrer* is both an act of connecting to country and responding to the power of the agency of country. If country is non-gendered, and has its own agency, what boundaries apply to gendered cultural practices including *nokegerrer*? Smith (1999, p. 151)

---

[1] The term *palawa* is also used by some to refer to all Tasmanian Aboriginal people regardless of gender.

argues that "[g]endering indigenous debates, whether they are related to the politics of self-determination or the politics of the family, is concerned with issues arising from the relations between indigenous men and women that have come about through colonialism". Therefore, explorations about the agency of *melythina* and its role in gendered cultural practices requires a decolonizing lens and methodology to "talk[ed] back to" (Smith 2012, p. ix) heteronormative settler conceptions of connections to country.

Queerness, as it relates to Indigenous identity politics in Australia, is centered on narratives around Sistagirls, Brothaboys and Blak Drag Queens (see Browning 2018; Burin 2016; Kerry 2017; Maxwell 2018), and their acceptance and access to cultural practices. This emphasis on identity politics, whilst being an important act of claiming Indigeneity, leaves unanswered questions relating to the potential theoretical construct of queering of country and how it may apply to agency of country. This raises the question of whether country may actually be gendered and, if so, does it command gendered cultural practices and can queer theory apply to agency of country? Can men weave baskets as a response to agency of country and if so, is this a decolonizing act of queering country? My questions challenge Western notions of country, as I follow Smith's (1999) view that "space has been colonized"; "compartmentalised with absolute parameters, qualities (including gender), and possibilities, that are dominated by mathematical constructs" Smith (1999, p. 51). By opening up the narrative of queering country, I am reclaiming an Indigenous world view of the agency of country whilst challenging the distorted Western spatial image of country (Smith 1999).

I use the term "Blaq" when referring to myself only, as it allows me to self-determine my Queer Blak female body while decolonizing and reclaiming both the terms "Queer" and "Black". I follow Ku Ku/Erb/Mer visual artist Destiny Deacon in her original creation of the term "Blak" as a "vehicle to express identity and subvert the racist notion that Aboriginal people are 'black', or rather are only identifiable as having 'black' skin" (Baylis 2015, p. 16). As I identify myself as "Blaq", I do so whilst respectfully acknowledging that "BlaQ/BlaQueer" is used by "people of Black/African descent and/or from the African diaspora who recognize their Queerness/LGBTQIA+ identity as a salient identity attached to their Blackness and vice versa" (Petersen et al 2020, p. 3). Recently in Australia, the term "BlaQ/blaq" is being used by some Aboriginal and Torres Strait Islander LGBTQ+ people to define their identity (see Sullivan 2020), with hashtags such as "#blaqMobs #blaqAs #BQmob #BlaqOut" emerging in social media (see BlaQ 2021). When I use the term "Blaq" I am doing so in the context of belonging to my Queer Blak Aboriginal mob in Australia.

As a Queer Dharug woman with kinship connections with *palawa*, responding to the agency of *lutruwita* country, I use Indigenous methodologies to set the conditions for gay *palawa* men who dream of weaving baskets and developing their own *nokegerrer* practice. In this essay I problematize the question, "Can men weave baskets?" As I work through the problematic, I investigate the proposition of "what does country think about men weaving baskets?" by applying critical and political theory to country itself. My methodological approach is critical and reflexive (Nicholls 2009) and intersects Queerness and Indigeneity (Fotopoulou 2012). I use my own Blaq body and connection to *lutruwita* country and kinship with my gay brothers to investigate the key intellectual curiosities surrounding this question, by exercising my Indigeneity and culturally framed understanding of myself, others and country (Kunnie & Goduka 2006; O'Sullivan 2017). I do this carefully, recognizing that the hyphen in "self-other" is present as I approach this research as both an insider and outsider (Nicholls 2009; Smith 1999) and as I collaborate with *palawa* and *lutruwita* country to create this counter-colonial research. I am seeking out what priorities for research methodologies are required to tease out the tensions surrounding the prospects for the male practice of *nokegerrer*. As I decolonize the position that men cannot weave baskets, I am propositioning what we can expect under an Indigenous view as a response to and from country. I will use the term "club" as a metaphor for the research methodologies that I will apply. Country is a reflection of our body (Bawaka Country et al 2014; Evans 2019; Lee 2017) and thus I use clubs to reflect how our body works in country.

As I enter into this investigation, I pay respect to *nokegerrer* practitioners past and present. I do not hold a critical view of the cultural knowledge shared by others nor do I wish to offend those who hold the position that men cannot weave baskets. My intention is to respectfully explore the possible gender boundaries for *nokegerrer* practice as it relates to the agency of country. I am highlighting the tensions around gendered and non-gendered approaches to the *nokegerrer* practices not for the purpose of resolution, but to provide an alternative interpretation for the agency of country and how it might relate to cultural practice. I am concerned about individual acts of decolonization and the exercising of Indigeneity for people, not just Blaqness. My purpose is to place the power of cultural practice *in country, from country, of country* and away from colonized cultural institutions.

Before I commence my investigation, I wish to situate myself within Professor Linda Tuhiwai Smith's seminal work, *Decolonizing Methodologies: Research and Indigenous Peoples*. Like many Indigenous scholars before me, I embarked on an academic career in my mid-forties, having proven that I could produce research within the expected Western scientific norms. Throughout my PhD journey, I had many questions that laid unanswered, such as "where am *I* in all of this, why can't I find literature that explains and supports my findings, why do my supervisors have not much to say about Indigenous business, methodologies and knowledges, and why are the methodologies I have to use so limited?". It wasn't until I started being employed as a research fellow, when I had full academic freedom to seek what I knew was missing, that I found Linda's work. Understanding the depth and breadth of what decolonizing methodologies are, and can give, became a watershed to how I conceptualized myself as a researcher and my research practice. I quickly found a deep meaning to my work, and a sense of agency which had been latent, waiting to be set free. Reading *palawa* Elder Uncle Jim Everett's words referenced in Linda's "twelve ways to be researched (colonized)" (Smith 1999, p. 102) gave me confidence in knowing that my place in the world has not been ignored and that I too can have a voice. Since then, I often return to Linda's work for inspiration, finding new strength in my Indigenous and decolonizing research by "researching back" to the academy, and "recovering" myself (Smith 1999, p. 7) through deploying my own Blaq scholarly practice.

Background: genderization of *nokegerrer* and country

For millennia, *nokegerrer* practices have provided necessary vessels for carrying resources that are borne of country from the natural fibers produced (Gough 2009). Although temporarily interrupted by colonization via British invasion in 1803, *nokegerrer* practices in *lutruwita* have been revived by *loonner*, and now "represent in themselves the carrying onward, the continuation of culture" (Gough 2009, p. 3). Like *lutruwita* country, the *nokegerrer* weaving method is unique and uses an s-stich that is a mirror of the z-twist basket weaving technique used in other parts of Australia (Gough 2009). *loonner* are coming together to weave this unique stich again, to connect with the old people and have "restored to the hands of Tasmanian Aboriginal women, secure in the knowledge that they are the custodians and owners of this traditional practice" (Gorringe 2009, p. 39). Country determines cultural practices in *trouwunna*[2] (Cameron 2016) and can

---

[2] Some *palawa* prefer to use language for the place name of Tasmania as *trouwunna*, which is sourced from Plomley (1976), while others use *palawa kani* (TAC 2013), which is *lutruwita*. I respectfully use the term *lutruwita* whilst acknowledging that the name *trouwunna* is also used.

geographically confine practices via distribution of resources and is therefore an agent in creating and maintaining traditions. The act of *nokegerrer* is a signal and connector to and from country, "weaving . . . identifies movements in the country or on the land . . . first discovering the plant, to then discovering more about my own people" (Frost 2009, p. 27).

Whilst *loonner* are reviving *nokegerrer*, what is the certainty that it is exclusively women's business and has always been so? Until recent times, the written accounts of basket making were singularly penned by non-Aboriginal males (Gough 2009). Historic accounts of gendered business in *lutruwita*, concentrated on *panner*, were prejudiced in colonial anthropography and subverted the economic, spiritual and socio-cultural contributions that *loonner* made (Cameron 1994). *lutruwita*, at that time, was like many other colonized places where "white men whose interactions with indigenous 'societies' or 'peoples' were constructed around their own cultural views of gender and sexuality" (Smith 1999, p. 8). French explorers (see Baudin 1754–1803; D'Entrecasteaux 1739–93, cited in Plomley 1983), British invaders (see Robinson 1829–1834, cited in Plomley 1987) and English missionaries (see Backhouse 1838) feminized basket making and ownership. Although they admired the high craft, observing its perceived value, documenting its construction and use and the *loonner* reluctance to trade the objects (Backhouse cited in Plomley 1987; Baudin [1802]1974), they did so through their colonizing eyes and androcentric view. *terri* became desirable objects; romanticized and sexualized as exotic feminine primitive curiosities, and accordingly were traded, stolen and acquired (Gough 2009). The connotation that basket making was "the work of the females" (Backhouse cited in Plomley 1987, p. 244) can also be inferred by the observation of the *loonner* market at Wybalenna from 1836 to 1838, where 30 *loonner* sold *terri* during their post-contact incarceration (Gough 2009). During this time, basket making on Flinders Island was one of a few government-endorsed cultural practices (Gough 2009). The insinuation that basket making was a women's only business by virtue that only *loonner* were present dismisses the economic reality of post-contact production by the surviving women. This contested history is a reality for contemporary Indigenous communities, where their oral traditions and ways of knowing are disputed against colonizer accounts and culture is en-gendered and objectified (Smith 1999).

Cameron (2016) provides a refreshing antidote to the question of exclusive genderization of *nokegerrer* practice: "Collection bags were woven out of fibrous plants … the women undertook many other roles … most of these tasks were undertaken by the women alone and were probably considered as being outside the interest or ability of males"(Cameron 2016, p. 43). Cameron's approach cuts through colonizing narratives, turns the purview away from an anthropological lens, makes space for the realities of *palawa* life and situates gender roles. *terri* have agency: "the baskets are not empty. They are full of makers, their stories, their thoughts while making. The baskets are never empty. All of the thoughts jump out of the baskets onto all of us" (Nichols 2009, Frontispiece, para. 1). Country is the power medium to which *nokegerrer* practices and *terri* are a response to, and product of, and therefore are unaffected by perceived gender roles.

The relationships that country holds with Indigenous Peoples have been extensively documented and are multidimensional and complex (Ganesharajah 2009). Western scientific paradigms fail to explain the deep interconnectedness between and within life-forces that Indigenous knowledges provide (Graham 2009). "Many indigenous creation stories link people through genealogy to the land, to stars and other places in the universe, to birds and fish, animals, insects and plants. To be connected is to be whole" (Smith 1999, p. 148). Connection to country is often interpreted as human agency contextualized to place through ecological knowledges and is used as a trope for the biophilia hypothesis (Kingsley, Townsend & Hendersen-Wilson 2013). The biophilia hypothesis asserts that humans have an innate attachment to nature and its life forms (Wilson 1984). Discourses cover extensive terrain and grapple with the notion of connection to and understanding of country using human-nature theory, post-nature theory, posthumanism, kincentric ecology, Indigenism, Indigenous expressivism, eco-feminism, ecopluralism, Dreamings, connectivity, anti-colonial critiques and decolonizing methodologies (see Bawaka Country et al 2013, 2014, 2016; Bignall, Hemming & Rigney 2016; Curry 2008; Jaimes Guerrero 2003, 2004; Kingsley et al 2013; Lee 2017; McGrath 2015; Plumwood 2003, 2010; Rose 2000; Salmon 2000; Samson 2001; Weir 2012).

In contrast to the positivist and reductionist Western academic explanation of connection to country, Indigenous Peoples interpret and value the human and non-human forces of the world as interrelated and holistic (Champagne 2015). "Connecting is related to issues of identity and place, to spiritual relationships and community wellbeing" (Smith 1999, p. 149). The restoration of rituals and practices by people on their traditional lands can be healing (Smith 1999). Everett (2017, n.p.) describes the action of being connected to country from a *palawa* perspective as a matter of philosophy: "[it's] very holistic; you're connected with the total-ness of country, everything that makes up the universe that you know you live in; and they're reciprocal ... all the animals and the plants, the waterways, the seaways and the heavenly universe".

Country can be understood beyond human–country dualisms and acknowledged as a life-force within its own right that has agency, co-created with humans (Bawaka Country et al 2013, 2014, 2016), "[it] is not a passive background but an active presence; it grows you up, teaches you, misses you, and calls to you" (Neidjie, Davis & Fox 1985; Rose, cited in Plumwood 2006, p. 127). In country relationships between human and nature, culture and species are entwined, emanating laws and practices (see Kinnane 2002; Langton 2002; Rose 1996, 2000; B.R. Smith 2005; Stanner 1979; Weir 2012). Country holds inscriptive and interpretive practices that are able to be retrieved from the landscape and are not constrained as binaries (Rumsey 1994). The metaphysics of country extend beyond such practices to a vast world-and-life view that has powerful agency able to elicit Dreamings, totemic geographies, embedded knowledges and non-linear deep time (see James 2015; McGrath & Jebb 2015; Moreton-Robinson 2003; Paton 2015; Rose 2000; Tonkinson 2011; Weir 2012) that can be independent from colonization.

Given that country is an entity with its own right having powerful agency, my interest lies on the question of the genderization of country and if country commands gendered cultural practices. There is gendered men's and women's business; for example, reproduction, anatomy, ceremonies, taboos, hunting, conflicts, access to country (Maher 1999; Robertson, Demosthenous & Demosthenous 2005; Rose 2000; Toussaint 2004) that provides distinct gendered social division. Country facilitates connections to the past, to ancestors, and triggers physical and emotional responses and determines cultural practices (Cameron 2016; Lehman 2006; Torpey Hurst 2015), some of which can vary between and within genders (see Breen & Summers 2006) and can be influenced by gendered sacred landscapes (Evans 2019; Liljeblad & Verschuuren 2019). Cultural practices that create cultural objects can embody a sense of gender roles (Lee in Cockerill 2018) and in *lutruwita* country; for example, shell necklace and basket weaving traditions are the domain of *loonner* (Greeno & Gough 2014; Nichols 2017; TMAG 2009). Although gendered country, men's and women's business and gendered cultural practices exist (some of which are traditional and some revived), there is a danger of taking an essentialist view of the genderization of country and cultural practices. Even though Indigenous Peoples perceive an alternative rendering of the use of essentialism relating to connection to country (Smith 1999), space must be given for decolonizing modes of recreation of culture. Cultural practices and customs impart knowledge of country when the holistic philosophy of connection to country is understood (Everett 2017).

Methodology: casting decolonizing clubs on country

As I decolonize the position that men cannot weave baskets in *lutruwita* country, I acknowledge that my own Blaq Dharug body responds to the power and agency of country in a way that may not conform to *palawa* norms. I recognize that the application of critical and political theory can be complex and contradictory (Smith 1999) and that the deconstruction of fixed notions of gender through queering may have implications for those where gender differences matter (Johnson & Hendersen 2005). As I apply critical and political theory to country and *nokegerrer* practice, I am decolonizing my mind through my methodology as an ethical, ontological and political exercise (Ndlovu-Gatsheni 2017). I am exercising my Indigeneity, self-determining how I identify as a Queer "First Person" and pursuing my culturally framed understanding of country and *nokegerrer* practice (Kunnie & Goduka 2006; O'Sullivan 2017). As I use an Indigenous methodology, supported by kinship and agency of country, to collaborate with *palawa* and *lutruwita*, I am facilitating culturally appropriate narratives (see Evans 2019; Verschuuren 2019) about Queer Indigenous identity. Through this decolonizing enquiry, I am reversing cultural metanarratives and deconstructing the cultural discourse (Arnold 2018) of *nokegerrer*, so as to grapple the problematic whilst respecting the position of *palawa* and myself in this research (Cariño 2005; Pulani Louis 2007).

In order to employ a decolonizing methodology to respond to the proposition that men cannot weave baskets, I will apply critical and political theory to country, whilst reflecting on the cultural safety of gay *palawa* men who desire developing their own *nokegerrer* practice. My enquiry is a wicked problem (see Brown, Harris & Russell 2010; Sheehan 2011) caught in the tensions between decolonizing aspirations for some to restore traditional roles, rights and responsibilities (Smith 1999) and others who wish to decolonize the Queer Native body and recover their specific tribal gender and sexuality (Clark 2015; Driskill 2010; Finley 2011). Wicked problems require multiple tools and perspectives to disentangle colonial foundational concepts and elucidate Indigenous values (see Brown et al 2010; Sheehan 2011). I will use "clubs" (critical and political theories) as tools to create perspective as I explore my proposition. In *lutruwita* country, *panner* and *loonner* use clubs to hunt, and thus it is an appropriate non-gendered metaphor.

Country is a reflection of our bodies (Bawaka Country et al 2014; Evans 2019; Lee 2017) and clubs reflect how our bodies work in country. My decolonizing methodology involves testing what clubs may be used to frame up the proposition that men can weave baskets and, if so, can they be ranked in their applicability? As I use these clubs, I will align them as they may lie in country, as a method for teasing out decolonizing insights. It is important for me to reflect on the pluralism of country (see McGrath 2015; Rose 2000). Country has distance and perspective (see James 2015; Paton 2015); therefore, I need distance and perspective to answer the question. My methodology is about positive relations to country (see Kinnane 2002; Langton 2002; Rose 1996; B.R. Smith 2005) and using inclusive clubs to identify potential boundaries where colonization intersects with country. I am using my Blaq body as orientation for the clubs, and country as a mirror to both my body and the clubs. In addressing this wicked problem, I will cast the following clubs on country: queer theory, queer ecology, ecofeminism and nature conservation using my decolonizing and Indigenous methodologies.

There are many examples of ways in which the diverse Indigenous Peoples of the world use decolonizing methodologies to redress the colonizing effects on their sovereignty and Indigeneity. Decolonizing methodologies have been used to empirically investigate the effects of heteronormative and heteropatriarchy settler-colonialism on queer theory and queer politics (Greensmith & Giwa 2013). Decolonizing discourses on sexuality have been used to challenge heteropatriarchy and biopower by aligning Native and Queer studies (Finley 2011). Queer theory has been applied to extend understandings of colonialism and Indigenous sexualities in Australia (Clark 2015). Further, there has been an invitation for Native studies scholars to expand their work to integrate queer theory and to interrogate Queer and Queer of color critique, as it has the potential to unsettle settler-colonialism (Finley 2011; Smith 2010). Viewing country through a postcolonial lens, the expressivist philosophy of Ngarrindjeri Yannarumi or "speaking as country" has been operationalized to deliver nonhumanist nature conservation (Bignall et al 2016, p. 457). As country is "continually co-created by both human and non-human agents", the application of more-than-human nature research can expand the conception of how country co-produces knowledge (Wright et al 2012, p. 39).

As I proceed into this enquiry I visualize my methodology as a form of weaving. I see the longitudinal threads of critical and political enquiry (warp) being tested and shaped by the weft of the clubs. The action of my weaving creates a mixed voice of academic enquiry and my reflexive Blaq body as I use the clubs to explore my playing field.

Results: queering the clubs and country

I now turn to my first club, queer theory, and cast it on country. Queer theory has been called out as needing reinvigoration to reclaim its potential to spark surprise (Halperin 2003). It is the role of queer theory to dislocate binaries of personhood, and value conceptual elasticity, whilst rejecting labeling philosophies and recognizing that language fails to definitively represent phenomena (Adams & Holman Jones 2008; Hird 2004; Nicholas 2006; Smith 2000; K. Watson 2005; Yep, Lovaas & Elia 2003). Queer theorists revel in symbolic disorder, pollute established social conventions and diffuse hegemonic categories and classifications (Baudrillard 2001; Haraway 2003). Simultaneously, queer theory revels in the political commitment required to deconstruct the natural and normal by focusing on how bodies may serve as sites of social change as they grapple with power systems (Kong, Mahoney & Plummer 2002; Smith 2003; Yep & Elia 2007; Yep et al 2003). Queer theory is a politic of transgression that is anti-foundationalist and working to oppose fixed identities (Alexander 2008; Baudrillard 2001). "Queer involves the open mesh of possibilities, gaps, overlaps, dissonances and resonances, lapses and excesses of meaning (that occur) when constituent elements of anyone's gender, of anyone's sexuality aren't made (or *can't be* made) to signify monolithically" (Sedgwick 1993, p. 8). Others extend queer theory to embrace Queer inhumanism: a process of dehumanization of self so as to reconstruct what it means to be human, a blurring of line between self and the other to open up myriads of alterities (Anzaldúa 2012; Luciano & Chen 2015; Stone 1991).

This club flies deep into country, ricocheting off established norms and shaking the foundations of cultural revival from a traditional viewpoint. It is difficult to see where this club will settle and eventually lie in country. On one hand, it speaks strongly to the notion of country as an entity that is non-binary, inclusive and inviting of human interactions that care for and acknowledge its power and interconnectedness. On the other hand, it wields a strong and noisy trajectory into what some would see as the heart of country: Indigenous identity. Perhaps this club lays on the margin between non-gendered Indigeneity and Indigenous identity underpinned by gendered cultural practices. This margin is a slippery one, the moving site of colonization where Blaqs chose this club to decolonize themselves either individually or collectively. However, this club opens up the interiority of country for possibilities for engagement, reciprocation and co-creation of agency. The queer theory club is a distinctive club, one that may work for some and not others, or one that may be chosen on the basis of identity that is free from gender and sexuality. This club does not need to be colonized: it is already decolonizing by nature.

The second club that I will cast on country is queer ecology. Queer ecology aims to develop sexual politics and theory as a constructive corrective to redefine the intersections between sex and nature, where the influences of sexual relations, environmental politics and the natural world collide (Schnabel 2014; Seymour 2015). Queer ecologies can "bring unique insights on who or what expresses agency and counts as a subject" (Schnabel 2014, p. 11). Queer ecology pushes the boundaries on subject–object dichotomizations, strives for greater inclusion, and privileges discursive and linguistic notions of agency to the neglect of material relations and processes (Schnabel 2014). The hierarchy of humans over animals is challenged in queer ecology where "natureculture" is viewed as inseparable, therefore providing scope for subjectivity and agency formation (Schnabel 2014, p. 12). Further, queer ecology contests Western heteronormative subjectivities so as to express the potential queering of "natureculture" and its agency (see Mortimer-Sandilands & Erickson 2010). In queer ecology, Queer identity is perceived as discursive; bringing unnecessary human action and identity into the landscape and conceptualizing and weighting human relations (Alaimo 2010; Schnabel 2014). The exploitation of Indigenous Peoples and the environment at the hands of heterosexually driven capitalism is critiqued in queer ecologies; followed by the corrective requirement for recognition of the important role Indigenous People have in addressing environmental change (Schnabel 2014; Sturgeon 2010; Unger 2010).

The queer ecology club is attracted to the openness of country and supports its agency and inclusion of others who may want to weave their own personal response to country. But this club is not interested in material relations, particularly gendered and/or cultural practices and may not be supportive of Queer identity on country. The queer ecology club may be deficient in human Indigeneity, weighted with strong interests in restorative aspects of nature conservation or conditional values that Indigenous People can bring to such restoration. This club also does not travel far in country and falls a little flat in its trajectory, as it does not have much power. The undervaluing and dismissal of cultural practice and identity inhibits this club, and does not provide the muscle required for it to fly in the wide-open possibilities that it has for country. However, the queer ecology club may be useful for those who are truly free in their Indigeneity and not concerned about gendered cultural practice. This club may work for those who are responding to the agency of country individually or with those who support them. This club works for the "free spirits" who may not be concerned with cultural safety or require support to develop cultural practices as their identity is not creating a barrier for them. I am not sure that queer ecology club is one suitable for Blaqs, as we have vested interests in country and identity. Although, country may be open to this club, if those that throw it can bring their own decolonizing power to it.

I will now cast my third club on to country, ecofeminism. Ecofeminism is feminist environmentalism: a philosophy that is concerned with the epistemologies that avoid dualistic divisions between human and non-human life whilst rejecting the commodification of biodiversity (Cannella & Manuelito 2008; Plumwood 1991). Concerned with the connection between women and nature, ecofeminism implicates Western enlightenment along with patriarchy and colonialism as culprits for the exploitation and plundering of nature and women (Shiva 1995; Wane & Chandler 2002). Contemporary ecofeminism investigates the deep conceptual divides between female/male, body/mind and spirit/matter to comprehend how gender contributes to the roles of culture and economics in ecological crises (Plumwood 2003). Within the ecofeminism discourse, there is a counter narrative (spiritual ecofeminism) that embraces Indigenous values such as "Mother Earth" where women are perceived as having closer bonds to Earth than men through their shared reproductive abilities (Wilson 2005). Critics argue that spiritual ecofeminism has appropriated Aboriginal culture and spirituality, therefore deepening the commodification and exploitation of Indigenous Peoples and their culture (Smith 1993, 1997; Wilson 2005). Ecofeminism is a contested philosophy.

Spiritual ecofeminists, who choose to embrace women and nature connections, disagree with social ecofeminists, who maintain a separation between woman/man/nature/culture and argue that these categorizations are social constructs that perpetuate the devaluation of women and nature (Wilson 2005). Ecofeminism also incorporates "native feminist spirituality" that combines Indigenism and ecofeminism. Native feminist spirituality advocates for native women's cultural rights, challenges male-dominated tribal politics and supports native women to exercise their subjective agency and reclaim their historical matrilineal/matrifocal roles (Jaimes Guerrero 2003).

The ecofeminist club is complicated, contested and unbalanced. On a fundamental level, the calling out of colonization and its neoliberalist plundering of nature, cultures and women is a powerful aspect of this club. However, the ecofeminist club becomes problematic involving its disagreements relating to the woman/nature binary/non-binary and Indigenous misappropriation. Further, the native feminist spirituality aspect of this club may not be helpful to

Blaqs as their identity and desires to patriciate in specific cultural practices may be counter to historical revivalism of matriarchy. Although, this club may be useful if Indigenous matriarchies were agreeable to share cultural practices with those of other Indigenous gender identities. I am not sure if the ecofeminist club even gets air as it is unstable. Country may see this club as too humanistic, noisy and jarring in its incongruent interests.

The last club that I will cast on to country is nature conservation. Nature conservation is a broad philosophy and ecologically based movement that aims to conserve nature and biodiversity. As a political theory and ethic, it has disparate value sets that can range from biocentrism to anthropocentrism, and thus creates space and tension for the contestation of human/nature/culture interfaces. It is recognized that Indigenous Peoples hold an environmental ethic and philosophy that is Indigenous, and have different needs and abilities to conserve country and its biodiversity from those of colonists (Langton 2003; Nietschmann 1992). Caring for country, caring as country, and speaking as country are vital ethical actions for Indigenous People, where responsibilities and obligations to belong, co-become and love country continue to happen (see Bawaka Country et al 2013; Bignall et al 2016; James 2015; Rose 2000). The unique relationship and interactions that Indigenous Peoples have with country that enhance and preserve ecosystems have been theorized as "kincentric ecology"; a philosophy of traditional conservation (Salmon 2000, p. 1328). Kincentric ecology illuminates the interconnectedness between Indigenous People and their country, by extending and situating ecology and its ecosystem to include all life, ancestors, kin, nature and their interactions (Salmon 2000). Despite the recognition that Indigenous Peoples have philosophies and means to conserve country, mechanisms to conserve nature through protected area management continue to socially exclude and marginalize Indigenous Peoples worldwide, and are enabled by historic and perpetuating colonization (Colchester 2004). There is a strong critique of the failings of nature conservation to recognize and fully engage with Indigenous Peoples and our values. There are multiple discourses on the failings of global conservation institutions, conventions and movements to recognize post-colonial power relations that limit Indigenous agency (see Dowie 2009; Liljebald & Verschuuren 2019; Reimerson 2013). In *lutruwita* country, the politics of nature conservation are embedded in wilderness values and stubbornly adhere to human/nature dualisms and attempts to co-opt *palawa* and *palawa* cultural heritage in arguments for selective conservation efforts (see Evans 2016, 2019; Evans, Kirkpatrick & Bridle 2018; Lee 2015, 2016a, 2017).

The nature conservation club is divisive and conditional. If this club is thrown by Indigenous people, free of colonizers and colonizing agents, allowing the love for and from country to flourish, this club may work. Under the right protected area management and decolonizing conditions, this club may facilitate full Indigenous relations with country. However, the nature conservation club is silent in its answering of the question about cultural practice, its genderization, or the genderization of country. This club may not be of much use to Blaqs. Perhaps the kincentric ecology philosophy aspect of this club may be beneficial; however, it currently lacks definition in relation to the boundaries for gender, cultural practices and traditionalist revivalism. Although the nature conservation club has positive qualities such as addressing biodiversity loss, enhancing sustainability and closing the human/nature gap, it is a very dangerous club in the hand of colonizers, as it perpetuates colonizing effects. I doubt that the nature conservation club could be decolonized, as it is proliferated with the vested interests of colonizers.

Discussion: can men weave baskets and is country Queer?

By casting the clubs (queer theory, queer ecology, ecofeminism and nature conservation) on to country, I queered and decolonized them. I am left with no definitive answer as to which club is most suited to answering my proposition that men can weave baskets as they are all inclusive in some way. However, the queer theory club has potential for men to weave baskets if supported by cultural safety. Similarly, the ecofeminist club may support men weaving baskets if they can gain the support of Indigenous matriarchies. The queer ecology and the nature conservation clubs are the least useful. Middle ground can be found by respecting all clubs and recognizing that the process of casting them on country has been useful in highlighting that country is decolonizing in itself. Country only cares about your connection, your kinship and reciprocity. There is no right or wrong in the seeking out of what country thinks of the proposition of men weaving baskets, as country neither cares about my proposition, nor feels that it has been queered. Country gives the fibers from the grasses that it grows; the growing of grasses and collection of them for fiber used in *nokegerrer* are not predicated by gender. Country is all about love; burning country is a reflection of this love. We know country as Blaqs, Blaks, as colonizers, as decolonizers and as Queers, but do we know country as Queer?

Country is trans-dimensional and complex, as is its agency and its relations with the Dreamings (Moreton-Robinson 2003; Samson 2001). In country, a powerful creator and ancestral beings both shaped and are the land, are omnipresent, and provide potent ongoing impacts (McGrath 2015; Neidjie et al 1985; Plumwood 2010; Shiva 1995). The Dreaming has intricate ontologies, is metaphysical and dynamic (James 2015; Rose 2000; Stanner 1979). "Dreaming is the source which makes possible all maps and celebrations – life in its variety, particularity, and fecundity" (Rose 2000, p. 44). The Dreamings tell of ancestral beings changing form and gender and creation stories where the supernatural powers of flora, fauna, landforms, spirits and ancestors interconnect (Lehman 2006; Moreton-Robinson 2003). Dreaming law requires that "no species, group, or country is 'boss' for another; each adheres to its own law" (Rose 2000, p. 45).

The colonization of *lutruwita* has produced "gross dispossession, disempowerment and disruption of traditional Aboriginal culture" (Lehman 2006) and has impacted on the knowledges and sharing of the Dreamings and creation stories. The Dreaming story of the creation of *palawa* man and all the country by the creation spirit *Moinee* was told by "clever-man" Woorady and recorded by colonizers at contact (Lehman 2006; E. Wilson 2008). Given that the initial written accounts of the Dreamings and creation stories of *palawa* are those by male colonizers, how can we be sure that "clever-women" did not orate Dreamings and creation stories relating to *loonner* or gender fluid creation spirits, landscapes or sacred geographies? Although the transference of *palawa* Dreamings and creation stories has been impacted by colonization, in contemporary contexts the Dreamings are open to interpretation and change by individuals through their own dreams and lived experiences (Moreton-Robinson 2003).

I suggest that country, through collaborative and personal Dreamings can be queered and is able to invite Queer connections and relations with it. Country has characteristics that are consistent with the principles of queer theory. Country, and its relationship with the Dreamings, are complex phenomena (see Ganesharajah 2009; Graham 2009; Rose 2000) and, consistent with queer theory, language fails to definitively represent its complexities, conceptual elasticity, non-binary, more-than-human qualities (Adams & Holman Jones 2008; Hird 2004; Nicholas 2006; Smith 2000; K. Watson 2005; Yep et al 2003). Country allows our bodies to connect to it and deconstruct ourselves by focusing on our bodies and our unique Dreamings as sites of social change as we grapple with power systems that dictate cultural practices. Country is open to possibilities, allowing our Queer identity to come in, and invites a Queer connection. Country is a place where the lines between human/country are blurred and receptive to alternative connections – a Queer connection. Country, therefore, is a place where men could seek to weave baskets.

I now turn to the proposition that men can weave baskets. *panner* participation in and development of *nokegerrer* practices as an enactment of identity may be more important for some than exercising Queerness, or vice versa. In order to decolonize *nokegerrer*, *palawa* regardless of their gender or sexual identities or Queerness may seek out opportunities to make baskets. If a *panner* practices *nokegerrer*, under the support and direction of a *loonner*, with cultural safety, then they are both challenging the colonizing paradigm that *nokegerrer* is a closed female practice, and thus are committing a decolonizing act. This can also be interpreted as a Queer act since it is removing binaries, allowing fluidity of gender and reinforcing decolonized valuing of matriarchy. This is possible if *loonner* chose to do so. *loonner* have the power to decolonize through their own agency as Blak females. There is precedent for such powers as argued by Aunty Dr Pasty Cameron: "*palawa* women are the sole custodians of our cultures, stories and spirituality, and due to colonization our community has emerged as predominantly matriarchal society" (Cameron 1994, pp. 65, 66). *palawa* matriarchal authority is also positioned by Matson-Green (1994, p. 70): "*palawa* women have had, as a matter of right, a great deal of power, both in traditional and contemporary society".

There are cases of males learning basket making from *loonner* elders in *lutruwita* country (see Elliot 2018; Nichols 2017). Aunty Verna Nichols, when questioned about the appropriateness of males learning basket making (kelp baskets), gave the following account:

> They say there's women's business and then there's men's business, and while I agree, I have grandchildren, but they are nearly all boys, and so how am I going to show that family because there are no girls? So, I have asked a group of women when we were together how they felt about it because I had shown a grandson how to make water carriers and why I had shown them. They agreed that they had felt that it was alright because we have to retain it we can't let it slip back and go to sleep again. If we don't have the girls, I really don't mind the men knowing how to do it. It's important and there are some really great basket weavers – men in other Aboriginal communities. That is a must, I don't care what practice it is; the elders need to pass it on and that's how it goes. And I suppose maybe it doesn't have to be the elders as long as it's instilled in our young fellas and we continue to make it and that way our ancestors are not forgotten. We make them

proud and they can look back and in acknowledgement of what has been passed
down and feel proud that they have this object.

Nichols 2017, n.p.

Aunty Verna's view makes it possible for *panner* to not only make baskets but
to participate in other cultural practices with or without eldership guidance.
However, her position brings caveats, that objects are made with respect for the
cultural practice itself and in honor of acknowledging the ancestors with the
intent of keeping cultural practices alive. The opening of cultural practices to all
gender identities (*panner* or *loonner*) perhaps is a predictor for its survival. For
example, basket weaving on Norfolk Island has been a Pitcairn women-only
craft, inherited from their Polynesian foremothers (Mühlhäuser 2015; Reynolds
2019). The craft has recently been opened to Pitcairn men to save the practice as
few women remained. Men openly weave and plait and now one of the Island's
finest weavers is male (Mühlhäuser 2015; Reynolds 2019). Like *loonner* weavers,
Pitcairn weavers feel connections and a sense of continuity with their ancestors
when they weave (see Grace, cited in Greeno 2009; Kleiner 2009; Shaw, cited in
Greeno 2009; TMAG 2009).

The obligation to honor ancestors is important in the continuation and revival
of *palawa* cultural practices. Country is the power source and medium, co-
created with *palawa* – inviting connections with the ancestors and country (see
Evans 2019). Uncle Jim Everett eloquently explains the production of cultural
practice predicated upon connection to country: "Cultural practice is really the
product of what people understand of their philosophy [country] and how they
enact that. So, philosophy [country] is the core, culture is really the product"
(Everett 2017, n.p.). Aunty Vicki West's account of her *nokegerrer* practice
reflects this ethic of making, being and connecting to country and her ancestors
"the country sort of informs you, it's part who you are and it's also important to
connect back with your ancestors" (West 2017, n.p.).

Conclusion: the Blaq voice

This essay has not set out to provide a definitive answer of whether men can
participate and develop their own *nokegerrer* practice. Rather, it is precursory to
establishing the explicatory boundaries for men to develop their own *nokegerrer*
practice in *lutruwita* country. This essay sets the conditions for the proposition
that men may weave baskets by using critical scholarship to frame its potential

theoretical thresholds. Within this task, I have been mindful of matters of cultural safety and the contemporary discrimination of Queer Indigenous People (see Browning 2018; Burin 2016; Chisholm 2018; Kerry 2014, 2017; Maxwell 2018; Wriggs 2007). At the outset, I intended to interview my gay brother to bring his Queer voice to this exploration, but realized that it was not culturally safe for him or me to do so as conditions for theoretical approaches had not been met. Therefore, I acknowledge that the voice of Blaqs (beyond my own) is absent in this enquiry and requires further attention. There is a missing club that should be cast onto country in future research: the voices of Blaqs and those who wish to pursue gendered cultural practices outside their cisgender.

I propose that country has qualities that are Queer, and agency is able to invite Queering of oneself and Queer connections to it through personal Dreamings. However, for cultural safety, Queer *panner* and *loonner* may need to reach out and connect with other Blaqs globally, and seek support to develop non-cisgendered cultural practices as First Peoples. This way *panner* and *loonner*, like all Indigenous People under the United Nations Declaration on the Rights of Indigenous Peoples (UNDRIP), Article 1, would be discovering, recuperating and self-affirming their Indigeneity (Verschuuren 2019). However, it is paramount for individuals to be culturally safe on country and in their cultural practice. The Dreaming may be the mechanism by which individuals locate themselves in country and within their practice. Here through their Dreamings, men may weave baskets respectfully whilst acknowledging the ancestors and with the intent of keeping the practice of *nokegerrer* alive.

Part Two

Violence and Safety

3

Black panopticon: who wins with lateral violence?

Jacinta Vanderfeen (*trawlwulwuy*)

We have a history of being put under the microscope, in the same way a scientist looks at any insect. The ones doing the looking are giving themselves the power to define.

Mita 1989, p. 30

Introduction

Colonization brought with it real consequences and impacts for my people, the *trawlwulwuy* people of *tebrakunna* country. Our people were subject to great sorrows; our colonization was of the worst order and in the aftermath of our genocide the injury to us continued, as our status was declared extinct across the world. *lutruwita* (Tasmania, Australia) was inhabited by our people for more than 40,000 years prior to British invasion in 1803 (Ryan 2012). As a *trawlwulwuy* woman from *tebrakunna* country, from the north-east coast of *lutruwita*, I position myself as an insider, as a proud *pakana*[1] woman whose past, present and future situates me. As an Aboriginal early career researcher, I honor with deep respect our people, and our culture. While I cannot speak on any of my peoples' behalf, I can speak for my own.

I know that our people were dispossessed and murdered as we resisted colonization (Ryan 2012). Violence and bloodshed were extensive and brutal, as was the loss of our lands and the impacts on our traditional economies. The colonizers encroached on our hunting lands, cleared native bush and dramatically

---

[1] *pakana* and *palawa* are terms used to describe Tasmanian Aboriginal people as a collective, I identify as a *pakana* woman and will use this term throughout this essay.

altered our traditional landscape and Country (Cameron & Miller 2011). The deliberate and systematic disempowerment of *pakana* conceded almost every part of our lives, leading to our dependency on the colonizers for food, clothing and shelter (Reynolds 2012; Ryan 2012). Within a short period of less than 50 years, only 47 of our people were recognized as survivors of our obliteration from point of first contact (Reynolds 2012). Our ancestors were held on Wybalenna, an offshore prison located on Flinders Island (part of the group of northern Tasmanian off-shore islands known as the Furneaux Group), specifically built by the colonial government to house our families as the remnants of war (Cameron & Miller 2011; Ryan 2012).

At the same time as the physical assaults on our bodies are occurring, there are assaults within our minds that reflect the invisible colonizing structures that reinforce our lack of humanity and amplify violence in its space (Marks 2013). These colonizing structures are buttressed in our minds and recognized in our social interactions, where we take on the perspectives of the others (the colonizers). It is in this prison of our minds that we anticipate the actions of the colonizer and thus adjust ours accordingly – this is our oppression. Yet these structures do not hold our values of moral and ethical worth – these are owned and dispensed by the colonizers.

By removing us from our homelands, taking our families and isolating us from our cultural practices, our colonizers inserted surveillance into the devastation they had already caused. As they built their fortress infrastructure to underpin their superiority, through making and keeping records of us, we became the objects of enquiry, intrigue, monitoring, scrutiny and observation, and not sovereigns in our own lands. Surveillance brings to mind Jeremy Bentham's prison architecture of the *panopticon* in the late eighteenth century, with the structure described as an "all-seeing place" (Jesperson, cited in Mungwini 2013, p. 344). This all-seeing place, the panopticon, has been used by philosopher Michel Foucault (1979) to illustrate the power relationships between discipline, control, space and surveillance. Wybalenna, then, became a matter of the panopticon principles of surveillance and power intersecting with the structures of colonization to further the control over *pakana* lives. However, the panopticon is not generally thought of as a tool with a specific edge honed especially for Indigenous Peoples. There is a gap in the literature as to knowing the localized effects of surveillance and power on colonized people under the panopticon gaze. I want to raise in this essay a case study of my people – the people of *lutruwita* – regarding the impacts and outcomes of a *black panopticon*.

Colonization maintains a hierarchical model of power that allows the dominant society to impose upon minorities a series of networks that invests itself in every aspect of people's lives (Foucault 1979; Marwick 2012). This form of oppression, creating inequality and marginalization (Acker 2006), manifests itself as a loss and abuse of – and re-distribution of power relations against – *pakana* people. This iteration of power has enabled lateral violence to surface as a direct result of colonization, which is a form of violence exercised internally between colonized Indigenous Peoples (Bennett 2014; Clark, Augoustinos & Malin 2017). Lateral violence is characterized as silent and unassuming, public and private (Fforde et al 2013), overt and covert (Langton 2008), debilitating and toxic (Koch 2011). In *lutruwita* lateral violence is present, yet its underlying mechanisms are yet to be investigated. Cameron and Miller (2011) allude to *lutruwita* lateral violence, by sketching out the effects of power imbalances portrayed in familial inter-relational conflict.

However, I wish to go further and characterize lateral violence in *lutruwita* by defining the concept of the black panopticon and how it has operated in communities to reinforce the structures of colonization among ourselves. I do this by first describing the concept of lateral violence and how this is viewed from the lens of a black panopticon using a decolonizing framework, setting out to illustrate how the black panopticon is a Western construct, embodying white colonial power and control relations. I then define the black panopticon by applying decolonizing theory to reveal its colonizing impacts and lift the veil on lateral violence between *pakana*. Once defined, I then characterize the experience of lateral violence in *lutruwita* and describe the exclusion and oppression within the spaces of the black panopticon. Next, I proceed to expose the impacts of lateral violence on Aboriginal identity validation and the role that colonization plays in identity politics and its ongoing processes. Finally, I suggest Indigenous methodologies to decolonize lateral violence and its habitation in the black panopticon by embracing the axiology of Whiteness Theory and Indigenous Standpoint Theory.

As I work through peeling back the complex layers of lateral violence, to expose its colonizing effects, I am also centering and defining the term "black panopticon" to reflect power dynamics that occur between Indigenous Peoples as we confront our dispossession and inequity. I do this to differentiate the subtle power relations unique to the black panopticon, compared with the familiar Western (white) panopticon (Manokha 2018). I believe that the black panopticon houses unpredictable power and deficit discourses that are exercised between Indigenous Peoples. This is distinct from the stable power of white surveillance in the white panopticon (Galič, Timan & Koops 2016). My purpose here is to characterize lateral violence and how it is shaped, disseminated and sustained under the black panopticon in order to identify methods to decolonize it.

Defining the black panopticon

In the eighteenth century, the English philosopher, jurist and reformer Jeremy Bentham worked for many years designing the physical prison structure of the panopticon and refining its architectural and psychological intent (Semple 1993). In his sketches the prison is a circular building composed of cells on the outer walls and an observation tower in the center of the building, designed to facilitate eternal surveillance of those placed in the outer rooms (Bozovic 1995). The occupants in the outer wall cells were also invisible to each other, which inferred that inmates self-regulated their behaviors, as they were constantly unaware of when or who was watching them (Semple 1993).

For Foucault (1979), the occupants located in the outer wall cells were the object of surveillance and information, meaning that those in the cells never really knew who was exercising the central power from the observation space. This notion of never knowing by whom and when one is being surveilled is designed to be oppressive (Garland 1995). This form of visibility was described "as a trap" (Foucault 1977, p. 200), whereby the "all-seeing power" is organized for the dominant, overseeing gaze (Foucault 1980, p. 152).

Decolonizing the panopticon is a way to understand how colonization has given lateral violence a platform in Tasmanian Aboriginal communities. The curved walls of Bentham's physical prison are replicated in the spherical gaze generated from within the black panopticon. In decolonizing the panopticon, I describe the inner sanctum of *lutruwita* communities. Power is programmed in the asymmetry of the panoptical gaze, encasing *pakana* people in the outer wall cells, as well as in the central control tower. The central tower can be monitored by us, and equally it can be controlled by us. The dual function of power demonstrates that both those in the outer cells and those in the central tower are watched, and Foucault describes the genius of its design as a "mechanism of power that is reduced to its ideal form" (Foucault 1979, p. 205).

In *lutruwita*, *pakana* are the entirety of the population within the black panopticon. Just as in Bentham's original design, we are both prisoners and keepers, the seeing and the surveilled all housed together. However, the difference between a Western and a black panopticon is that the formulative control is still with the colonizers and outside of us. Power still lies with the colonizer. The purpose of the Western panopticon was to manage self-abnormality, or deviance, among its own population (Monaghan 2013). Thus, the black panopticon provides another layer of control from its ability to reinforce colonizing structures. By this, *pakana* populations are policing ourselves, not to correct or manage deviance, but rather to aid and perpetuate white control over us. The black panopticon thus works as a promise to favor some Indigenous Peoples – the observer guards – while exposing that lie through colonizing gains of total control of both the *pakana* observer and the observed.

The process of colonization inflicts new violence: people in unequal societies trust each other less and increased identity violence becomes common as people's sensitivities and requirement for safety are unmet through the trauma of colonization processes (Wilkinson 2005). Oppression thrives under the rule of colonization, amplifying the power of the panopticon, in the centrality of its surveillance in which it is housed (Galič et al 2016). Surveillance-as-oppression is given a fresh dais when *pakana* mimic colonial forms of control over each other. Colonization has created mistrust between *pakana* peoples, while furthering cultural disruption that dislodge our traditional cultural ways of being, knowing and doing. Under the colonizing gaze, the panoptic purview allows the controller to "see everything, everyone, all the time" (Foucault 2006, p. 52). Everyone can and will be watched; this is how lateral violence can be perpetrated in black communities.

The Western panopticon is the governing and roving eye, the constant stare at marginalized people that pushes us to the periphery of Australian society. In the black panopticon, surveillance is turned upon us by ourselves to inflict oppression against each other. As *pakana*, it seems our only choices are to act collectively or individually to subject other *pakana* to a form of disciplinary power and its constant use of control, surveillance and supervision (Foucault 1979). The black panopticon is powerful, extending into the whole social body, and exercising a range of extensive networks catching and entangling many, consistent with Foucault's (1972) understanding of surveillance power. Surveillance power, as discipline, is perpetrated through denial, exclusion and marginalization (Foucault 1972). In other words, lateral violence is a result of internal black surveillance that gives power to the colonizers by producing the illusion that we are governing our own norms and behaviors rather than embedding white ones. Monaghan (2013, p. 492) would refer to this as "racializing surveillance" that "fulfils prefabricated stereotypes and prejudice by colonial authorities and produces a social hierarchy defined by normative standards and signifiers of whiteness".

The black panopticon becomes a vehicle for power relations that manifest into lateral violence. Lateral violence is then best described as the action of Indigenous Peoples expressing their anger to those who also are the victims of unequal power relations. The outcome of lateral violence is oppressed people turning on themselves and violating each other with overt physical and emotional violence and/or covert, inward deflection ("black gaslighting") (Bailey 2020; Clark et al 2017; Langton 2008). The matrix of the panopticon pushes the panoptic eye to become embedded within communities. This pervaded community gaze is conditioned from the wider sets of power and knowledge used by colonizers to shift the gaze to self-surveillance, as individuals and communities begin to subject themselves and others to scrutiny.

Living inside the black panopticon ... lateral violence

Lateral violence is a core means of discipline under the black panopticon. It is important for us to understand the foundations of lateral violence as part of the suite of colonizing tactics against us. It is equally important that this understanding be found by us, not for us. Lateral violence has been defined to describe the violence and disruptive practices that occur within oppressed groups and is directed towards each other (see Clark et al 2017; Fforde et al 2013; Roberts, Demarco & Griffin 2009). Colonizing spaces carve out the power and control that creates exclusion and oppression of *pakana*, where Koch (2011) argues that governments have created an environment for the conception of lateral violence through their lack of recognition of Indigenous rights and turning marginal groups against each other. Lateral violence has emerged as a subject of academic interest (Clark & Augoustinos 2015; Dudgeon, Garvey & Pickett 2000; Langton 2008), as its prevalence, drivers and impacts within and between communities are yet to be fully defined. Although, evidence has revealed that lateral violence impacts the social and emotional wellbeing of Aboriginal people (Clark et al 2017; Memmott et al 2001).

The former Social Justice Commissioner Mick Gooda (2011a) has called out lateral violence as a difficult conversation (even for himself), but necessary for communities to increase wellbeing and understand the effects of colonization. Such conversations can and should be occurring within our communities, allowing the experiences of our people to be illuminated to understand the debilitating effects of lateral violence and how it is conceptualized and dramatized in everyday life. Part of the exercise of responsibility towards sharing these experiences compels me to share mine: as an insider, a *pakana* community member, I have witnessed lateral violence.

There are three main ways in which lateral violence is created, used and leveraged through identity by *pakana* that distinguish the black panopticon. The first is the *questioning, governing and undermining of identity*; the second is the *guarding of identity by an Indigenous elite*, while the last is *denial of identity* (see Harris, Carlson & Poata-Smith 2013). Lateral violence in Tasmania is grounded in the effects of colonization, particularly the physical dispossession from Country from 1803 onwards – the wholesale removal of Indigenous People by white people from mainland Tasmania onto off-shore islands, such as the settlement at Wybalenna on Flinders Island (Ryan 2012). Colonial policies incurred further movements of *pakana* back to mainland Tasmania in the mid-1800s, although some families stayed behind on Flinders (Ryan 2012). Families, since colonization began, have been divided by geography, policy and physical restraint.

Questioning, governing and undermining identity

The fractured nature of physical dislocation and genocide often inhibits the ability to conduct accurate genealogy to show proof of identity or demonstrate cultural practices or even retain the knowledge of *pakana* ancestry, such that *pakana*'s colonization experience was so horrific as to be falsely declared extinct as peoples in 1876 (Lee 2019). Into this picture, *pakana* suffer the questioning of identity from both black and white. From the white, the question of whether *pakana* could exist, given that schools all over the world taught of our false extinction (Reynolds 2006), has been a double burden as it asks to prove existence and identity at the same time. From the black, whether we have the right to our fullest lives in all their diversity.

Aboriginal contemporary identity is a construct of the black panopticon, because of its multi-faceted, complex interactions with social and historical constructs (Paradies 2006). The very question of identity and the politics of authenticity have "deep roots within colonial racism" (Sissons 2005, p. 43). Aboriginal identity has been used by governments to help guide and direct policies and actions for *pakana* people. Identity thus continues to be a political and legal platform, whereby implicit social approval is then given to the right to question it (Assante 2005). Monaghan (2013) goes further and suggests that the way governments govern identity is to achieve a "logic of elimination" (Wolfe

2006, p. 387), whereby colonization requires the removal of all traces of Indigenous People and culture in favor of colonizing narratives of dominance.

The Tasmanian example highlights what Monaghan (2013) sees as an endless process of Indigenous People either subject to or voluntarily engaging in Western societal rules, where the winner is always the colonizer. By this he explains that the purpose of a black panopticon and associated surveillance tools is to separate out blacks as either "good" or "bad", where the "good" can become enculturated as whites, while the "bad" are deemed to be unworthy of humanity: "Sorting between good and bad conduct based on racial distinction between whiteness and others, racializing surveillance simultaneously confirms notions of indigeneity as abnormal and illiberal, while disaggregating within Indigenous populations between worthy and unworthy life; those who can be transformed and those who can be killed" (Monaghan 2013, p. 492).

On this basis, lateral violence is a mechanism used by ourselves and learned through colonizing behaviors to sort ourselves into "good" or "bad" blacks. Those who are "bad" further suffer through the governing of identity, as it is the *pakana* responsibility within the black panopticon's central tower to now wield the power of conferring identity and acceptance – or taking it away. There is a link here between non-identity, or denial of it, and death noted by Monaghan (2013), where lateral violence is the weapon of both black and white to extinguish and sever a person's connection to family, place and community. This is the isolation of the outer walls – while we are all together within the arena of discipline, power and oppression (Foucault 1977), the effect of questioning and governing an identity enforces a separation of ourselves from each other and to our own identities.

In Tasmania, the black panopticon is an outstanding success. The level of distortion and dysfunction within the government policies that govern identity – known in Tasmania as an "eligibility" policy to participate in government-funded and sponsored programs that directly apply to *pakana* (Tasmanian Government 2020) – was of such gross magnitude that even the white conservative government addressed the imbalance of the policy in a sweeping change to the direction of Aboriginal affairs in Tasmania. On 21 January 2016, the former Premier of Tasmania, Will Hodgman, declared that "(s)omething is very wrong here" (Hodgman 2016, n.p.) when he referred to the issue of identity and recognition among our people. His speech went on to state that the "most recent Australian Bureau of Statistics from 2014 reported 25,845 Indigenous people in Tasmania. Yet, under the current Tasmanian Government policy, it's estimated that there are just 6,000 Indigenous Tasmanians" (Hodgman 2016, n.p.).

The governing of identity allows for a Western panopticon to set the vague rules as to what constitutes a *pakana* person to qualify as eligible (Tasmanian Government 2020). A veneer of Indigenous self-determination is then applied by allowing *pakana* organizations the right to choose and approve the individuals who want identity confirmed to participate in funded projects (Tasmanian Government 2020). The devolution of identity governance to *pakana* communities then becomes the tool and pathway to enable government-aided lateral violence or the bricks of the outer wall of the black panopticon that isolates *pakana*. This is achieved through black elitism.

Black elitism

The particular cruelty of lateral violence is that it is a colonizing tool that is un/consciously used by *pakana* to favor not any of us, but rather white privilege and control. The means of using ourselves to oppress our identities and rights also means that a *pakana* elite is created and maintained – those in the central tower who act to enforce a colonizing control through closely governing identity. In Tasmania, this control and power from the black panopticon's central tower has largely been exercised by an organization called the Tasmanian Aboriginal Centre (TAC). The TAC is the oldest and best-known organization for *pakana* rights, being first engaged with rights advocacy in the 1970s (Flanagan 2002; Ryan 1996).

However, in recent years some Aboriginal people and community groups, known and affiliated with the TAC, prided themselves on knowing exactly how everyone fitted into its network of extended family groups, and started the narrative of identity judgement. As funds from the Tasmanian government started to flow into communities to establish Aboriginal programs and services, the TAC offered incentives for people to "identify" as Aboriginal, according to their invitation (Marks 2013). *pakana* who tried to do so, and who were not affiliated with the TAC-aligned families and groups at this time, began to feel the pinch of ostracism as "contested" Aboriginal people through denial of identity and corroborating documents. Elder Aunty Patsy Cameron confirms the oppression by stating that that "many people had oral history but no documentary evidence of their Aboriginality. I just can't come to terms with the notion that people would want to claim Aboriginality when they are not" (Shine 2017, n.p.). Many people who come from familial lines that are contested by the TAC feel that they are "frozen out" and labeled as "paper blacks" (Marks 2013, p. 184).

Key activist and past leader of the TAC, Michael Mansell, has determined that in order to be recognized as a *pakana* person, they must: "show that ... their families, from every generation back to tribal, have always maintained their connection with being Aboriginal. So that excludes people who undoubtedly have Aboriginal descent but who have been brought up as white people.... If there's been a break in the generations, where someone lost contact, the Aboriginal community's view is ... you can't revive it" (Mansell, cited in Marks 2013, p. 185).

This position of elitism to choose whose experience of colonization counts and whose does not has been contested by the *pakana* academic Dr Greg Lehman, who acknowledges that his family did not identify for many years. Lehman argues that TAC identity recognition may at times be based not so much on a person's ancestry, or their family history of identification, or even their warrior credentials, but is rather based "on the opinions and interests of powerful people within the community" (Marks 2013, p. 185). Elder Aunty Patsy Cameron argues:

> that even someone who hasn't been active in their culture or in the politics of the day ... it doesn't make them any less Aboriginal. Anyone who can show their lineage, and their extended family, and acknowledges them as part of that family, we should be embracing them. We should be embracing our people who have been lost, rather than chasing them away and doing to them the exact thing that non-Aboriginal people have done to us in the past: denying us our rights, our identity.
>
> Cameron, cited in Marks 2013, p. 191

Black elitism guards and protects lateral violence to diminish a person's identity, and leaves them labeled as a "tick-a-box black" as portrayed in popular media (Berk 2017; Denholm 2015; Hunt 2016; Ratcliff 1997; Shine 2017; The Advocate 2017). The black panopticon works by leveraging the right of gaining an identity in exchange for following the norms and behaviors that black privilege (the surveillance class) dictates to suit the political climate (Marks 2013).

However, it is the power of the colonizer that manipulates both the perpetrator and the victim of the black power struggle for white gain. Identity politics and its laterally violent behaviors in *lutruwita* reached peak notice among the wider community in Tasmania in 2016 (ABC 2016). At this time, black elitism and the governance of identity were so distorted as to replicate the original extinction myths of colonial Tasmania of the mid-1800s – widespread denial of any *pakana* identity outside a chosen few decided upon by the TAC. The emergence of new Aboriginal organizations in the late 1980s and beyond throughout *lutruwita* gave some *pakana* an alternative voice to the TAC, but this gave rise to compounding lateral violence from identity politics, as community organizations become the arbitrators of identity (Carlson 2016). Lateral violence then extended beyond individuals to community organizations and institutions as the spaces for internecine disputes of oppression.

Identity denial

Oppression is the purest form of power; it creates an "us" and "them" divide between black and white, and targets Indigenous People for restriction, ridicule and marginalization (Smith 1999). Lateral violence means that we do this to each other as a "black and black" divide. Returning to the Premier's speech, he gave examples of what outright denial of identity looks like as a form of violence. In drawing attention to the statistical mismatch between those who self-identify as *pakana* on a census and those who are accepted for eligibility through *pakana* organizational legitimacy, Hodgman (2016) punctuated his speech by putting a focus on the cultural impact of denial.

Denial means the limiting of opportunities to pass on knowledge and practices: grandparents, who are recognized by the TAC, cannot share with their grandchildren, who are not, the rights to culture, as the Premier heard and recounted (Hodgman 2016). The Premier then segued from this experience to one where only two of three sons from the same parents are recognized, and the family is left to fight a bureaucratic battle on behalf of the other that should be common-sense (Hodgman 2016). Identity politics are often attributed to the misallocation and appropriation of federal and state government funding initiatives to *pakana* organizations, as some organizations are not considered "Aboriginal" by others (Lambie 2016). It is the institution, the people or the entity with the most dominant power that wins over as the recognized *pakana* organization most deserving of funding. These forms of identity denial prevent *pakana* gaining recognition of heritage and exclude some *pakana* from taking part in their cultural traditions. This oppression adds another layer to the haves and have nots in our community that is already too often marginalized.

Community lateral violence regarding identification and confirmation processes for the determination of Aboriginality are wreaking havoc in families, organizations and communities. Elder and author, Aunty Patsy Cameron, suggests that historical Tasmanian colonization outcomes continue to shape our futures, particularly negative impacts such as lateral violence on our wellbeing (Cameron & Miller 2011). The exclusion of some people regarding their Aboriginality divides families, creates levels of disproportionate trust, has people doubt their own identity and the identity of others, and the power of self-determination is removed from families. This speaks to Foucault's (1980) analysis of power where everyone can be involved, touched by or caught up in by its effects – both the oppressors and the oppressed. Foucault (1980, p. 39) also describes how power affects the "grain of individuals, touches their bodies and inserts itself into their actions and attitudes, their discourses, learning processes and everyday lives". It is this immersion of mistrust, self-doubt and conflict, that the politics of identity play a pivotal role in the saturation of lateral violence in *pakana* communities.

Gooda (in Koch 2011) describes lateral violence as internalized colonization, where the anger and fear of oppression can only be vented to those who are closest to us. Those with power try to maximize the impacts of lateral violence and, in doing so, diminish the rights of others (Stilwell 2017). Identity politics are perpetrated through lateral violence in both overt and covert ways (Langton 2008), where the organizations and individuals can assert elitism to ill effect on our people. In *lutruwita*, the descendants of relations borne of colonial circumstance, means that "whiteness" is often inferred to those who do not "look black enough" (Frogley 2018, p. 38), a view also shared by colonizers past and present. Thus, the right to claim identity, and community and cultural belonging, is complex, as both *pakana* and colonizers have power in passing judgement. Levels of prejudice and racism experienced by Indigenous People working in higher education settings have been reported by the National Tertiary Education Union (NTEU). They found that a considerable component of prejudice relates to "being black" as much as it does to "not being black enough", with both non-Indigenous and Indigenous People exercising prejudice towards those they perceive as the latter (Frogley 2011).

Identity is shaped and framed within the external (colonizers) and internal (*pakana*) constructs of the black panopticon. There is no equilibrium for how we as *pakana* negotiate identity; it is still framed within colonial power. We need to challenge the power construct and take formulative control of who we are. Distinguished Professor Maggie Walter in Carlson (2016, n.p.) summarizes the governance of power and how it continues to rule *pakana* through: "The continuity of the oppressive obsession of the colonisers and their twentieth century descendants with defining and containing Aboriginal identity to suit their own racially infused purposed into the present, where Aboriginal people and organisations are sometimes co-opted into continuing this damaging task." In *lutruwita* our communities have been co-opted, but also the perpetrators. In this manner, decolonizing work must occur for both black and white to rid our communities of this scourge of violence.

Decolonizing lateral violence and the black panopticon

The case study of *lutruwita* demonstrates the severe magnitude of lateral violence, where even a white premier rallies against its effects on our people. While this essay has gone some way to provide an example of how lateral violence functions, through the understanding of surveillance power as a black panopticon, I have yet to explore the methods of repairing the harms we have caused ourselves through being colonized. My contribution to decolonization studies, through characterizing lateral violence within *pakana* communities, is supported by an exploration of how and why we should decolonize our own spaces of identity.

I believe that healing is an essential component of decolonizing work. Decolonizing methodologies and practices, whether they are to break white privilege or black elitism, should be a force for good. Therefore, healing is both an outcome and impactful to the core processes of decolonization. For example, Canadian research has provided empirical insights into how lateral violence may be managed (Archibald 2006). Narratives of community healing, with education sessions to identify cultural interventions, therapeutic repair and reclaiming history, have been implemented in attempts to stamp out lateral violence for their First Nations populations (Archibald 2006). In this manner, Professor Linda Tuhiwai Smith (1999) is right when she describes how decolonizing methodologies are an opportunity to re-claim, re-name and re-write our own narratives based on our lived and learned experiences.

Healing begins with recognition of the problem – what are the conditions that create lateral violence and racialized surveillance? We need to find strength and replace harms with cultural values that place our people central to their own stories of family and community through surviving colonization. Professor Smith's (1999) work focuses on how Indigenous methodologies build a research practice to assist in our struggle for dignity and rights, away from the control and forces that the black panopticon pervades into our lives. In our attempt to decolonize we must engage with colonial policies and practices from the past, which will create a pathway for us to have a "space" where we are able to express our unique identities, and our ways of knowing, being and doing (Strelein & Tran 2013). Through processes of resistance, we can challenge the phenomenon where non-Indigenous people assume authority and expertise to speak on our behalf through enabling lateral violence over identity (Kesseris 2006).

Indigenous methodologies allow me, as an Indigenous researcher, to confront the limitations of Western research, by challenging the exclusion and denial of us and our knowledges, instead privileging the experiences of *pakana* and validating our cultural practices and traditions (Nakata et al 2012). Indigenous methodologies are useful for framing the experience of lateral violence from an insider view (Clark et al 2017); I am able to center myself and my worldviews, applying this knowledge to critical thinking and the act of decolonizing the research as much as the lateral violence. Indigenous methodologies, therefore, allows me to assert my own cultural authority and identity to participate in repairing the harms of lateral violence and see outside the black panopticon.

Indigenous Standpoint Theory provides a platform that can allow my Indigenous epistemology to be privileged over Western ethnocentric norms (Ardill 2013; Bamblett 2013; Foley 2003; Nakata 2007). It aids me as an early career *pakana* researcher to consider lateral violence in *pakana* communities: *pakana* knowledge that is learnt, shared and retained becomes part of the body of knowledge for the *pakana* community. I, therefore, am able to speak from my own cultural position, assisting in the maintenance of cultural protocols by sharing my own epistemological "truth" and attempting to produce a more inclusive, holistic and culturally acceptable and respectful form of knowledge and ways of knowing, being and doing.

As I work through finding and sharing my voice from an Indigenous standpoint, I am aware of the negotiation of power needed to navigate the discursive practice within the black panopticon. This power can be used for good and bad, as can the discourse that we use to negotiate lateral violence. These power relations are complex and create unstable processes where the narrative of lateral violence can be both an instrument and an attractor of power. In the case of lateral violence, the negative discourse transmits and produces power as it permeates itself within and outside the black panopticon. Western power reinforces it but, in doing so, it also undermines and exposes lateral violence, and renders it fragile and unable to work effectively (Foucault 1998). The deficit discourse of lateral violence continues to keep us "colonized", whilst undermining our model of identity.

Indigenous and decolonizing methodologies are buttressed by critical theory that concerns itself with race, racism and power (Writer 2008), occupying the spectrum from Whiteness Theory to Indigenous Standpoint Theory (Malagon, Huber & Velez 2009; McLaughlin & Whatman 2011; Yosso et al 2009). These schools of thought are invariably concerned with power relations and the discourses that drive those into dominance (Foucault 1979). We need to change the narrative, eliminate the negative discourse of lateral violence and bring useful power back to our communities. Through decolonizing the Western panopticon to reveal the characteristics of the black one, we see how lateral violence can be framed as the black elite trying "to feel powerful in a powerless situation" (Phillips 2009, n.p.).

Through the decolonizing process we can see the birth and maturation of lateral violence, how it is rooted in colonization, and the by-products such as disadvantage, discrimination and oppression that it brings. The social and economic inequity in preserving a black panopticon that serves Western ends of discipline (Roithmayr 1999) requires an honest and forthright acknowledgement of the underpinning power and control of the colonizers and enacted by their black envoys (Nakata 2007). When we can see *pakana* as lateral violence victims created by our own guardians and brick walls, we can then begin to target the remedy to the cause, rather than be torn between different competing discourses (Frankenberg 1993). But from here we need to focus on the dominance of white social constructs, to allow us to shift the attention away from us as the marginalized and disadvantaged group, to question and investigate the behaviors of the dominant colonizer (Bonilla-Silva 2009; Frankenberg 1993; Habibis & Walter 2009).

Conclusion

The black panopticon contributes scholarship to defining how lateral violence looks in communities. Using my Indigenous methodological lens, in my own community, I have seen what the structure of the black panopticon looks like. The black panopticon provides opportunity to explore the colonial fortress of power that continues to encase us in contemporary *lutruwita*. Challenging lateral violence requires a multi-disciplinary approach to provide insight, affect change and commence healing. We need to find a safe space within the panopticon, which will allow us as *pakana* to lead how we can change the narrative framing our communities and lateral violence. Through storytelling, we can re-enact the wisdom of our Old People, bring together our collective and cultural knowledges to progress ourselves, our way, and not in the current form with oversight from the colonizer. Our ontological ways of being, and our epistemological ways of knowing, should be a force that brings good and allows our voice to the forefront. The intersection between Western and Indigenous methodologies can create a platform for discussions. We need to give voice to the myriad of daily negotiations we make in colonized contexts to free ourselves from the black panopticon. This way, we can create a path for understanding and explaining how our Indigenous subjectivities are continuing to be constituted within colonial relations of power (Nakata 2007). We need to enable the white lens of colonization to be deconstructed and analyze our own knowledge of what is lateral violence, and how is it affecting and informing our wellbeing as *pakana* people. An important step in challenging these colonial power relations is to expose lateral violence and its colonizing effects through educating *pakana* of the continuing unequal distribution of power that is perpetuated amongst our communities. I echo Smith (1999, p. 28), when she states, "we want to write our own stories, in our own way, to give testimony to our history". It is the structure of the black panopticon, not the people, that needs changing, as identity is constructed and conformed by power.

4

Blak & Salty: reflections on violence and racism

Donna Moodie (Gomeroi), Kelly Menzel (Ngadjuri), Liz Cameron
(Dharug) and Nikki Moodie (Gomeroi)

Introduction

The Māori concept of *iwi* loosely translates as "tribe" and encompasses many different communities (Smith 2012, p. 139). Smith explores the utility of tertiary qualifications to *iwi* in the context of treaty settlements, but warns of the risk of poor quality or unethical research: "any sign that secret deals have been made, or the traditional processes have been overridden, can result in a halt to further work and a schism in the tribe" (Smith 2012, p. 221). However, in thinking through the implications of Indigenous governance of Indigenous education, Smith also notes how "the processes of consultation, collective meetings, open debate and shared decision-making are crucial aspects of tribal research practices" (Smith 2012, p. 221). The university then is a site of tension and risk, its purpose and modes of operation creating challenges for tribal governance and Indigenous Peoples' political projects. Yet, simultaneously, the university provides an opportunity to elaborate and practice tribal governance within the confines of the colonial institution, allowing a degree of appropriation, revision and remix – a tribal methodology for institutional engagement that may enable new Indigenous futures, if not decolonization. However, in pursuit of greater cultural fidelity between Indigenous peoples and academic institutions, we experience the refractory imprint (Wolfe 2006) of practices that have incorporated the violence of settler-colonial racism. We speak back to this lateral violence as a collective of Indigenous women storying our own healing journeys, together, as both method and meaning-making (Smith 2012).

The historical behavior of researchers and research institutions is not unknown to us, and thus we bring our knowledge of this treatment as we enter tertiary systems – as students and as staff. We take up Smith's (2012) discussion of the ways in which tribal governance systems manage and take up the promise of research of tertiary education and extend that discussion to expectations of Indigenous relationality in the way Indigenous matters are arranged inside universities. For example, Indigenous student support centers or Indigenous Education Units (IEUs) have long been recognized as "a haven of understanding" (Page & Asmar 2008, p. 112) for our students. These units have, for a number of decades, provided a constellation of emergency, personal, financial and academic support in a culturally safe and relevant manner (Behrendt et al 2012). Indeed, these centers have been integral to improving completion rates for Indigenous students (Asmar, Page & Radloff 2011): "universities with more complex Indigenous support and research infrastructure demonstrate higher Indigenous student completion rates" (Pechenkina, Kowal & Paradies 2011, p. 64). Often IEUs include identifiably *Indigenous* governance structures and leadership strategies that center Indigenous cultural values, for example by employing Indigenous People in positions of power, hosting Elders-in-Residence or running healing and cultural programs. However, it is the case that we often find ourselves working outside of IEUs or within IEUs that do not have a high degree of cultural match between the governance structure adopted and the staff employed there. We suggest that culturally appropriate governance within universities, which attends to relationality, Country and wellbeing, is a well-recognized strategy to combat lateral violence (Gooda 2011a).

In this essay, we use an Indigenous Methodological (IM) approach from Kovach (2010a) to story our experiences and interpretation of Smith (2012), from our perspectives as Indigenous women engaging in Indigenous women's business in the Australian university sector. Culturally we represent an intergenerational view and a network of relationality that is often invisible in academia. We are provoked by questions that ask "what is Indigenous women's business inside the Academy?". Smith (2012) asserts that settlers (or outsiders) view the issue of contestability within Indigenous communities – internal or external to universities – as proof that infighting is rampant. Thus, we four Indigenous women discuss our experience of this outsiders' view. Smith (2012, p. 221) contends that some "insiders" tend to view outcomes, defending a lack of culturally appropriate processes, as driven by the academy and government agenda as "settlement at any cost rather than a reflection of traditional practices". This essay illustrates how multiple generations of Indigenous women *do* Indigenous research in the white Australian academy and indeed questions *if* we can, in a way that respects our cultural specificities as Indigenous women, as Gomeroi, as Dharug, as Ngadjuri. Initially, Donna approached us and asked us to describe our experiences and address and explore issues such as internalized micro-aggression and lateral violence, often termed "mobbing" and "bullying". In highlighting our experiences, we four Indigenous women bring our ideas together to support better processes regarding safe cultural spaces in the academy.

Mobbing and bullying occur in many workplaces, and academia is no exception (Twale & DeLuca 2008). Yet we suggest that the phenomenon of lateral violence at once includes mobbing and bullying and also goes beyond these behaviors to include a racialized dimension. These behaviors create imbalances and inequities and have ongoing ramifications that reiterate and reinforce the policies and practices associated with colonization. It is argued that both *internalized racism* and *intraracial racism* intersect with racism in academia and continue to reinforce colonial practices (Evans et al 2014). What does this mean for Indigenous women academics from our perspectives? And what of the disgruntlement and intolerance within Indigenous communities? We could consider this as possible evidence of the *tall poppy syndrome*, so common in Australia, which in this context might actively discard Indigenous People working with the academy as being seen as *gone white*, as *coconuts*, or "flash blacks" (Smith 2012, p. 138). Yet many Indigenous students, academics and professional staff see higher education employment as a career pathway, along with supporting and advocating an obligation to give back to community in order to make positive change (Behrendt et al 2012). This essay explores and defines culturally safe practices and process, based on our reflections on the role of the university in engaging with First Peoples. While our individual storylines capture individual experiences that encompass truth through experience, commonalities between us are evident.

Positioning

We write as four Aboriginal women, a Gomeroi mother and daughter – Donna and Nikki; a Bohemian Ngadjuri woman – Kelly; and a Dharug woman – Liz. We come together with the collective aim of understanding the university as a site for the articulation of historical and contemporary Indigenous identities, to strengthen ourselves and each other, and to assert the role of institutes of higher education in the resurgence of Indigenous knowledge. We have each negotiated universities as mechanisms for the reproduction of Western elitism, where we – and our programs of work – have struggled to survive in the face of overwhelming hostility towards our identities and knowledges (Smith 2012). We begin this essay with a discussion of lateral violence and proceed to relate our experiences within the Australian university system. In disclosing our personal experiences, we seek less to provide evidence of the existence or impact of lateral violence and racism, and rather more to assert the survivance and reinvention that higher education can support, when we are brought into a relational framework that creates cultural security (Gooda 2011b).

Lateral violence

Lateral violence is often described as internalized racism, a phenomenon that occurs when oppressed peoples damage their own communities (Gooda 2011b; Royal Australian College of General Practitioners [RACGP] 2014). That damage may manifest as gossiping, bullying or shaming others in an organization or in the wider community, or in direct efforts to socially isolate or exclude other people. Families are often most at risk of extreme physical acts of violence, and this includes the risk of self-harm and injury (physical, psychological and spiritual) as a result of these experiences (RACGP 2014). Recent research suggests that "lateral violence is inescapable, intense and chronic within Aboriginal and Torres Strait Islander communities" (Clark & Augoustinos 2015, p. 24).

Clark and Augoustinos (2015) discuss the need for specificity in the use of the term *lateral violence* because of the risk of stigma associated particularly with the use of the word *violence* and persistent racist representations of Indigenous People as inherently volatile (and thus incapable and deviant). These authors conducted a qualitative research project with 30 Aboriginal participants on the prevalence, description and naming of the phenomenon of lateral violence. Participants in that project describe how the phrase allowed them to feel a sense of relief when their experiences could be interpreted using this language. The term *lateral violence* both includes and is more expansive than other descriptors often used in the research literature, like *bullying* or *infighting*.

More recently, Paradies (2018, p. 4) writes how lateral violence describes the intersection of both *intraracial racism* and *internalized racism* and is often focused on: "indigenous authenticity (e.g., skin color or cultural knowledge), manifesting as innuendo, exclusion, insults, sabotage, undermining, scapegoating, backstabbing or failure to respect privacy". Paradies (2018) discusses the result of a 2011 survey conducted by the National Tertiary Education Union (NTEU) on Indigenous Peoples' experiences of racial discrimination in Australia's university sector. The report defined lateral violence as "the harmful and undermining practices that members of oppressed groups can engage in against each other as a result of marginalisation" (National Indigenous Unit of the NTEU 2011, p. 1). A total of 172 members completed the survey, which found that only 24 per cent of respondents had never experienced lateral violence (National Indigenous Unit of the NTEU 2011, p. 18). In contrast:

- 60.6% had experienced lateral violence in the workplace.
- 57.9% stated that colleagues at work were the main perpetrators of lateral violence.
- 8.6% stated that their employer attempted to address lateral violence in the workplace.
- Of this, 5.7% stated that their employer took positive actions to address lateral violence,
- 10.0% of respondents stated that their employers were somewhat successful in addressing lateral violence at work (National Indigenous Unit of the NTEU 2011, p. 4).

The research conducted by the National Indigenous Unit of the NTEU reinforces the landmark Social Justice Report released in the same year by Aboriginal and Torres Strait Islander Social Justice Commissioner, Mick Gooda (2011b). The 2011 Social Justice Report included an extensive discussion of lateral violence as a phenomenon that affects colonized peoples particularly, emerging as it does from the challenge of maintaining a collective identity in the context of ongoing oppression.

The overwhelming position of power held by the colonizers, combined with internalized negative beliefs, fosters the sense that directing anger and violence towards the colonizers is too risky or fruitless. In this situation we are safer and more able to attack those closest to us who do not represent the potent threat of the colonizers (Gooda 2011b).

In the broader Australian context, a tall poppy is someone who is both successful and held in contempt by virtue of their success (Peeters 2004). Australian egalitarianism – as a cultural mode of interaction rather than political commitment to equity – manifests as an aversion to conspicuous success; or perhaps more specifically as an aversion to the sense of entitlement that leads some to engage in egotistical or self-indulgent behavior as a result of their success (Peeters 2015). In education, sport and public life, high performance and enthusiasm are routinely denigrated, to the extent that the tall poppy syndrome and the inevitable "cutting down" that follows, have been described as Australia's national sport (Peeters 2004, p. 12). If, then, "taking someone down a peg" or cutting down a tall poppy is such an established social practice, how might we understand the intersection of racism and colonialism that combine to create an oppressive system of disenfranchisement for Indigenous People in Australia? In the broader settler-colonial context of Australia, the act of "cutting down tall poppies" is the exercise of a powerful social norm that seeks to limit the expression of pomposity, braggadocio or conceited entitlement. Yet Indigenous Peoples' experience of lateral violence – whilst similarly a powerful leveling social norm that aims to standardize behavior – includes both a racialized dimension and a manifestation internal to our communities that marks it as a fundamentally different phenomenon from the tall poppy syndrome (Clark & Augoustinos 2015).

Lateral violence raises the specter of violating an identity rooted in survival that masks the internalization of colonial stereotypes about Indigenous being and potentiality (Hallinin, Bruce & Burke 2005). For example, being labeled a *coconut*, or *flash*, can indicate a violation of a collective identity developed out of a need for safety in opposition to non-Indigenous Australia (Moodie 2014). Moving away from one's own community to study or get a higher paying job can not only be seen as a threat to the cohesion of the family and community and a rejection of one's own identity, it can also be seen as an investment in a society that condemns and denigrates Indigenous People (Sonn, Bishop & Humphries 2000). As such, statements about the ability of Indigenous People to succeed in particular domains, or the likelihood of poor employment prospects and comments on the disloyal, inauthentic nature of People who choose to engage in mainstream institutions seem to involve two movements: first, a critical assessment of the historical chances of success for Indigenous People in colonial institutions; and, second, an internalization of the dominant cultures' negative beliefs and stereotypes regarding Indigenous People (Moodie 2014).

Regarding the first, neither the male life expectancy gap, nor the incidence of tertiary qualifications amongst Indigenous People are expected to close for at least another century (Altman, Biddle & Hunter 2009). Non-Indigenous people are four times more likely (24 per cent) than Indigenous People (5 per cent) to have attained a bachelor's degree or higher (Australian Bureau of Statistics [ABS] 2011). Given these objective circumstances, and the violence perpetrated against

Indigenous People by colonial paramilitary forces (Nettelbeck & Smandych 2010), the police (Royal Commission into Aboriginal Deaths in Custody [RCIADIC] 1991) and the welfare and education systems (Human Rights and Equal Opportunity Commission [HREOC] 1997), the barriers preventing equitable outcomes for Indigenous People are historic, systemic and ongoing. This is not to overlook the substantial achievements of our Peoples, nor the work of those engaged in resurgence and self-determination. However, it is safe to say that any discussion of Indigenous identity and social norms within Indigenous communities must include a discussion of Indigenous history, which in Australia, as in most colonial nations, is one of violent dispossession and ongoing oppression (Moodie 2014). An assessment of the objective chances available to Indigenous People must acknowledge the reality of poorer outcomes, particularly with regard to incarceration and child removal. We can objectively state that some things are getting worse, not better (ABS 2018; Dean 2018).

Second, the evolution within Indigenous communities of social norms that construct education as buying in-to, or compliance with, mainstream values involves a collective internalization of the beliefs of the dominant culture of Indigeneity as deficient (Moodie 2014). Sarra (2006, pp. 78–79) describes workshops, conducted as part of his doctoral research, in which he asked participants to relate words and concepts that describe how mainstream Australia views Indigenous People:

> At every forum, the participants reported that mainstream Australia perceived Aboriginal people as alcoholics, drunks or heavy drinkers. It was also widely held that Aboriginal people were privileged or that, in some way, they "got it good". Aboriginal people were regarded as "welfare dependent", "dole bludgers" and "lazy people who wouldn't work". On every occasion, many considered that mainstream Australia used pejorative terms such as "coon", "nigger", "boong", "black cunts" and "black bastards" in relation to Aboriginal people. These were the names my brothers and I were called at school.

In a study examining barriers and pathways to schooling and vocational education and training (VET) for Indigenous young People, Alford and James (2007) identify not only a lack of family support for Indigenous students, but also a perception held by non-Indigenous interviewees that Indigenous families were dysfunctional. Whether held by community members and teachers, or perpetuated in the media, stereotypes of Indigenous inability and disengagement exist and are entrenched. In conjunction with the historical experiences mentioned above, these contemporary racist attitudes form part of the world in which a young Indigenous person is socialized (Paradies & Cunningham 2009; Sarra 2006; Wall & Baker 2012). The internalization of negative expectations of Indigenous People leads not only to the normalization of low academic achievement, but also to the belief that participation and excellence in mainstream institutions are antithetical to the cohesion of Indigenous communities (Moodie 2014). This obviously has significant implications for the development of career aspirations and an academic self-concept (Craven 2005). These norms and manifestations of lateral violence create yet another hurdle to overcome in the pursuit of wellbeing and cultural safety (Moodie 2014).

Entering the university

Taking into account the discussion above, what then drew us in to universities, and how have our expectations met with reality? Donna posed us the following questions:

- Why did we want to work at university?
- What did we foresee or envisage as our employment?
- Were our expectations fulfilled?

Kelly   I always wanted to work in a university. I was 26 when I won my first academic job. I was so excited. Like stupidly excited and enthusiastic to be the best I could be. I left a full-time, permanent position working in community for a 9-month contract, with the aim of learning as much as I could and making myself indispensable. I was asked to stay on. Although I am not sure it was because I was indispensable, rather I was cannon fodder, because I never had the opportunity to fulfil any potential. I tried to engage with the more experienced scholars in my school. I wanted to learn from them. I would ask them if we could work on things together. They would say yes. I would arrange a meeting to discuss project ideas or mentoring support. The people I invited would not show up to the meetings. This happened regularly. I still do not know the lesson I was supposed to learn from that. In the end, all I ended up doing was teaching. All the units to do with culture, Indigeneity and rural communities (because apparently that is where all black people live) fell to me, and it kept being piled on. Until I burned out. I was excluded from engaging in any scholarly activity within the school. I witnessed this happen to other young women who joined the school. I also saw young non-Indigenous men being fostered through the ranks. They were supported, mentored by the senior women in the school and invited to join projects, from the day they commenced. I did not realize this actually occurred in real life. I thought it was the stuff of textbooks and of past times, until I saw it first-hand.

Liz I entered university through chance and a sequence of unplanned events, rather than having set goals of a career pathways. After undertaking post-graduate studies in Indigenous social health I applied for a professional position that led to an academic role in later years. Since then I have worked at four universities.

Initially, I felt disoriented and overwhelmed by the policies, procedures and academic language. I felt inferior. I was astonished to find few Aboriginal and Torres Strait Islander academics engaged in teaching and research, and a noticeable absence of senior leadership roles. I witnessed many Indigenous units being taught by non-Indigenous academics that led me questioning cultural standards. I became aware of the inequities surrounding Indigenous academic workloads and Community Engagement activities compared to other peers who did not experience such overwhelming and demanding roles. I found there was little understanding or recognition of student and extended kin support needs and no comprehension from other senior university executive staff on the holistic nature of service provision. Yet, personally connecting with Indigenous students is essential for their success. On par with cultural protocols, introductions and negotiating kinship connections provide more meaningful exchanges, yet are often in direct conflict with university processes, as taking the time to deeply know students is not encouraged or made obvious by dedicated time allocation in workloads. It is argued that knowing students allows for a deeper richness of connections to flow into the learning environment, as diverse cultural understandings can be used as examples and case-related studies. Perso and Hayward (2015) state that knowing individual students is imperative in considering large numbers of diverse cultural groups, each with different languages and cultural customs, as a means to prevent stereotyping Aboriginal people and culture (Harrison 2011). Such engagement is largely undocumented and therefore "invisible" yet immense (Page & Asmar 2008).

Nikki I didn't want to work in a university until well after I started my PhD. I had been building a career in the public service until a health issue forced me to reconsider entirely what my working life looked like. I didn't know at that point that I had severe endometriosis, but it had begun to take quite a toll on my body with fatigue and pain that was diagnosed as all sorts of other things. So until my late twenties I was focused on working in government and community, to put into practice everything I learned in my undergraduate degree. But after a few years in the public service I was approached by my honors supervisor with an invitation to apply for a PhD scholarship. It seemed like a good way to further my career and have a change of pace to focus on my health.

Through my candidature I had a sense of how hard it was to find permanent, full-time academic employment and even towards the end of my PhD was still focused on returning to government. I was offered a short contract teaching Indigenous Studies whilst I finished my thesis and still remember coordinating classes, lecturing and writing whilst actively looking for jobs back in government. It wasn't until I had submitted my thesis, been awarded the doctorate and had a permanent, ongoing teaching and research position in a university that I allowed myself to think this might offer a stable future.

In many ways my experience of universities has not been typical. I have enjoyed immense privilege and security that I do not see available to many other academics – either Indigenous academic staff or non-white people and women or gender diverse early career researchers. In part, this is because a large slice of my childhood took place in universities whilst Donna attended as a mature-aged student and single mum. So I knew many academics growing up and I got to know the feel and function of a university from an early age. I always knew I would go to university, maybe even do a PhD, but I didn't know I would end up working in them. The value of a tertiary education for our mob is clear, and the great privilege of working inside a university is clear, but there is a large cost to be paid if the work is disconnected from our communities and our expectations of cultural fit between our home and work are not met.

Cultural safety

The idea of *cultural safety* appears variously as a research mode and methodology, as a condition for identity, and as management strategy in higher education. According to Rigney (1999, p. 116), Indigenist research has been defined as "culturally safe and culturally respectful research that is comprised of three principles: resistance as an emancipatory imperative, political integrity in Indigenous research and privileging Indigenous voices in Indigenist research". The landmark Social Justice Report (Gooda 2011b) later discussed how *cultural safety* and *cultural security* offer antidotes to lateral violence by creating opportunities for personal growth and achievement and then the entrenchment of those opportunities in policy and procedure. As Mick Dodson noted in his 1994 Wentworth Lecture, Indigenous Peoples' relationship to our own identities is mediated by our relationship to the past: "the repossession of our past is the repossession of ourselves.... Our peoples have left us deep roots which empowered us to endure the violence of oppression. They are the roots of survival but not of constriction. They are roots from which all growth is possible. They are the roots which protected our end from the beginning" (Dodson 1994, p. 23).

In a university context, *cultural safety* is often described as synonymous with *respect, sensitivity* or *competency* (Universities Australia & Indigenous Higher Education Advisory Council 2011). We separately consider how our workplaces offer cultural safety or security by responding to the question:

- Do you feel that the university, faculty or school that you work in is overall a culturally safe environment?

Liz   No. I have continually witnessed "Aboriginal matters" being seen as "the problem" with a tendency to ignore, push aside or reject claims of safety. I have seen senior staff run in fear over Indigenous issues, seeing us as a "problem" through suggestive "here we go again" gestures. I have witnessed a great deal of passive racial victimization in "saving" the poor black fella that Tatum describes as "white superiority to improve Aboriginal and Torres Strait Islander livelihoods" (1997, p. 11).

Kelly   No, I do not think the wider university is culturally safe. I am almost hyper-vigilant when I step outside of my safety zone. Because I have experienced the feeling of being attacked, thus forced to defend my professional conduct and the performance of the students (which I discuss further below) I find I always keep my wits about me. Having said that, I do not always feel unsafe in the wider university, but I have certainly come to learn where is safe and where is not.

I have made an interesting observation during my time at the university. I was originally recruited to work in the wider university, but I moved into the Indigenous space after 18 months. My colleagues knew I was Aboriginal (the only Indigenous person on staff) but it was not until I moved into the Indigenous space that I noticed they began treating me differently. Nurses are always prepared to micro-manage and scrutinize each other, but it was not until I moved that I began to feel a deep sense of distrust from staff in the wider university school. The dynamic changed so significantly that I felt and still feel as though I am not believed, my abilities are not trusted, my knowledge is not trusted, my expertise is not trusted and that I somehow work in a lesser environment.

Nikki   I think there are spaces inside universities that tend to be more culturally safe than others, and that I'm lucky to know many colleagues who understand the challenges of being blak (Munro 2020; Thorner et al 2018) in a white colonial institution. But I often struggle with the idea that universities could ever be truly culturally safe. Universities in Australia do not have the same history as in the United States with tribal colleges or historically black colleges and universities (HBCUs). Simultaneously, the idea of self-determination in Indigenous education that we've been permitted to hold is particularly anemic. The idea of an Indigenous university has never been seriously entertained in this country yet is established in Canada, the United States and New Zealand. Our right to determine our own education systems is recognized internationally and exists within the countries Australia compares itself to. So when I think about what *would* be culturally safe, I think about institutions that are designed within Indigenous cultural systems, to hold and grow Indigenous knowledges, and teach Indigenous students. That's the benchmark that actually exists, so how could we ever expect a white, colonial institution that has been built on the exploitation of Indigenous peoples and knowledges to ever take the place of self-determined Indigenous institutions?

Mobbing

Mobbing is a form of group behavior and in the workplace is defined as "a malicious attempt to force a person out of the workplace through psychological terror, unjustified accusations, humiliation, general harassment and emotional abuse" (Shallcross, Sheehan & Ramsay 2008, p. 57). Workplace mobbing is a type of bullying behavior where perpetrators work together collectively to cause psychological, sexual and other forms of injury (Mulder et al 2013). The damage is done through malicious gossip, rumor, hearsay and unfounded accusations. Perpetrators are generally part of the dominant group and targets are often isolated and blamed as the one at fault (Branch, Ramsey & Barker 2012). The intent of workplace mobbing is often to destabilize another employee or to force them out of their workplace or job. Perversely, perpetrators often accuse *their victims* of being bullies, as those perpetrators realize the benefits or security of claiming a victim status (Shallcross 2019). Shallcross (2019) suggests that victims of workplace mobbing are often high achievers, whistle-blowers or change-agents. We respond to the question:

• Have you seen or experienced "mobbing"?

Liz　Yes. I have seen this in a variety of settings and have had my own personal experiences. I have witnessed underhandedness, deceitful activities and undermining within a black space. My experiences of mobbing include sudden isolated feelings where distinct groups give you the silent treatment, or being given no opportunity to communicate (*silenced*) and shut down. Vindictive and disruptive attacks lay prevalent in Indigenous centers that Denenberg and Braverman (2001, p. 7) refer to as a "concerted effort by a group of employees to isolate a co-worker through ostracism and denigration". From a personal perspective, this has also included indirect secretive character assassinations and direct criticisms where I was left questioning my abilities and capabilities. Davenport, Schwartz and Elliott (2002) refer to such scapegoating and personal targeting as being forms of intimidation through persistent hostile behaviors to undermine one's integrity. One of my particular challenges involved the secretive nature of such behaviors as publicly the attackers frequently appeared to be cooperative employees (Lee & Brotheridge 2006).

I have listened to many stories of Indigenous staff continuously being exposed to a historical legacy of internalized mobbing, that has resulted in poor health and wellbeing. Other responses include a desire to leave the organization as they felt there was a workplace disease. Richardson and McCord (2001, p. 2) state that the resulting consequence of mobbing "destroys morale, erodes trust, cripples initiative, and results in dysfunction, absenteeism, resignations, guilt, anxiety, paranoia, negativity, and marginal production" and a loss of professional reputation. It is well recognized within Indigenous academia that the more one advances their career, the more likely they will be targeted from other Indigenous individuals and groups. This additional individualized pressure is not recognized nor supported by universities, leaving the individual battling it out on their own. Universities are also recognized in using scapegoating as a means to quickly solve the "Indigenous problem". Westhues (2003) describes how, at an organizational level, scapegoating provides a tension release for universities by focusing the stress and blame on the target instead of examining and redressing the wrongs perpetrated against workplace mobbing. This results in the offenders more often facing no consequences. Interestingly, Namie and Namie (2009) further argue that the silencing of witnesses helps assure the permanence of the offender within the organization and the scapegoating continues towards others.

Kelly I have experienced mobbing. In one particular situation, I was reprimanded by a manager for not doing something she directed me to do. Now, I know I must not be the easiest person to manage. I am loud, slightly bolshie and I do not always do what I am told, however I had a perfectly rational reason for not doing what she had directed me to do, but that was apparently irrelevant. As part of the "punishment" she allotted, she directed me to stand up in a management meeting and publicly apologize (atone) for my "failure to follow a directive and my poor performance". She also instructed me to go to each of the executives and privately apologize for my indiscretion. I knew what she was doing. I understood at an intellectual level what was happening to me but I felt there was nothing I could do about it. I weighed up the pros and cons of not following her directive, but I believed the backlash of not doing it would have far outweighed any feeling of satisfaction I would have gotten from standing my ground. I felt as though my employment was at stake and, at that time, I was the only income earner in my family. I did not feel as though I had the luxury of protecting my ego from a public shaming. So, I apologized. It felt terrible. I felt sick, powerless, and full of shame and embarrassment. Not one of the management team or the executives ever questioned this.

Donna I have experienced mobbing. In fact, it was mobbing "upwards" that included Indigenous and non-Indigenous women and two men. The head of the Indigenous Education Unit (IEU) was quite unwell. This should not have been a problem, however. As their health deteriorated, this person became to rely more and more on personal assistants, administration staff and professional officers. Academic staff became the target. Gossip, rumor and innuendo became the staple conversation, particularly amongst the "smoking" group who would spend quite a lot of time talking with each other outside. I was privy to these conversations at first, but became ostracized when I called the group out for targeting another professional officer and a couple of non-Indigenous academics. These people had total access to the head of the IEU, and it was made quite clear who was in favor and who was out of favor. Those of us who were the aim of these vitriolic conversations noticed that the head of the IEU was actually believing the gossip and many of us were called upon to explain these rumors, which were untrue. Then came the micromanagement and intense scrutiny on time spent in the office. It was obvious where this was originating from and it was the upward motion of this mobbing that was then strategically forced on the target of the mobbers, Indigenous and non-Indigenous academics and professional staff. For many of us it became too much and we moved on to other academies. Many who endured became quite unwell with diagnosed stress symptoms. Some just could not leave and many were eventually "performance managed" out. After much collateral damage this university did however take up the issue of "mobbing", and the human resources department instigated a policy to create awareness of what actions and behaviors constituted the behavior. And unlike some other academies that I have been employed at, at least this university conducted "exit interviews" for those of us who chose to leave.

It seems to this writer that these universities only act when the IEU haemorrhages staff or issues become public or legal options are taken up. And then many questions are not asked by senior management. It seems to me that it is easier to let the divide and conquer mentality rule. In many instances and in my experience our own people use the tools of the colonizer with potency. This needs to be called out. We are calling on all academies, institutions and universities to understand what is continuing to occur in the post-colonial turn and create opportunity and policy positions that insist on respectfully engaging with blak staff to make safe the lives of blak academics and professional officers, and those of our colleagues who are non-Indigenous who walk with us.

Indigenizing

Historically in colonial discourse, research was "done" on Aboriginal communities and presented our families and communities as "objects of curiosity and subjects of research, to be seen but not asked, heard or respected. So the research has been undertaken in the same way Captain James Cook falsely claimed the eastern coast of the land to become known as Australia as *terra nullius*" (Martin 2003, p. 203).

We four Indigenous women researchers challenge this dominant discourse. We are Indigenous women and cannot be anything other than Indigenous women. This is our standpoint. Moreton-Robinson (2013, p. 340) states: "Indigenous women's standpoint is ascribed through inheritance and achieved through struggle. It is constituted by our sovereignty and constitutive of the interconnectedness of our ontology (our way of being); our epistemology (our way of knowing) and our axiology (our way of doing)." Thus, our ways of being, knowing and doing include the way we research and the way we manage information. This has been taught to us by our ancestor creators and our Elders, and enables us to navigate the space between two worlds whilst maintaining our connection to Country and cultural practices. Indigenous women's standpoint acknowledges Indigenous women's experience and knowledge as it relates to dominant, white patriarchal paradigms. Due to varied levels of oppression, Indigenous women's ways of being, knowing and doing are affected by individual experiences along with collective, shared experiences of colonization that have emerged "under social, political, historical and material conditions that we share either consciously or unconsciously" (Moreton-Robinson 2013, p. 340). Martin (2003, p. 206) argues: "Indigenist research must centralise the core structures of Aboriginal ontology as a framework for research if it is to serve us well. Otherwise it is western research done by Indigenous people."

Further utilizing an IM approach is holistic and guided by an Indigenous Knowledge Paradigm. As a paradigmatic approach to research, IM influences the types of methods of data collection, and how the data are interpreted and analyzed (Kovach 2010a). The perspective of the *relational*, the way in which two or more people or things are connected, is an important aspect in IM. In Western methodological frameworks the relational is viewed as biased and therefore not included in the research. In contrast, "Indigenous methodologies embrace relational assumptions as central to their core epistemologies" (Kovach 2010a, p. 42). An IM perspective views the world, things both seen and unseen, holistically. It is about the whole, entire research process, not simply data collection and analysis (Kovach 2011). Kovach (2010a p. 42) suggests that IM must proceed from an Indigenous belief system, which in turn "has at its core a relational understanding and accountability to the world". Indigenous Methodologies proceeds from Indigenous epistemologies and often prioritize orality, or oral transmission of knowledge, as well as collectivist traditions (Kovach 2010a). It is located in and based on respect, reciprocity and collectivity (Martin 2003). Subjective information is valued and the contextual aspect of the data, the place from where it comes, is valued (Little Bear 2000).

It is our desire to conduct our research in the most culturally safe way possible, and we offer our stories here as a demonstration of IM and of Indigenist research. Indigenist research must be undertaken in a culturally safe, respectful, and competent manner. Further, Indigenist research must privilege the voices of Indigenous Peoples, and be a site of political resistance, integrity and moral responsibility (Rigney 1999). This is what we aim to do. All of this supports Smith's (2012) call to disrupt the rules of the research to move towards practices that are more respectful, ethical, sympathetic and useful and no longer the racist practices and attitudes, ethnocentric assumptions and white, patriarchal exploitative research that has been conducted in the Western academy.

Conclusion

We came together to write and reflect on our experiences of lateral violence and cultural safety in academia to help us heal together, to story and survive together (Smith 2012). Our vignettes tell stories of different encounters and responses, modeling Bishop's (1999, p. 5) "diversities of truth", yet each contributes to a collective narrative in which we each have an important and valued voice. Our experiences can be violent, traumatic, ambivalent, hopeful, but because we tell our stories together, we are able to make meaning of our histories together, and see possible futures for collaboration, community and survival.

We began by asking what is Indigenous women's business in the academy? We conclude by suggesting that our task is twofold. If lateral violence emanates from the racism that exists in the very air we breathe, then combating racism in all its forms – new, old, internal, institutional or interpersonal – must be our first priority. Second, creating spaces and practices in the academy that have a high degree of cultural fidelity with Indigenous Peoples who exist/resist in these spaces requires an ethic of radical inclusion from the institution. An agenda of radical inclusion prioritizes not only the teaching and research function of universities, but Indigenous aspirations as defined by Indigenous collectives both inside and outside the institution.

Our experiences of lateral violence in the academy prompt us to consider the ways in which Indigenous governance practices are supported in university environments. As universities begin to cede space and authority to Indigenous People and knowledges, appropriate resourcing becomes critical to give life to institutional policies and procedures intended to deliver cultural security. Yet, as Gooda (2011b), Dodson (1994), Martin (2003) and Moreton-Robinson (2013) all suggest, our healing and our orientation to the future is based on our roots in the past. From these roots we grow and re-emerge and re-(de)-fine our Indigeneity and our obligation to each other, and we take up Smith's (2012) call to tell our stories well, thus moving beyond and healing from many types of violence experienced in our communities and workplaces.

Part Three

Wisdom and Knowledge

5

Kei hea au e tū ana? Reflections on a journey

Kelly Ratana (Ngāti Tūwharetoa, Ngāti Rangiwewehi)

Ko wai au?

Ko Tongariro me Tiheia ōku maunga,
Ko Taupō-nui-a-Tia me Te Rotorua-nui-a-Kahumatamomoe ōku roto moana,
Ko Waikato me Te Awahou ōku awa
Ko Te Heuheu me Tawakeheimoa ōku tūpuna
Ko Te Arawa te waka
Ko Ngāti Tūwharetoa me Ngāti Rangiwewehi ōku iwi
Ko Kelly Ratana ahau
Ko au tēnei e mihi ana

I have chosen to introduce myself through my pepehā,[1] which links me back to the ancestors and places of my origin in the central North Island of Aotearoa, New Zealand. While I am most connected to my taha Māori (Māori ancestry), I also want to acknowledge my taha Pākehā (English and Scottish ancestry), and the knowledge, practice and beliefs they have both contributed to who I am. In doing so, I acknowledge that I am more than the sum of these disparate parts: I descend from the unique places, contexts, practices and beliefs of my ancestors, of those who came before me and will be part of the legacy of those who come after. This is a great responsibility, but one that keeps me grounded, accountable and moving forward. By acknowledging these dual beginnings, I hope to highlight a central theme of this essay – "bridges". I am a bridge between the two cultures from which I descend.

---

[1] A tribal saying that outlines the mountains, waterways, important ancestors and tribal affiliations of a person. This saying locates me and my place in the world.

In my very existence, I am a bridge.

As we progress through this essay I use Professor Smith's book *Decolonizing Methodologies* (1999), in which she interrogates the role of research and researchers in Indigenous Peoples' lives, as a touchstone to reflect on my own journey. Professor Smith (1999, p. 5) wrote:

> A growing number of . . . researchers define themselves as Indigenous, although their training has been primarily within the western academy and specific disciplinary methodologies.

I am one of these researchers. I began my training in the Western academy at the University of Auckland in 2005, where I completed a conjoint Bachelor of Science majoring in Biology, specializing in Marine Science and Bachelor of Arts majoring in Māori studies. After a brief working break, I continued on to complete a Post-Graduate Diploma in Marine Studies at the (then) Bay of Plenty Polytechnic, in Tauranga during 2011. Progressing naturally through the Western academic system, I was offered the opportunity to spend time in Hawai'i and complete a Master of Science in Marine Science at Hawai'i Pacific University from 2012–2014. My academic career, while successful in many ways, was always fraught with tensions, both seen and unseen, as I struggled to find my place between Te Ao Māori and the Western scientific academy. It now strikes me that throughout my entire academic career there was no sign of *Decolonizing Methodologies* or notions of Kaupapa Māori methodologies in any of my lectures, tutorials or even discussions amongst my peers. In seven-and-a-half years, at three tertiary institutions, across two continents, these important ideas were entirely absent.

Perhaps this was a sign of the times; an indicator that although Professor Smith had asked questions of Indigenous Peoples, research and the colonizing frameworks of Western academies that prompted the academy to question itself, her work was still situated outside of the mainstream in fields such as marine science. Regardless of the reason, these two parts of my world seemed to be at odds. I continually wrestled with the ideas and concepts at the interface of my Indigeneity and Western scientific training. In fact, I continue to wrestle with these same ideas in my professional career but have, perhaps, become more accustomed to this particular wrestle. In pursuing a career that places me at this interface, I embody a bridge between both Māori and Western scientific knowledge systems.

In my work, I am a bridge.

Not only did Hawai'i provide me with an opportunity to advance in the Western academy but, looking back, it was a significant turning point of my life and academic career. Although I did not come across *Decolonizing Methodologies* and its theories, my experiences exposed me to the strong desire to decolonize my practice, which I had never before recognized or acknowledged within myself. I have written about my time in Hawai'i as a pivotal part of my journey later in this essay, but this brings me to another bridge. A bridge that perhaps pinpoints my apprehension to write this essay at all. When beginning my career in earnest as a science researcher, I was introduced to *Decolonizing Methodologies* as a text and the concept of Kaupapa Māori research in various forms. I saw the immense impacts that Professor Smith's work had made on so many, impacts that rippled through space and time. Yet, when I thought about writing this essay, I felt unqualified to reflect or comment on the thought leadership *Decolonizing Methodologies* represents, especially given my lack of interaction with it. I felt disconnected from the theories, with the view that my research was applied science and yet I had been challenged by fellow researchers about whether my work (using science knowledge systems to support and create outcomes for Indigenous communities) was actually Kaupapa Māori research. Despite these feelings of unease, I contemplated what I might have to say, spoke with mentors and friends, and decided to do it anyway (obviously). In agreeing to write this essay, facing my own insecurities head on, I hope to highlight the way in which we as Indigenous researchers in science do not have to re-articulate, or re-theorize what Professor Smith so masterfully articulates, but we are instead a bridge between these theories and their practice.

In my approach to my work, I am a bridge.

Throughout the rest of this essay, I have provided *whakataukī* or traditional proverbs. They are, where possible, credited to the source, or area of origin, but in some cases it remains unknown who was first to utter them. These words of wisdom handed down from my ancestors and those of my Hawaiian family serve as a reminder that we are part of a legacy. These proverbs have at various times guided and shaped me, propelled me forward, connected me to those who came before me and those who will come after me.

A bridge through time.

Ahakoa he iti, he pounamu
(Although it is small, it is precious)[2]

As an Indigenous science researcher I want to highlight some of the challenges and opportunities being "a bridge" presents. While to some my essay may be a small contribution to the discussion about where we are 20 years on from the first publication of *Decolonizing Methodologies*, I hope it will also be a precious contribution to another Indigenous person navigating a career in science, technology, engineering and maths (STEM). I hope that in some small way it inspires more Indigenous science researchers to occupy this space with confidence, because our contributions are invaluable.

On writing this essay

Tū whitia te hopo, mairangatia te angitū
(Feel the fear and do it anyway)[3]

This whakataukī encourages bravery. It implores you to forge ahead in spite of fear. I draw inspiration from this because, in order to write this essay, I am required to open myself up: to share my story, my journey with any and everyone who might take the time to read it, so that you may see where I stand today. To do so, I must be comfortable with being uncomfortable, with being vulnerable.

Part of this uncomfortableness comes from the very process of creating literature and ensuring that *how* it is written conforms to what is expected. I wanted to reflect on this process of creating literature, and in particular the requirements upon us as Indigenous writers to reference other written literature. Given the often oral nature of knowledge transfer, teaching and learning embedded in Indigenous cultures, this simple act can sometimes be uncomfortable, alienating and compromising. For example, how do we as Indigenous researchers acknowledge and reconcile non-written sources, such as the multitude of songs, stories, visual arts, people, places and experiences that have influenced and shaped our practice and thinking? How do we conform to (in my case) scientific writing conventions that do not allow us to accommodate our training and teachings from both within and outside of the Western

---

[2] For a further description see Mead and Grove (2004).
[3] For a further description, see Pihama et al (2019), pp. 47–48.

academy? How do we build on available published academic discourse in written form when it so rarely reflects us or our Indigeneity? It is perhaps these same questions that pinpoint why Professor Smith's work has been so important to so many.

In order to think critically about how *Decolonizing Methodologies* has impacted on my personal journey, I must bring forward and reflect on a collection of experiences, conversations, interactions and learnings that span people, place and time, that for the most part are situated outside of my academic training. These have no published records from which I can reference to adhere to the requirements of writing convention. In an attempt to overcome this limitation, throughout this essay I will attribute teachings to those experiences, individuals and communities that have shaped my perspectives, the times and events that provided me with growth and learning, and the places that challenged and molded my outlook on my work and practice. I do this in an attempt to acknowledge the legitimacy of this collection of experiences, people and places and how they have contributed to the position I write from, and in an attempt to further decolonize this process.

Hawai'i

In 2011, I applied to Fulbright New Zealand for a Fulbright Science and Innovation Graduate Award. The Fulbright award provides New Zealand graduates the opportunity to study in the United States of America. Passing up the opportunity to study at Scripps Institute of Oceanography (which I was told was quite a prestigious center for marine sciences), I chose to complete my master's degree at a lesser known, private university in Hawai'i. The reasons for this decision were both practical (resourcing) and personal. I wanted to experience another culture not unlike my own, within its unique context, practice and beliefs (Woodley 2002) and knew that I would grow more as a person in doing so. At this point, I had no idea how much this decision would shape my life or my work – how much this experience would be life-changing and perspective-altering for me. While my academic journey continued along much the same vein as my previous academic wanderings, what was remarkably different from what I had experienced up to that point in time were the people, places and practices that I was exposed to. It is impossible to summarize this time in my life in this essay alone, but I have attempted here to share some of the key moments and how they have influenced my career and practice.

"Cuppa tea time" and "talking story"

Professor Smith (1999, p. 5) writes that:

> Many indigenous researchers have struggled individually with the disconnections that are apparent between the demands of research, on the one side, and the realities they encounter amongst their own and other indigenous communities, with whom they share lifelong relationships with, on the other side.

This "outsider within" dynamic (Collins 1991) was something that I had never encountered in my work before, made even more complex by the fact that I was an Indigenous foreigner in another Indigenous Peoples' land. The added complexity of navigating not only the American Western academy, as well as a cross-cultural research divide, was incredibly difficult and I made mistakes.

Initially, responding to the demands of my research, papers and proposal defense, I tried repeatedly to engage with Kanaka Maoli (native Hawaiian people) for the purposes of my research. I would send emails and make phone calls to no avail. I was in contact with a group of Kanaka Maoli within the Heʻeia watershed, and in particular those restoring Pihi (also known as Heʻeia) Loko Iʻa (Fishpond[4]) through the non-profit organization Paepae o Heʻeia. As my research began to fall behind my supposed timeline, I contemplated why I had not made much progress with this community in regards to my research, especially given I was an "Indigenous researcher" with genuine intentions for my research to be relevant. A comment from a good friend while flying to New York together abruptly delivered an answer to this question and the first important lesson that this experience gave me:

> Kelly, if you were going to do work with our kaumātua (male and female elders) at home [in New Zealand] would you send emails and call them?
>
> Painting, I., Flight to New York, 2013

Without even realizing it, I had given in to the colonial structures of research and its communication and somehow forgotten a key research principle implicit in Professor Smith's writing: the principle of *kanohi ki te kanohi* (face to face). The essential act of repeatedly showing up, in person (which in retrospect seems painfully obvious) and being accountable within the teachings of my own Indigeneity, was missing from my approach. As this realization dawned, my response to my friend was simple: "No, I would take some biscuits and have a cup

---

[4] The Hawaiian "loko iʻa" is translated as "fishpond", which is an English term for the ancient aquaculture ponds constructed by native Hawaiian people. Heʻeia Fishpond is run by a non-profit organization Paepae o Heʻeia, and is a rock wall fishpond set on a reef-platform at the mouth of the Heʻeia Stream.

of tea." This same concept is described in Hawai'i as talking story. Alongside the fact that my research had not been grounded or grown from a place of mutual benefit with the He'eia community, my subsequent approach to engaging them into my research in the first place was flawed. This is something that Professor Smith talks about where, as beginning Indigenous researchers, we often experience these failures, flaws or lessons organically and in process as we try to navigate the insider/outsider dynamic (Smith 1999, p. 10), in my case without knowing it. While having a "cup of tea" on the surface seems arbitrary, what this methodology represents is far from arbitrary, including: repeated face to face interactions, listening genuinely, thinking slowly and understanding the needs of the communities you wish to work with and for. The multitude of these "cups of tea" form the basis of the lifelong relationships that bind me as an Indigenous researcher to all communities that I work alongside. They help us navigate being the "outsider within" *alongside* and mentored by our Indigenous research relationships.

When I returned to my research, my approach to working with the He'eia community changed substantially. With this realization, and the coincident arrival of another Māori scholar and her partner interested in working alongside the He'eia community, I began to spend my time volunteering at He'eia Fishpond and wetland workdays, working alongside the people with whom I would form that lifelong relationship. Without having encountered *Decolonizing Methodologies* at the time, I was practicing what Professor Smith was talking about. My relationship to He'eia Fishpond, the staff and extended community of Paepae o He'eia grew into a feeling of deep connectedness that transcended time and place and persists today. The many experiences that resulted from this relationship transformed my approach to research, causing me to question deeper my work as a scientist and the role of institutional science, and created an unyielding willingness to seek outcomes with and for the communities we are privileged to work alongside, and to go about it in the way that resonates both with the communities I work with and myself as an Indigenous person first and foremost.

"Not a museum piece"

When talking with my friend and kumu (teacher) about traditional fishing techniques, he told me of a remote historic fishing village not far from his hometown and how their ancestors used to live before they were removed by the American government. He talked about how his generation would travel there in season to gather resources and restore different parts of the village. He said it had been unoccupied for many generations, and that he had been asked to help lead the restoration of the hale va'a stone wall (the wall of a thatched house used to store canoes) in the village. Before accepting this, he asked why it was being restored, and what it would be used for. When prompted, he explained that:

> If it is only to look at for the tourists, then we should leave it as is, because I don't wanna build a museum piece and just be half done. If we're gonna do it, we should follow through. With the rock wall comes the hale (thatched house), with the hale comes the va'a (canoe), with the va'a comes the keiki (children) and then everything becomes alive and starts living again.
>
> Flores, P., Waimea Valley, Kaua'i, 2014

This intrigued me, and as I reflected on all of the experiences that my kumu had shared with me, I began to understand the significance of this particular comment. In his everyday work, he drew on the teachings of his ancestors. He *practiced* his culture, traditions, ceremonies, language and spirituality, irrespective of whether he had thought deeply about it, written about it, researched it or even obtained a degree from the Western academy. I thought about my encounters and experience with my own culture and how different it was from his. Most of my teachings about my culture had come from literature.

In my work, research as an endeavor is often filled with spaces to theorize, test and write about what we think and see. However, oftentimes research can lack practical and tangible outcomes, particularly for Indigenous communities. In his practice, my kumu was drawing on ancestral knowledge, thinking through issues, observing change, and adapting as his ancestors did, a different kind of "research" with immense value. This experience taught me many things, but most of all it taught me that as "a bridge" between cultures, both personally (because of my whakapapa (genealogy)) and professionally (because of my work), means that I need to create space for ways of being, knowing *and doing* that come from both Māori and Western academic beginnings. It highlighted for me that, in my own journey, I had unknowingly nurtured and sought out not only theory and knowledge (as opposed to practice), but also Western academic theory and knowledge. The words of my kumu hung heavy with me, and to this day guide the way I think of my own culture.

"You will know"

I was raised by parents who were not allowed to nurture or grow the part of themselves that was Māori. They were of the generation subject to the colonizing and oppressive laws that punished children for speaking te reo Māori (the Māori language) in school. My parents were denied the knowledge and tools required to immerse their children in our culture and language at home. Despite this, they always ensured we knew we were Māori, made sure to take us to events at the marae (complex of buildings including the traditional meeting house used for gatherings of importance), and used what te reo Māori they could each day. I was lucky my parents saw the value in our culture, language and practices even though they had not had many opportunities to pursue it themselves. Understanding the importance of sharing our language and culture, but knowing they could not provide it, they chose to set me on a pathway into Te Ao Māori, for which I am forever grateful. My secondary school education, and in some ways first concerted step into Te Ao Māori, ironically began at a Catholic Māori girls' college. Although it was a special character Māori girls' college, the school curriculum was mainstream, taught in English, and only occasionally reflected the substantial knowledge system of my ancestors. As a result, I began to seek this knowledge outside of the classroom. Those lessons came in many forms including my peers, elders and even experiences (e.g. attending gatherings and in many cases funerals on the marae). Seeking to deepen my understanding of Te Ao Māori and my own Indigeneity continued into my tertiary studies and throughout my Bachelor of Arts (Māori Studies) in particular. To this day I remain a student on this journey. As it should be.

Beginning my research career in Hawai'i and realizing how much of my work was to bridge gaps in understanding, in methods, in communication – and with much less knowledge and understanding of Te Ao Māori/Indigenous teachings than I would have liked, I was often left feeling inadequate. On one occasion, as I sat with a friend and mentor at Huilua Fishpond in Kahana Valley, O'ahu, looking at the fishpond rock wall needing some repair, we talked about how overwhelming things can seem not only in research or fishpond restoration, but in life. She reminded me of a Hawaiian proverb that I had heard many times working alongside her and others:

> *Ma ka hana ka 'ike*
> *(In doing you will know/learn)*[5]

When I talked to her about my feelings of inadequacy especially when it came to practice of culture and creating space for what I did not know deeply into my work, she told me:

---

[5] For a further description, see Pukui and Varez (1983).

You do not need to know everything, as long as your intentions are genuine,
your kupuna (ancestors) will guide you and it will come. Just start . . . one step at
a time . . . you will know.

Wallace, K., Huilua Loko Iʻa, Kahana, Oʻahu 2014

This was a timely reminder for me, that as a researcher I often get caught up in
intellectualizing and rationalizing my work, my culture and my place in the
world. She reminded me that nurturing our knowledge is important, but that we
must not forget to practice it. As I continued my research, I endeavored to apply
this approach, spending time with the community, being present and "doing". I
talked with the community (outside of my research), built trust and respect on a
personal level, and found that from this organic relationship, my research was
invited to be shared.

When I reflect on this approach, despite my perceived inadequacies in
Indigenous knowledge and teachings, and without having read Professor
Smith's work, I realize that the people, places and experiences I shared in
Hawaiʻi had shown me decolonizing methodologies in action. Hawaiʻi was
where I first encountered the concept of Kaupapa Māori, or (in this case)
Indigenous Hawaiian methodologies without having ever come across it in a
textbook.

In doing, I had learned.

Hawaiʻi was a turning point in my life in many ways, some of which I have
shared above. I would like to now move away specifically from my time in
Hawaiʻi, although you will see it continues to permeate into how I have perceived
and received many other experiences as a science researcher. In many ways, my
experiences have become a benchmark for how I want not just my work, but
my life to unfold. However, this also means that I sometimes struggle to attune
my professional work reality with a space that enables practical and tangible
outcomes, accommodates and promotes diverse knowledges and where our
communities are leading science research.

Diverse knowledge

One of the challenges for Māori researchers . . . has been to retrieve some
space – first, some space to convince Māori people of the value of research for
Māori; second, to convince the various, fragmented but powerful research

communities of the need of greater Māori involvement in research; and third,
to develop approaches and ways of carrying out research which take into
account, without being limited by, the legacies of previous research.

Smith 1999, p. 183

Retrieving space is a large part of my work.

As Māori "scientists" among our communities, we are often looked to as experts by those communities, as people who know *more* than the communities we work alongside. I am always trying to reiterate to our communities that their knowledge and understanding of their place is far superior to mine, that they are in fact the experts in their place and critical in achieving their research aspirations. Too often I hear "I don't know much" before a two-hour long interview that examines the rich history of use and practice embedded in the places and spaces our communities instinctively and naturally occupy. In this way we are not just retrieving space to convince our communities that research has value, but that *their* knowledge, Māori ways of knowing, being and doing, have value. As Professor Smith highlights, research is often implicated in "denying the validity for Māori of Māori knowledge, language and culture" (Smith 1999, p. 183). The legacy of science research (and research in general) with our communities includes practices of knowledge extraction and the systematic reliance on institutionalized scientific data. This legacy has meant that among some of our Indigenous communities, there is a disbelief that what they know matters. This is when the approach that we as Indigenous researchers take to working with our communities is crucial. In my work, with and for our communities, I aim to share the journey completely, from engagement, to co-creating and co-identifying the question/s, to gathering the data, to analyzing, interpreting and articulating the findings in multiple ways.

Pursuing the journey together can be uncomfortable, challenging and yet immensely rewarding. In some recent work with Ngāti Maniapoto, we have developed a project to map and collate their mātauranga of repo (swamps) and puna (springs) to support a hapū-driven and strategic prioritization of restoration efforts for their wetlands. During the introductory circle of our first wānanga (workshop), one of the participants began to ask questions about the project's relevance and how it would tangibly benefit him. He spoke at length of the issues that he was facing in his rural community and how this project (while of interest) was not going to be helpful. As I stood in front of him, all I could do was agree with his assessment of the multi-faceted challenges that him and his whānau faced, and in that moment I felt helpless. One small question has stayed with me and continues to reinforce the importance of research that has relevance:

What's the point?

Workshop Participant, Kāwhia 2017

This small question carried a heavy burden. This was probably the second time I had been confronted with directed cynicism towards research (not just my own research), and the first time that the multiple realities that many of our communities are dealing with really hit home. Our people are busy, really busy, dealing with multiple responsibilities, multiple jobs (paid and unpaid) and just trying to live in today's society. Add to that the responsibility of carrying our rich knowledge system into the future, the many research projects and researchers asking for their time, and you begin to see just how resilient our people are. During the break of our workshop, I was in tears as the weight of his comments sunk in and I began to realize that I had failed to consider these perspectives.

I took a moment, pulled myself together, and our workshop resumed. To my surprise, as we continued, and despite his conviction that the work was less than useful to him, this participant worked seemingly enthusiastically to map wetlands known to him, sharing knowledge we were privileged to receive. I cannot pinpoint when the shift happened, or why he stayed, but something about the process managed to break down those barriers. Perhaps it was because we were inside the whare tupuna (the carved meeting house, the realm of Rongo – the deity of peace) or perhaps it was his way of testing me and, somehow, I had passed. Regardless, throughout the whole project this participant remained engaged from start to finish. Sharing our journey, multiple cups of tea, thinking slowly through the process and ensuring that we could be both respectful and honest about the benefit of spending his time with us, we saw a shift in his perspective that was so rewarding. Watching the delight when he and the other participants saw their knowledge represented on maps and in a tool to support decision-making (for and by the whānau) was hugely satisfying and humbling. I share this experience because there are three key things that story highlights:

1. Research priorities are one subset of a much larger set of priorities (e.g. treaty settlement[6]) that each of our whānau, hapū and iwi is striving to achieve – and we must be patient with that.

---

[6] The Treaty of Waitangi is an agreement, written in both Māori and English, that was made between Māori rangatira (chiefs) and the British Crown in 1840. This document is the basis through which iwi are undertaking treaty settlement that seeks redress for historical breaches of the treaty.

2. When we as Indigenous researchers enter a community, we are often expected to shoulder the criticisms and injustices of a legacy of research that has not prioritized our communities' questions, knowledge or culture.
3. We are all on a journey together and it is shared experience that builds trust, accountability and life-long relationships.

To put it in the words of Professor Smith (1999, p. 5):

> Indigenous research is a humble and humbling activity.

Working alongside Māori communities, there are two key messages that I reiterate; that science from the Western academy is one source of information and one set of tools available to us (and the source I am most qualified to talk to); and, that mātauranga Māori (and all Indigenous knowledge systems for that matter) remain another powerful and valid source of knowing, understanding, describing and experiencing the world. Something that I have come to realize in my journey is that, as Indigenous Peoples, we have our own knowledge systems, intimate understanding of the land and waterscapes – ways of seeing the world. As such, we are uniquely able to draw on, interpret, discuss and utilize that ancestral, traditional and contemporary understanding in our search for answers. It is for this reason that we have such a valuable contribution to make, especially in environmental science and research. While I may not know or understand the depth and breadth of Te Ao Māori, it is not my job to. Rather, my role has been creating the opportunity and space for our communities to access all available knowledge and tools to achieve their research aspirations.

The tension that exists at the interface of these two knowledge systems is highlighted in *Decolonizing Methodologies*; the idea that the Western academic institutions cannot and should not monopolize the power and economy of knowledge. I believe, as Indigenous Peoples, only we have the power to realize the potential of our unique knowledge systems. There is some discourse in the literature that debates whether Indigenous ways of knowing and being are, or should be, called science or "Indigenous science" (Catton 2009; Hikuroa 2017). When discussing this idea with a good friend, mentor and a tertiary educator from Hawai'i, she spoke specifically about the act of naming science:

> When talking about science we need to be specific in our references especially when talking about institutional (Western) sciences. When we speak of "Science" (institutional) with an assumption that it is THE science we continue the belief that there is only one science AND that it is all powerful. Institutional science is one very valuable way to explain and define the world around us, BUT so is

Hawaiian Science [or] Māori Science.... Referring to Institutional science as "the" science also leads "others" to assume and continue to believe the lie that other cultures and people do not have science AND we most definitely do.

Andrade, P., Whāingaroa 2018

This idea that we might inadvertently empower institutional Western science knowledge by the mere act of calling it "science" is important for us to consider. It is especially important when considering the policy context which is most often driven by "science or evidence-based" decision-making. The question of what is, or rather whose "science" and "evidence" decisions are being made, becomes a key driver of much of the work that we as Indigenous science researchers do.

Almost 15 years ago, the government of Aotearoa New Zealand released the "Vision Mātauranga Policy" (VM Policy), which was to be applied to all science, research and technology funding (New Zealand Government 2007). This document talks about "unlocking the potential of Māori people, resources and knowledge for the benefit of New Zealand", and has forced the prevailing science system to look deeper at the relationships between itself, research and Māori in Aotearoa. While the intent of the policy is attempting to embed space for Māori knowledge systems and people in the science funding system, almost 15 years on the application of the policy continues to evolve, driven largely by Indigenous researchers who are working to untangle what "unlocking the potential" looks like in practice. The VM Policy has been successful in creating a shift in science research funding, but it is still reliant on the genuine intentions and open-mindedness of researchers (both Indigenous and non-Indigenous) to create the required space and explore new horizons driven by and together with Māori communities. This is an ongoing challenge that we as Indigenous researchers must continue to work on.

Direct and indirect impact

Professor Smith's work is arguably one of the most heavily referenced texts by Indigenous researchers world-wide because of the articulate, relevant, thought-provoking and familiar narratives that it lays out. Although I did not encounter this narrative until beginning my professional career, I am fortunate. I am fortunate because my personal journey has developed my approach to my work through ongoing experiential learning, a multi-cultural amalgamation of teachings, and a deep desire to *be* Māori in the work that I do. I think this story will be familiar to many walking this path in STEM, and in many ways is exactly what Professor Smith wrote about. From where I stand, one of the key outcomes of *Decolonizing Methodologies* was the emergence of academic literature, theory and methodologies specific to Indigenous Peoples. The formalization of Kaupapa Māori research in this text was a landmark for many Indigenous researchers, in that this articulation of research methodology finally reflected the way in which we *already* operate instinctively. This created space for Indigenous researchers such as me, to do the work we do, *how* we do it, with just a little less justification required. It enabled the ability for me to "stand on the shoulders of giants" and reference literature (in a system so focused on referencing literature) that placed an emphasis on an Indigenous methodology, and centered our experiences operating as Māori researchers in its critique of the research process. In this way the impacts of *Decolonizing Methodologies* have been direct.

However, *Decolonizing Methodologies* has also impacted me indirectly and in some instances challenged my perspectives on myself and the work I do. When I first started my career in research, I was still getting comfortable with the, at times, uncomfortable nature of working at the interface of knowledge systems. I was still learning to navigate how to be a bridge between Western notions of science and ensure I made space for mātauranga Māori. As that bridge, my work was often to find the tools and approaches that would best achieve the outcome sought by the community I was working with. Sometimes those tools and approaches were derived from Western science and sometimes they were derived from Te Ao Māori. At the time, the question about what exactly Kaupapa Māori research meant was raised many times. Most often, the response I heard was that it was research with Māori, by Māori and for Māori. As a researcher (who is Māori), working alongside Māori communities to create positive outcomes for Māori, I identified as a Kaupapa Māori researcher – until I was challenged on this belief. I was questioned by another Māori colleague about whether the use of Western science methodologies alongside Te Ao Māori methodologies was still Kaupapa Māori research. At the time I was quite confronted by this, mainly because (as is hopefully evident) I was (and still am) advocating for our Indigenous knowledge systems to be *enough*, to be legitimate and valid, and yet much of my work drew on Western scientific tools and approaches. I was also confronted because it felt as though my integrity as a Māori (researcher) was being challenged. How could I claim to be a Kaupapa Māori researcher, when what I do is Western science? I rationalized that my work was still "with Māori, by Māori and for Māori" as described by so many as the definition of Kaupapa

Māori and found peace in that, but this challenge always weighed heavy on my mind. In discussion with mentors who have spent much longer working in the space in which I found myself, I also gained strength in the notion that utilizing Western scientific methodologies was not so much a cop-out, but actually strategic. As I was once told:

> You refer to yourself as a bridge builder, but you still need someone to decide that a bridge is needed.
>
> Tipa, G., 2019

Further to this, when I am humbled by the communities that I work alongside to be invited back, and receive positive feedback and gratitude, I know that if I wasn't there, if we as Indigenous researchers weren't there, then no one would be pushing these boundaries alongside our whānau, hapū and iwi. We are in the position to be able to take the best of what Western science has to offer to support delivery of Māori-focused outcomes. For many of our Indigenous communities, Western science approaches have been seen as a necessary tool to support the communication of what their Indigenous knowledge systems and assessments tell them to be true, to external audiences such as local councils and central government agencies. The difference (and perhaps imperative to seek out Western science) is that within the prevailing narrative of "evidence-based" policy and decision-making, Western science (as opposed to Indigenous ways of knowing, being and doing) is still privileged and is the most common "language" that is listened to. Until this paradigm shifts and Māori understanding, ways of knowing, being and doing are recognized and listened to, I believe we are no less Māori by utilizing Western scientific tools to our advantage in order achieve the outcomes we seek. This concept is echoed in the following whakatauākī (proverb) by Sir Āpirana Ngata:

> *E tipu, e rea, mō ngā rā o tōu ao; ko tō ringa ki ngā rākau a te Pākehā hei ara mō te tinana. Ko tō ngākau ki ngā taonga a ō tīpuna Māori hei tikitiki mō tō māhunga, ā ko tō wairua ki te Atua, nāna nei ngā mea katoa (Ngata, 1949)[7]*

In this proverb, Ngata encourages us to grasp the tools and approaches of the British[8] to support our aspirations, while also holding fast to the teachings of our ancestors that adorn and guide us. Embedded in this proverb is an affirmation

---

[7] Grow up, tender plant, to fulfil the needs of your world; your hand grasping the tools of the Pākehā (non-Māori settlers) for your physical needs, your heart centered on the treasures of your Māori ancestors as a plume for your head, and your soul to God who made all things.

[8] The British are referred to here as they were the dominant settler society established in New Zealand and represented the Crown as a treaty partner.

that we as Indigenous Peoples have the innate ability to be the bridge between these two knowledge systems, *and* to utilize both without compromising our Indigeneity.

Professor Smith (1999, p. 199) wrote:

> As Indigenous peoples we have our own research needs and aspirations. Our questions are important. Research helps us answer them.

I think this statement highlights an important point: that it is Māori research needs, aspirations and questions that drive Kaupapa Māori research. It is more about *how* we conduct ourselves in the research process, and less about what tools we use to achieve the outcome. To me, Kaupapa Māori research is about having genuine intentions and a shared journey to navigate the research within the unique cultural context of our communities. I have come to realize one of the most important parts of my work within a science institution is to be the person who can be the bridge for our communities because, if we are not here to do so, no one else will be.

Reflections

When I first set out to write this essay I wondered – would my journey have been different if I had come across *Decolonizing Methodologies* while I was at university?

Maybe, maybe not.

So much of what Professor Smith wrote is familiar to me, given the experiences I have had to date. I am not sure that 20-year-old me would have found such resonance. This process has highlighted that, with or without *Decolonizing Methodologies*, the teachings of my ancestors (that I am still discovering), the places that I have lived, the people I am lucky to have shared space with, and the communities that I am privileged to work alongside, have taught me to decolonize my methodologies.

Upon completing the essay, a mentor posed two questions for me to reflect on: what advice I might give to other Indigenous Peoples currently studying science and if I would recommend reading *Decolonizing Methodologies*. First, I would say, whether Indigenous or not, that reading *Decolonizing Methodologies* can only better equip you for working within the current science and research system in Aotearoa New Zealand, that it would not hurt to have a more in-depth knowledge of what might be encountered on your journey. In the same breath my advice to Indigenous students would be that ways to decolonize your methodologies cannot and should not only be found in a book, but in actively committing to research alongside your community. There will always be times when we stumble, maybe even fall, on the path but I can guarantee our communities will be there to set us straight. In doing, we learn the deepest, hardest and most meaningful lessons – so do not be afraid to try.

The second question posed was if I regretted my training to become a scientist. This one gave me pause. However, the short answer is no. I do not regret it at all. What I have come to realize is that I am a scientist with or without my training in the Western academy. Being curious, asking questions, observing changes and making life decisions were a common practice of our ancestors and it is also a part of mine. My training only provided me with another way to look at the world and be who I intuitively am. My career in science has created unique and beautiful opportunities that have changed my life and led me right where I need to be.

Each of us will walk a unique path – I only hope that in sharing this part of my journey, I can bridge space, time and culture to help another Indigenous scientist to navigate their own path.

I am a bridge.

6

A spoke in the wheel: Ancestral women's legacies

Angela Burt (*palawa*)

Introduction

I am a First Nations woman descended from a matriarchy who held together a sovereign people and have defied the odds by surviving. I am an Islander, a *palawa* woman of *trouwunna* (Cape Barren Island), an isolated island in the Bass Strait, the body of water that separates mainland Australia from *lutruwita* (Tasmania). Colonization is a tiny fragment of our story that dates back over 40,000 years to the last ice age, when *trouwunna* formed part of a larger landmass known as the Bassian Plain (Ryan 2012). As the sea level steadily rose and engulfed the landscape, *trouwunna* was realized and remains in place today (Maynard 1985). The term *palawa* is a collective term, a familial term used to identify and position First Nations Peoples of Tasmania. In contrast, most of what is written about us fails to acknowledge our identity, referring to us as the Aborigines of Tasmania.

The disconnect between how we are known, and who we are, is a problem that weighs heavily on the hearts of my people. The outside world has come to know us through the unnamed portraits of my family (Bonyhady & Lehman 2018) – spiritually and narratively held captive in the museum archives, through the catalogs that list cranial measurements and through the blood samples taken without consent – and are known through the physical bits that accompany the visual record of our colonization. The disconnect between "knowledge about" First Nations Peoples and "knowing" First Nations Peoples lies at the heart of our collective struggle for survival within settler-colonial states.

This essay tells a story that is not dissimilar to that of other First Nations Peoples globally who have been defined and known by events and acts outside their control. Positioned as subjects, sometimes as objects, these histories render

First Nations Peoples as voiceless "extras" whose presence is needed, but certainly not wanted. This story aligns with the basic premise of all colonial tales which position the superior against the inferior, with the colonizer victorious based on their intellect, superior resources and systems of governance. For First Nations Peoples of *lutruwita*, our tale of colonization was written prior to the British setting foot on the island, influenced by the sharpening of their tactics through other colonial battles. Our story ended with the supposed extinction of the "Aborigines of Tasmania" (Reynolds 2008; Ryan 1996), of our people discontinuing as a First Nations identity. From the arrival of the colonizers, it took just 30 years for the *palawa* population to fall by over 90 per cent and is a brutality unlikely to be seen again in the modern world (Reynolds 2008; Reynolds 2012; Ryan 2012; West 1852). My people have come to be known through quantifiers, our lives mapped out linearly, from existence to non-existence. Such reductive generalizations do not adequately represent Indigenous knowledges that are "theoretically sophisticated and robust" (Rigney 2001, p. 9). The language and terminologies used do not belong to us, the accounts of our actions are not our own, our silence and our inability to respond is not our choice. Whilst we have no control over the marginalization of our knowledges within these colonized spaces, our knowledges, which are inherited and influenced by our relationship to Country, our people and our ancestral creator beings, refuse to be silenced (Moreton-Robinson 2013). Through the voices and actions of our women, in particular, these matriarchal knowledges are challenging the ways in which we are known.

In writing from a position that is both *palawa* and female, my existence disputes the generalized knowledge about *palawa* by inserting contrasting knowledge: knowledge that is not white or male. Therefore, I tell the story of one of the women in my family and how her story influences my work, while I, in turn, strive to reclaim her place in colonizing space. This is an exploration of how women are woven through my family tree as part of Country and belonging, where their voices are a "powerful form of resistance" (Smith 1999, p. 34).

I share with you the story of my Great Aunty Molly – Dr Mary Maynard Mallett – a published author, Elder and advocate for children. In her text, *My Past – Their Future: Stories from Cape Barren Island* (Mallett 2001), Aunty Molly combines her experience, academic knowledge and culture to expose and refute the knowledge generated about *palawa* through the 1939 Harvard – South Australia University Anthropological Expedition to Cape Barren Island. In doing so, Aunty Molly becomes a framework for future generations of *palawa* women to decolonize the knowledges that define, limit and silence us. I use this framework as a guide to further interrogate the conditions that enable knowledge to be created about *palawa*. I also use the text of Aunty Molly as a case study to reframe the normative narratives of Western knowledge systems and create a space for female Indigenous knowledges and ways of knowing. Drawing upon the theories of First Nations and other scholars including Linda Tuhiwai Smith (1999), Gayatri Spivak (1988) and Aileen Moreton-Robinson (2011), I expand this framework to include global perspectives and, in turn, bring the voices of *palawa* women to this global dialogue.

Our knowledges

For First Nations Peoples our ways of knowing, being and doing, when compared with Western knowledge systems, are classified as naïve, with no scientific basis or cognitive credibility (Foucault 1980). This classification has less to do with the integrity and legitimacy of our knowledges and more to do with who has the power to decide what constitutes knowledge (Fanon 2008; Foucault 1980; Moreton-Robinson 2011; Spivak 1988). The established rules that dictate whose knowledges are most valued are deeply rooted within and influenced by imperialism and colonialism – both predicated on Western superiority (Smith 1999). This superiority was strengthened as Western explorers and researchers traveled the globe, growing the empire and collecting evidence that strengthened their status, whilst controlling the discourse about First Nations Peoples (Bourdieu 1986; Foucault 1980).

It is important to recognize the pivotal role that research played in the subjugation of First Nations knowledges (Said 1978; Smith 1999; Wolfe 2006). Professor Linda Tuhiwai Smith goes so far as to say that research is one of the "dirtiest" words in the vocabulary of Indigenous People (Smith 1999, p. 1). Colonization, among many other things, brought to First Nations people a menagerie of "researchers" – crew, convicts, free settlers – all collecting knowledge about the "natives" (Smith 1999). Their opinions were sent back to the Empire, shaping the way that the outside world would forever know First Nations Peoples (Smith 1999). The only people who were not contributing to this growing body of knowledge were First Nations Peoples themselves (Mallett 2001; Manne 2003; Smith 1999; Watson 2007). "The significance of travelers' tales and adventurers' adventures is that they represented the Other to a general audience back in Europe which became fixed in the milieu of cultural ideas" (Smith 1999, p. 8). These travelers' tales represented First Nations Peoples as primitive beings, more animal than human. Women were excluded from these tales, which were spread back home through church sermons, newspapers and by word of mouth. Imperial thoughts were normalized and unchallenged, fitting comfortably within the global discourse (Smith 1999; Wolfe 2006). Thus, we are known in the ways that support a Western narrative of intellectual superiority, while our knowledges are always the Other and decrepit (Gramsci 1971; Said 1978).

Spivak (1988), in expanding Gramsci's (1971) subaltern theory through a focus on women, has examined what happens to the voices of oppressed and marginalized female outsiders when they speak within a space that is dominated and ruled by the elite (the insiders). In her essay "Can the Subaltern Speak?" Spivak (1988) asks whether it is possible for women of color and of lower-class, who inhabit the periphery of society, to speak or be heard. Spivak's view is valuable here; First Nations women are appreciated as more than just female objects in a settler state – they *are* the understanding of what subalternity looks like and does. In exploring whether marginalized women can speak, Spivak (1988, 1999) examined the value placed on the knowledge that these women have to share. In doing so, she shifted the spotlight away from the validity of female knowledge systems, moving it towards how knowledge is created about women and by whom (Spivak 1988, 1999).

For those Western men who control the production and dissemination of knowledge, First Nations Peoples are obviously marginalized away from centers of power. In particular, First Nations women are subject to further colonizing burdens (Smith 1999), such as erasure from the record completely, which create the conditions of un-belonging:

> The process of en-gendering descriptions of the Other has had very real consequences for indigenous women in that the ways in which indigenous women were described, objectified and represented by Europeans in the nineteenth century has left a legacy of marginalization within indigenous societies as much as within the colonizing society.
>
> Smith 1999, p. 98

The invisibility of our women from the record has a profound and ongoing impact. Spivak (1988) introduced the term "epistemic violence" to expand the work of Bourdieu (1986) and Foucault (1980) to include the ongoing impact of subjugation on the body, mind and spirit of women. By expanding people's understanding of the ongoing impact of knowledge subjugation, Spivak (1988) highlighted how imperative it is to not only understand the conditions that enable this subjugation, but to challenge them and interrupt this cycle of knowledge oppression.

Epistemic violence

Thus, one way that Western superiority is legitimized by its own power and knowledge is the enactment of an epistemic violence against First Nations women that renders us either silent or missing. Distinguished Professor Aileen Moreton-Robinson (2011), an Australian Indigenous researcher, looks closely at how subaltern conditions are created for our women, but more importantly how we emerge away from them. Moreton-Robinson (2011), in understanding that power comes through knowing and naming the conditions that subjugate our knowledges, opens a discussion about who is best placed to generate knowledge about us.

When we speak of epistemic violence it is important to acknowledge that this is an ongoing violence, which for First Nations women occurred through colonization, but is propagated through colonialism and patriarchal whiteness:

> Patriarchal whiteness operates possessively as a raced and gendered epistemological a priori within knowledge production as universals, dominant norms, values, and beliefs. Patriarchal whiteness is thus epistemologically and ontologically privileged but invisible within its socio-discursive regime capillarising through Australian disciplinary knowledges and modern colonial practices.
>
> Moreton-Robinson 2011, p. 414

In "The White Man's Burden" (2011), Moreton-Robinson highlights the ongoing subjugation of the knowledges of female First Nations scholars within Australia. The article responds to commentary made by white male academic Dirk Moses (2010) on the Northern Territory Intervention, a national emergency response to protect Aboriginal children in the Northern Territory from alleged sexual abuse and family violence (AHRC 2007). Within this critique, Moreton-Robinson draws attention to Moses' description of the work of First Nations women and criticizes the government's handling of the response as being "emotional and political in order to reduce its validity by discursively positioning himself as the embodiment of rationality and reason: the disinvested white patriarchal knower" (Moreton-Robinson 2011, p. 420).

Moreton-Robinson draws attention to the language chosen by Moses to describe Aboriginal women, language that he does not use when describing the work of Aboriginal men. Moreton-Robinson then goes further, applying the same logic to challenge Moses' credibility as an expert on Aboriginal affairs, an area in which he has no formal qualifications. In doing so, she draws attention to his white patriarchal belief that knowledge produced by objective white male experts will always trump that of subjective black female non-experts (Moreton-Robinson 2011). Within this, she further critiques his assertion that one can only become an expert through formal Western education. By highlighting that Moses attacks only the logic and credibility of black female academics, rather than black males, she exposes his belief that, regardless of education, title or social capital, black women and their knowledges will always remain on the periphery (Moreton-Robinson 2011). Moreton-Robinson's critique achieves its purpose to expose the white patriarchal beliefs that constrain knowledge production and dissemination about First Nations women, highlighting that the subjugation of female Indigenous knowledges that began in 1788 persists today (Applebaum 2010; Moreton-Robinson 2011).

Decolonization and justice

Based on the continuity of colonization, and its relentless shaping of First Nations societies, Patrick Wolfe (2006, p. 388) reclassifies settler-colonialism as a "structure", rather than "an event". It is for this reason that the inverse process of decolonization requires a supporting structure, or framework, and cannot be achieved through a single process/event (Smith 1999). In relation to the decolonization of knowledges, and knowledge production, sustained labor is required from First Nations Peoples living in settler-colonial states (Battiste 2000; Bond 2006; Moreton-Robinson 2013; Smith 1999; Watson 2007; Wolfe 2006). It is for this reason that Professor Linda Tuhiwai Smith challenges First Nations Peoples to consider whether *this* knowledge, one that controls, silences and erases, is of importance to who they are, and where they are headed (Smith 1999). This is both a valid and necessary question that First Nations Peoples collectively seek to resolve. In doing so, they must first locate themselves within these knowledges – a process that is both violent and traumatic (Simpson 2014). For some, the burden of this process is too much; and for others, who can bear the load, this process leads to further critical inquiry. In critiquing and deconstructing the romanticism that underpins anthropological work about them, First Nations Peoples can reveal the racial structures that protect and enable whiteness. In doing so, we can increase both our agency and power, which can be used by First Nations People to negotiate space for our sovereignty and truth (Coulthard 2014; Deloria 2003).

Smith's theory of decolonization speaks of the power that First Nations Peoples can gain from understanding the conditions that oppress and marginalize (Smith 1999). The idea of knowing where we have come from is central to our ability to have autonomy over where we are headed. Fricker (2013) refers to this as epistemic justice whereby epistemic subjects use their knowledge of the conditions that marginalize them to change their social condition. The purposeful movement of First Nations Peoples away from simply surviving colonization, to re-writing narratives and re-righting our position as sovereign peoples has gathered traction over the past 50 years as Smith (1999, p. 72) states, "Indigenous peoples want to tell our own stories, write our own versions, in our own ways, for our own purposes". The production of knowledges about First Nations Peoples from this perspective breaks the rules about how knowledge is produced about First Nations Peoples and by whom. "When the people we speak of speak for themselves, their sovereignty interrupts anthropological portraits of timelessness, procedure and function that dominate representations of their past and, sometimes, their present" (Simpson, 2014, p. 97). This is why our stories need to be told. Through voicing our narratives we are giving testimony to the injustices of our past and emancipating our people from the grips of colonialism (Dudgeon 2017; Fredericks & White 2018; Huggins 1998; Martin & Mirraboopa 2003; Smith 1999; Watson 2017).

A spoke in the wheel

palawa women are great initiators and fierce fighters, especially when it comes to protecting our own and fighting for justice (Cameron 1994; Felton 1989; Mallett 2001). As a result of the work of female Tasmanian Aboriginal academics (Cameron 1994; Cameron & Miller 2016; Mallett 2001; *tebrakunna* country & Lee 2017, 2019) we are changing the ways in which we are known. Through sharing our culture and our ways, we are claiming a space for Aboriginal voices that previously did not exist. Within this space we can develop our own methodologies and interrogate our contested knowledges, bringing our women and our knowledges back to a place that reflects and respects the matriarchy from whom we descended (Dodson & Cronin 2011; Watson 2017). The story of one *palawa* woman – Dr Mary Maynard Mallett (Aunty Molly) – provides a case study in how our women are using their knowledge and culture to find a form of epistemic justice. A self-described "spoke in the wheel" of colonialism and a strong matriarchal leader for my people, Aunty Molly's story puts into action the theories discussed in this essay and offers an alternative framework that is uniquely *palawa* and of *trouwunna*.

Aunty Molly

Mary Frances Maynard was born on Cape Barren Island in 1926 to James Henry Paul Maynard, a World War I veteran, and Augusta Lavinia Mansell. She had 11 siblings – with one being Baden, who is my grandfather. Known to everyone on the island as Molly, her childhood was idyllic, surrounded by her family, her people and her culture. She affectionately remembers attending school, caring for her siblings and mutton-birding with the community. As is common in our family, she could be a child, aware of, but not concerned with, politics:

> Those years on Cape Barren were wonderful times to look back on. We were free and there was so much love. We grew up without being surrounded by people who treated us as if we were inferior.
>
> Mallett 2001, p. 52

After leaving Cape Barren at the age of 14, and eventually moving to northern Tasmania, Aunty Molly later married, started her own family, and devoted her life to helping Aboriginal youth.

> That was something that I knew there was a need for and so I just went ahead and did it. My involvement with children went back to when I started to take "wards of the state children" in. I knew the need was there for these children to be cared for and better themselves.
>
> Mallett 2001, p. 63

After attending the first Aboriginal Child Survival Seminar in 1979, Aunty Molly decided that she would establish an Aboriginal childcare center in Tasmania (Mallett 2001). After sourcing funding and finding a suitable location on King's Wharf in Hobart, she began preparing the facility. With no money to employ contractors, Aunty Molly rolled-up her sleeves and proceeded to transform the derelict building. She went on to be the inaugural coordinator of the Tasmanian Aboriginal Childcare Centre and donated her salary back to the center to buy food and clothing. Once the center was operational, she became chairperson of the Tasmanian Aboriginal Education Council, a role which she filled for six years.

In 1998, in her role as Elder-in-Residence at the University of Tasmania, Aunty Molly returned to *trouwunna*. In 2000, she received an Honorary Doctorate of Letters from the University of Tasmania. In 2002, she was made a Member of the Order of Australia for her service to the Aboriginal community. She later published a book about her early life on Cape Barren Island titled *My Past – Their Future: Stories from Cape Barren Island.*

My Past – Their Future

Can't people see that the written history is not true? So many reports have been written about Cape Barren Island people.... Who starts this history? So much of it is malicious gossip. You've got to see and hear before you can repeat anything about us. I think we have enough educated Tasmanian Aboriginal people in today's society to be able to put a spoke in some of the wheels and write the truth about us.

Mallett 2001, p. 46

My Past – Their Future focuses our attention on the 1939 Harvard-Adelaide anthropological expedition to Cape Barren Island (*trouwunna*), one leg of a whirlwind tour of Aboriginal reserves in Australia. The purpose of the expedition was to examine whether race-mixing and hybridity presented a safety risk to the general population of Australia (D'Arcy 2007). To do this, it was necessary to collect data from a "half-caste" population that had existed in relative isolation from outside contamination, and Cape Barren Island was the perfect provider (D'Arcy 2007). At the time, the expedition was described as revolutionary; it is now described as an extreme practice of whiteness, superiority and control (Davis 2009). This criticism is based not only on the actions of the researchers, but on the racist policy of assimilation that underpinned and funded the tours (D'Arcy 2007; Hasluck 1961; Mallett 2001). Eugenics, the belief that more suitable races or strains of blood had a better chance of prevailing over the less suitable, while unconfirmed, was a silent partner within this research project (Anderson 2008; D'Arcy 2007; Davis 2009).

The tour group comprised two white male researchers – Joseph Birdsell and Norman Tindale. Together with their wives, they arrived on the shores of Cape Barren in January of 1939 (D'Arcy 2007; Tindale 1939). Over a period of nine days, the men extracted samples of blood, took measurements of body parts and photographic records (Anderson 2008; Birdsell 1939; Bonwick 1870; D'Arcy 2007; Malcolm 1920; Tindale 1939, 1941). The data were meticulously recorded and later cataloged as the Tindale Collection, which is held in the South Australian Museum Archives. The collection contains the genealogies of over 50,000 Indigenous People including thousands of photographic portraits (AIATSIS 2018).

In her book, Aunty Molly purposefully omits known facts about the expedition, knowledge that already exists, published by other non-Indigenous researchers. Instead, she includes first-hand recollections of events, anecdotal "non-scientific" data; knowledge that sits in stark contrast to that collected and collated by Tindale and Birdsell. She re-publishes the photographs taken by Tindale, but this time she adds captions and detailed descriptions of each person's interests, their mannerisms and other intimate knowledge. The knowledge that Aunty Molly shares is personable, her language is colloquial, these purposeful choices being the binary opposite to the way in which Tindale and Birdsell generated and presented knowledge about my people.

Of the collection of samples, Aunty Molly writes:

> I can remember as a young teenager getting undressed and standing in line with boys while we were examined by the scientists. I was very embarrassed, we were taught to never expose our bodies to the opposite sex . . . I cried all the time, I wasn't the only one who had their head measured, looked up nose, in ears, structure of cheek bone, hair, fingers, toes recorded.
>
> Mallett 2001, p. 43

In sharing this memory, from the perspective of a young vulnerable Aboriginal woman, she is humanizing the data, at the same time drawing attention to the unethical practice of the researchers and their agenda. This anecdote highlights that whilst she was physically present, through the dehumanizing process of research, her being was erased from the record (Spivak 1988).

Of the purpose of the expedition she writes:

> When Norman B. Tindale came to Cape Barren Island in 1939, he was looking for specimens for testing of an Aboriginal-European community. I learnt later that Tindale was looking for the scientific point of view. I did not expect to see such disgusting photographs. Why were we picked? We were human beings just like the rest of the people in the world.
>
> Mallett 2001, p. 43

In this excerpt Aunty Molly writes from the perspective of the "naïve" subject, but at the same time uses pointed language such as "specimen" and "disgusting" to allude to the more sinister motives of the researchers. Her use of the pronoun "he", and her refusal to use correct titles, draws attention to gender and the power that is afforded, without question, to white male researchers (Moreton-Robinson 2013; Smith 1999).

The juxtaposition of these anecdotes against the photographic samples taken by Tindale expertly highlights the disconnect between how our people have been known, and who we are. In addition, Aunty Molly reclassifies us from unknown to known. She takes knowledge (photographs) generated by a white male Western researcher and superimposes new knowledge (names and stories). In doing so, she demonstrates that there is more than one way to know our people and that it is possible for Indigenous knowledges to exist alongside Western knowledges. In writing her story, Aunty Molly has interrupted the stagnant representations of our people, animating, naming and humanizing them (Simpson 2014). The expert way in which she weaponizes her knowledge (and words) to draw attention to and diffuse the power structures that enable white male researchers to construct knowledge about our peoples is inspired. In her own words, Aunty Molly has put a spoke in the wheel, stopping the cycle of misrepresentation and misinformation of knowledge about our people:

> Previously they were just unknown black faces, no features at all, these wonderful people who were born on Cape Barren and most of them buried on the Island. These old people were our teachers, our Elders ... I feel that it is important for me to tell this story, and to bring dignity to my people who were treated with such disrespect by this researcher.
>
> Mallett 2001, p. 43

From subject to expert

The title of expert is afforded to those who possess the ability to produce objective and scientifically sound knowledge about a subject (Foucault 1980), and the rules that govern who can generate such knowledge are set by those with power and privilege. Thus, the title of expert seems unattainable by First Nations women, who remain marginalized and silenced by the dominant patriarchal power structures that govern knowledge production (Moreton-Robinson 2011; Spivak 1988). Within this space, our women remain passive subjects, with knowledge created about them, but never by them. This arrangement, though, is dependent on the cooperation of the subject to remain on the periphery – never speaking, thus never being heard. An arrangement that comes unstuck when our women change the rules, shifting from subalternity to an alternate place where black female voices can be heard, where they can assume the role of knower, rather than the known (Mallett 2001). The knowledge they generate within this space contrasts and, in the case of Aunty Molly, contradicts Western knowledges about them and draws attention to the white patriarchal ways in which it was generated. This, in turn, breaks the rules set by the patriarchy, opening debate around who is the expert and who is the subject.

Dr Mary Francis Mallett was just a girl at the time of the expedition; it was 60 years later that she published a book to rewrite and re-right the injustices inflicted upon her. Her purpose was to name, and make known, the unknown black faces featured in a series of photographs taken by the researchers. Aunty Molly's insertion of new knowledge to accompany the unnamed photographs contributed in part to the seismic readjustment of existing power structures required to transform First Nations Peoples from unknown to known. Through this sharing, Aunty Molly provided not only new knowledge, but also a valuable framework for decolonization: a framework based on sharp tools that are uniquely female and *palawa*.

In subverting the epistemic violence against her, the tactics Aunty Molly uses and shares within her text are not dissimilar to the tactics used by the colonizers when growing their empire. These tactics were based on the superiority of Western knowledges over all others. In this case, the obvious difference being that Aunty Molly's decolonizing tactics privilege female First Nations knowledges. The knowledge Aunty Molly draws upon within her decolonizing framework is sophisticated and robust, inherited and influenced by her relationship to Country and Peoples (Rigney 2001, Moreton-Robinson 2011). This depth of knowledge enables her to challenge the assumption that, as a First Nations woman, she is limited by the conditions of her subalternity (Spivak 1999). Whilst Aunty Molly acknowledges her subalternity within her experiences, she goes further in demonstrating how this can be shaped into a set of tools that can be utilized to dismantle the white patriarchal structures that marginalize and oppress black female knowledges (Moreton-Robinson 2011). Aunty Molly then demonstrates, through her writing, how to enact these frameworks to derive a form of justice, not as a subaltern, but as a powerful First Nations woman in her own right.

The title of her book is a reminder Aunty Molly has afforded me a form of justice that was unknown to her for much of her life. This justice gives me the space, confidence and freedom to continue to speak and push boundaries. I know this justice is conditional, and there will always be tension and struggle in how I am able to use her story to further our rights while avoiding crossing a line in appropriating her own experiences as my own. But I also know this justice is generational, and it is my cultural obligation to learn from Aunty Molly's story and discover new tools that I can gift to my daughter to continue this decolonizing work and fight for our family's right to belong.

Conclusion

The influence of power on the production and control of knowledges about First Nations Peoples is irrefutable. It has kept our people at the margins of society, limiting our ability to speak and, thus, be heard. For First Nations women, our marginalization is further impacted by the erasure of our beings by a patriarchal belief system that dictates who is best placed to generate knowledge about us. Our experiences as First Nations women living in settler-colonial states has provided us with an objective and intimate understanding of the relationship between power and knowledge. Our knowing, and the collective labor of First Nations women like Smith, Moreton-Robinson and Mallett has provided us with a framework that supports us to challenge the patriarchal structures by allowing us to share our stories and our knowledge in a way that privileges our voices and celebrates us as black women. Thus, we are enabling ourselves to be our own version of a spoke in the wheel of colonialism.

While Smith's decolonizing theory speaks of the power that comes from reclaiming and rewriting our stories, and Moreton-Robinson challenges us on how to dismantle the patriarchal structures that oppress, Dr Mary Francis Mallett – Aunty Molly – has provided me with a specific and familial practical framework that will equip my family's future generations to continue this decolonizing work. Aunty Molly becomes an anchor for many from *lutruwita*, who will grow our rights, while the Harvard expedition is left to float on a historical tide.

Part Four

De/colonizing Minds

7

Indigeneity, Indigenous feminisms and Indigenization

Lori Campbell (2-Spirit nēhiyaw āpihtākosisān)

Introduction

Indigenization has become a popular trend within academic settings in the place currently known as Canada (but which my people know as Turtle Island). Few post-secondary institutions developed Indigenization strategies – or rather, Indigenous-centered learning – before the turn of this century. Some initiatives, however, have been Indigenous-led, such as Manitou Community College in Manitoba, 1973, and the Saskatchewan Indian Federated College in Regina, 1976 (now First Nations University of Canada).

A sense of urgency for the more mainstream institutions to jump aboard was motivated by the release of the nation-state-led Truth and Reconciliation Commission's (TRC) report in 2015. Even so, many institutions struggled to understand just what Indigenization was, and in the process of defining it, they came up with sometimes similar and sometimes widely divergent definitions.

At my own post-secondary institution, amid committee discussions and consternations, I came face to face with trying to find out what Indigenization meant for me on a personal level. In that moment, I realized that Indigenization had something to do with Indigenous identity and, therefore, what was important for me was to define Indigeneity. This understanding made me critically confront and problematize the notion of Indigenization and determined that I center Indigeneity within all aspects of my life, including my work within the academy.

I propose, then, that applying Indigenization from a settler-scholar or settler-administrator experience is an attempt to recolonize Indigenous Peoples. The process of Indigenization thus becomes the colonized idea of what Indigenization is. And like the ceremonies, traditions and regalia of our ancestors, the Indigenous-centered concept of Indigenization now has also been stolen, interpreted, translated and repurposed into a colonized idea of what Indigenization should be. The colonized version is spat back out at us and, in a condescending, paternalistic act, we are told to believe that the colonized version of Indigenization is our own version. And so we are expected to implement Indigenization from the colonized perspective.

The premise that Indigenous People must Indigenize from the colonizer-centered perspective is a repeat of history and it is how I have come to see Indigenization as a recolonization project. My aim in this essay is to explore the concept of Indigenization within colonial structures that "Indigenize", generally without inclusion of Indigenous Peoples (Arvin, Tuck & Morrill 2013; Flowers 2015; Waterman 2018) and to determine how an Indigenous person might navigate the process successfully.

Situating myself

Because this search has become a personal quest, I begin by situating myself to contextualize my relationship to this work of Indigenization. I am a child of the 60s scoop, taken from my mother at the age of two, to be placed in a foster home until adoptive parents could be found for me. I have always known that I was adopted and known that I was Indigenous. But I didn't always know who I was or where I belonged. My ancestral line was broken because I had been forcibly and intentionally severed from it.

The 60s scoop was a government assimilation project that removed Indigenous children from their families and placed them in white homes with the hope that we could learn to be and behave "white". My mother, a nēhiyaw iskwew (Cree woman) who was 16 at the time, thought I was coming back. I never did. And later I was to spend many years looking for her and my siblings. Eventually, after 25 years of searching, I located all five brothers and a sister as well as my mother.

During the search for my birth family, I learned firsthand the far-reaching effects of the residential school legacy. I found that my siblings had not had the same opportunities that I did. They did not all end up in happy or safe situations and several did not complete high school. I, however, made my way into university, and, along the way, found many Indigenous scholars who would become my mentors. My life experiences have contributed not only to my understanding of Indigenous culture and issues, but also to my passion for education. I find strength in these experiences as I navigate the academy. They were important sources of knowledge that resonated for me when I began to do my academic research and helped to guide me to philosophies that have had significant influence on me. The first among them is feminism.

Looking at feminism

Without realizing the connections between political activism and feminist research methodologies, I was drawn to both early on. During my initial university years, as I was finding my identity, I became an activist because I was queer, I was a woman and I was Indigenous. I was raised in a non-Indigenous family and immersed in an education system where I was led to believe that all knowledge of value was borne of whiteness. In my youth, this notion contributed to my feelings of being unintelligent, incapable and "less than", as compared to my non-Indigenous peers. It never occurred to me, like too many other Indigenous feminists before me (Green 2007; Maracle 1996; Ross 2009; Tohe 2000), to name myself an Indigenous feminist.

I soon learned that feminism was something that belonged to white women. I became painfully aware that I was trying to take on a philosophy or way of knowing that did not belong to me. I tried many times to look through the eyes of the white woman to take up feminism for the good of all women, but I felt out of place in a feminism that ignored and erased my Indigeneity.

I concluded that feminism, as liberating as it sounded, was not for Indigenous women and it was not for me. As time passed, my connection to and understanding of my own intersecting identities as a 2-Spirit iskwew deepened, but it would not be until years later that I was exposed to Indigenous feminism and learned of its inherent connection to Indigeneity.

As a note of explanation, 2-Spirit (or Two-Spirit) is the term preferred by many of us. It better captures the Indigenous concept of gender fluidity than the word *gay* to denote that some people are born with an understanding and spirituality of multiple genders, rather than just one, and are in that way gifted people. *Iskwew* is the Cree word for woman, which was historically taken over by white colonialists and renamed *squaw*, to be used with a pejorative connotation. I am reclaiming that word proudly.

Discovering Indigenous feminism

During my master's program I read about Black feminism through Patricia Collins (2000) and bell hooks (1984) and found many corollaries of oppressions and cultural differences that rang true for me. And then, of course, I learned about intersectionality through Kimberlé Crenshaw's work (1991). I read biographies of Indigenous women's experiences: Maria Campbell (1973), Morningstar Mercredi (2006), Patricia Monture-Angus (1995) and Mary Young (2005). I also discovered Indigenous research methodologies through Cora Weber-Pillwax (2004), Linda Tuhiwai Smith (2012), Shawn Wilson (2008) and Margaret Kovach (2009).

It was not until I started my PhD studies that I was introduced to Indigenous feminism. I had not realized there was such a thing. But at the World Indigenous Peoples Conference on Education in 2017 I found myself attending a session with Stephanie Waterman that focused on the ways in which Indigenous scholars were engaging with Indigenous research methodologies while centering Indigenous knowledge systems, and voices, from a female perspective.

Waterman (2017) made explicit reference to the notion that feminism is predominately whitestream – oftentimes focused on equality of the sexes and discomfited with lesbianism. Conversely, Indigenous feminism engages foundational principles of inclusivity, responsibility and relationships. Waterman proposed that Indigenous feminism could be used as a tool to reinforce Indigenous sovereignty in research; but without the Indigenous existence there could be no Indigeneity and, therefore, we would only see through white-colored glasses.

That conference motivated me to explore the notion of Indigenous feminism in Indigenous scholarly work. Arvin et al (2013) state clearly that Indigenous feminisms are foundational to Indigeneity. From an Indigenous feminist theory perspective, they explore the problematization of settler-colonialism and the structures that uphold it as well as the explicit erasure and dispossession of Indigenous women, Indigenous feminist theories, and Indigenous ways of knowing in academia.

Flowers (2015) further problematizes conceptions of allyship in relation to those who purport to act in solidarity alongside Indigenous Peoples. In doing so, she unpacks the term 'settler' and clearly outlines that it is a relational term that signifies the settler's relationship to colonialism rather than an equivalent to the term 'non-Indigenous'. Recognizing that Indigenous Peoples have no desire to build a future that is fundamentally borne of a colonial relationship, she identifies solidarity as not a temporal event but rather a long-term commitment that supports and creates structural change. Flowers (2015) explains that co-existence through co-resistance is the responsibility of all settlers, and that for settlers to participate, they must be committed to dismantling their own systems of exploitation and extraction. She poses the question of whether motivation of allyship for some settlers, as colonial subjects, is the desire to receive recognition of the colonized. I have observed that settlers receive personal benefit for feeling good about feeling bad about the experiences of Indigenous Peoples. This self-gratifying emotional acting is about the 'witnessing' by the colonized of the colonizer feeling bad. That is, that by 'experiencing' the pain and suffering as they hear the testimony, they have in fact suffered too; if they did not experience pleasure, then they are absolved of guilt. This act, akin to charitable feelings and thus self-gratification, is not allyship. The colonizer takes no concrete action, nor even recognizes the relationships and of the concomitant responsibilities involved.

Flowers (2015) reflects upon the deep love that Indigenous women hold to one another as a shared rage that drives our resistance. It is this rage that settlers are not comfortable with because it forces them to look at their role in power and oppression. Flowers (2015, p. 33) develops strong arguments through critically examining and defining the terms "settler" and "ally". She clarifies that rather than simply denoting "non-Indigenous", the word "settler" carries with it a set of privileges and enjoyment of standing assumed by the colonizer, and that "ally" should contain the set of responsibilities that accompany such a standing, but often do not (Flowers 2015, p. 33). These terms effectively set up a binary of identities, establishing an "Other" of exclusivity on the part of the settler, encompassing an inclusivity and desire of recognition by the Indigenous. With the terminology made explicit, she explores the relationship between the terminology and the motivation of and benefit to settlers who choose to engage in allyship relationships. Indigenous philosophy teaches us that not all knowledge is for all people; and as Waterman (2018) highlights, knowledge is not power, it is a responsibility. Flowers (2015) suggests that not all settlers need to be allies in order to engage in good relations with Indigenous women. Further, they cannot claim Indigeneity through association.

Through the work of these authors, and many other strong Indigenous women, I have since come to understand Indigenous feminism as inherent to my Indigeneity. It is this learning that challenged me to consider how Indigenizing a post-secondary colonial system centered from Indigenous feminist theories might add to the discourse of Indigenization of the institution.

Defining Indigenization

Words carry power. Before I go any further, I need to talk about definitions. I first heard the term *Indigenization* some 10 years ago at the Aboriginal Caucus of the Canadian Association of University Teachers (CAUT) conference. I had just completed a second undergraduate degree and was working at a polytechnical institute where I was providing support services for Indigenous students.

This conference played an integral role in situating me where I am today because it exposed me to two things: it was the first time I found myself in a room with dozens of Indigenous scholars who held graduate degrees and were working within post-secondary institutions, and second, it was simply hearing this new word: Indigenization.

As an Indigenous woman, something about the idea resonated within me, and over the next few years I sought out as much scholarly work as I could to understand the concept behind the word. It all made sense at the time. And I came to the realization that I, too, could go to graduate school. The outcome for me, brought about by my exposure to that conference, was the completion of a master's degree and a great deal of research into the topic.

Simultaneously, I researched and participated in the development and implementation of an Indigenization strategy at the polytechnic where I worked. This activity is also what led me to where I am today. I continue working in the strategic area of Indigenization in post-secondary and I am now a doctoral student in the Social Justice Education program at the University of Toronto (UT).

Since that initial conference I have had opportunities to attend many more Indigenous education conferences, have had conversations with remarkable scholars, discovered several different Indigenization strategies, and advanced my career, my education, and my critical thinking skills. But as an additional outcome of these pursuits, I began to question whether an Indigenization strategy might achieve its intended goals, or rather, if it would or could achieve the goals that I now believe are critical.

A general definition of the concept of Indigenization, provided by Castellano (2014, n.p.), reads as follows: "Indigenizing education means that every subject at every level is examined to consider how and to what extent current content and pedagogy reflect the presence of Indigenous Peoples and the valid contribution of Indigenous knowledge." In my experience, this has not necessarily been the definition that was adopted at the onset of implementing, or even exploring, Indigenization within institutions, but it is more or less one that has persisted or grown to be accepted within the Canadian context as described below.

Indigenization has been adopted for implementation at several postsecondary institutions in Canada. Each has approached the strategy from their own perspective for their own needs. Jimmy, Allen and Anderson (2015, pp. 6, 9) "recognize that issues of social justice, oppression, and colonization are part of the very ways in which we navigate our worlds every day" and thus state that "Indigenization within academia is about challenging ethnocentrism through processes of decolonization and (re)centering Indigenous knowledge at the institutional level and within our own practice as academics and researchers."

The University of Regina has defined Indigenization as the:

> transformation of the existing academy by including Indigenous knowledges, voices, critiques, scholars, students, and materials as well as the establishment of physical and epistemic spaces that facilitate the ethical stewardship of a plurality of Indigenous knowledges and practices so thoroughly as to constitute an essential element of the university. It is not limited to Indigenous People, but encompasses all students and faculty, for the benefit of our academic integrity and our social viability.
>
> Pete 2016, p. 81

Ontario universities have chosen different paths; for example, the University of Toronto and Western University (WU) developed strategies that both name and include recommended actions that contribute to Indigenization, but they have both shied away from centralizing the focus of the plans in their entirety with the term Indigenization.

The problem is in viewing Indigenization as an end stage once the strategic actions are completed. Without specifically "Indigenizing", many related attempts have been made under well-meaning efforts such as *diversity, inclusivity, equity, culturalism* and *multiculturalism* – strategies that are all too familiar by now. Newer attempts have been made with *reconciliation* and even *decolonization*; however, these are yet to be understood, let alone achieved.

Problematizing Indigenization

The various strategies mentioned above have been applied in post-secondary institutions to work with and include "the Other". However, none of them have succeeded in infusing Indigenous knowledge and perspectives throughout the university's curriculum and daily operations – that is, considering Indigeneity on an equal basis as being white.

Sherene Razack (2015, p. 207) suggests that "universities are happy to promote courses on Indigenous knowledge, and individual students enthusiastically participate in smudging ceremonies" but they are less willing "to examine their complicity in ongoing colonialism". These actions have simply been layered over the colonial structure to appease Indigenous members, commonly with a "recommendation for cultural sensitivity training for white [people]" (Razack 2015, p. 207). This form of Indigenization merely replicates the surface work of culturalism (Jeffery & Nelson 2009), further upholding the structure of the dominant society by creating the idea that those with culture are designated as "Other".

An Indigenization strategy must consider how it will engage in reconciliation. Martin Canon (2018, p. 165) asks us to think about reconciliation and poses the question, "How might we restore right relations?" And in response to this, he stresses that "before reconciliation is possible, it is necessary to think about land" (Canon 2018, p. 171).

Many universities have taken steps through land acknowledgements at public events to recognize Indigenous Peoples whose traditional territory their campuses sit upon. Although this address may feel like an empty exercise, the potential is for those listening to become accustomed to the names of the traditional territories, the original inhabitants, and the Indigenous existence prior to colonization as common knowledge.

Nevertheless, Glen Coulthard (2007) expresses a concern that when we seek to be made visible through the acceptance of colonial institutions, we reinscribe the colonial as arbiter and validator, and recognize its authority to regulate and dictate Indigenous life. It is apparent that an Indigenization strategy must be understood and accepted by all those who make up the colonial institution, on the same terms as it is by Indigenous members. Tuck and Yang (2012, p. 19) warn us that too often, among academics, decolonization becomes reduced to efforts of "decolonizing the mind", ignoring the physical effects that colonization has on Peoples. In other words, we cannot leave this process as a merely intellectual exercise. It requires a will to do more than just talk about it or apply simple strategies such as mentioned earlier. It is, however, a first step leading to awareness, a precondition before action becomes meaningful.

Recognizing race and place in Indigenization

I suggest that implementing Indigenization from a settler-scholar or settler-administrator experience is a racist act of violence towards Indigenous Peoples.

My experience is that those who apply Indigenization as an add-on do not see their "work" as causing harm to Indigenous Peoples. In fact, they see their "leadership" as practical, relevant and appropriate. More important, they are being "benevolent", and do not see the irony in this approach, which merely perpetuates the dominance of their position.

Without confronting the racism of settler-led Indigenization, the institution is supporting a recolonization project, tokenizing Indigenous leaders in the position of modern-day Indian agents whose job it is to move forward the settler-centered institutional agenda and calm the "Indians".

The only solution that I see, is for me to "be" who I am and to create my own space within the academy. What I have experienced is that to be and think Indigenous, in whatever way that looks, in Indigenous student centers is generally acceptable. To be invited out of that space by the white people into the white spaces of the academy, for the purposes of being or "performing" Indigenous, is also okay. Therefore, a typical act of Indigenization commonly involves inviting an Indigenous person to provide a token contribution, such as the territorial acknowledgement at a campus event, in which the person has otherwise had no direct engagement in the planning, delivery or content.

Yet witness what happens when that Indigenous person thinks Indigenous when not invited to do so, especially at a senior administrative table. This was just the case recently at the University of Manitoba, where two very well-respected Indigenous leaders chose to walk away from their positions.

Vice-Provost of Indigenous Engagement Dr Lynn Lavallee (2019, n.p.) shared these words after her resignation:

> At the University of Manitoba, I found what I experienced as, deeply imbedded, systemic racism. I told myself on starting at the U of M that I was here to walk through doors and get things done, not break down doors. Given the open commitment to Indigenous achievement in the strategic plan, I believed I would not have to rationalize *why* Indigenous specific initiatives and responses were needed but work on *how* to implement.

When Dr Barry Lavallee (Kusch 2019, n.p.) (unrelated to Dr Lynn Lavallee) was asked why he resigned a few weeks later, he responded, "Because it is hopeless." Dr Barry Lavallee, by the way, is known internationally for his work in Indigenizing the curriculum in medical schools and had worked at the Winnipeg-based university for nine years.

These are clear acts of refusal – clear acts where Indigenous leaders are choosing not to become the modern-day Indian agent of Indigenous Peoples. If

Indigenous Peoples are not following the "rules" of the ivory tower, the ivory tower often concludes we are not doing our jobs correctly. There are people in those ivory towers, and although they may be inviting Indigenous Peoples in, they will only let you stay if the Indigenous People choose to think "ivory". These are the white naturalized spaces. It is imperative that I think about the ways in which racism is driving this behavior. Institutions are not racist. The people in the institutions make rules, policies, procedures that can allow racism to flourish. In this way, the people are explicitly given the rights to be racist because the institutional foundation allows it. Western education was built on it (literally on the lands).

I often choose, for several reasons, to not use the word racism in many of the white spaces that exist in the academy. One reason being that I have been socialized to exist "comfortably" in "uncomfortable" spaces. If I were to name racism each and every time I witness it or am the recipient of it, it would make others uncomfortable and then we would all be uncomfortable. I think sometimes I like to be around comfortable people and imagine myself as comfortable too. It does depend on the setting sometimes and it also depends on my energy level at times. Is it enough to just name something as racist when it occurs, but not take on having to explain the why? If it is named, can the conversation, the meeting, the social gathering continue? We are programmed to avoid discomfort.

But what is harmful to me, as an Indigenous person, the Indigenous community on campuses and those who will attend the campus in the future, is not paying attention to the violence of racism that comes when settler-centered people are leading, naming and directing "acts" of Indigenization. Over the last decade I have read most of the Indigenization strategies developed in post-secondary institutions. And I have concluded that it is an impossibility to center Indigenization from a colonial institutional place since "settler societies are designed to not consider place – [because] to do so would require consideration of genocide" (Grande, cited in Tuck & McKenzie 2015, p. 154). In the case of the academy, to do so would also require a looking inward to recognize and disrupt the foundational colonialism that is at the base of their roots and has grown them into the imposing structures they are today – ones that attempt to stamp out the Indigenous print that lays beneath their concrete foundations. Yet Indigenous People have created some cracks in that foundation and we are creeping in.

When I speak to those Indigenous student services leaders who made it through the cracks kayâs (*long ago*) they talk about how they finally had a small broom closet space in a far corner of the basement that became the Indigenous Student office. They had a place within the naturalized colonized space of the institution and the place was out of sight. Over the last 25 years we have seen these spaces make it up to ground level floors, spaces with light, into visible spaces. The cracks are spreading in the institutions and Indigenous People are permeating the structure. We are taking faculty positions and administrative positions and we are sending out new roots. Our strength from within Mother Earth is increasing and we are in the process of germinating through those cracks.

More and more it seems that Indigenization has become a recolonization tool. It would be smart for the settler-academies to target Indigenous Peoples to become their own Indian agents. There may have been a time when the notion of Indigenization meant something to, and was a good vision for, Indigenous Peoples in the academy but now that the academy has started to take it over it has become a weapon to be used against Indigenous Peoples. It has become the colonizer's tool to further acts of racism and displacement: a tool to assimilate and recolonize.

What I have seen is that Indigenization has come to be accepted by the academy as getting Indigenous Peoples to behave in an approved way within the settler space. And if we do not or cannot conform, we become the "unsettled native, left to unsettle the settled spaces" (Watson 2007, p. 15).

I aim to take up that role proudly. If we consider that Indigenization is an education process, then the university is an appropriate forum for developing an Indigenization strategy. Pete (2016, p. 81) asserts that Indigenization is possible but requires an "institutional reform [that] must be undertaken on multiple levels". Everyone within the institution plays a role and will experience pushback from colleagues who feel that naming our work "Indigenizing" is a political act, if decolonization is part of the process. Yet how can it not be?

According to Eve Tuck and K. Wayne Yang (2012), Indigenization implies adding something in, whereas decolonizing requires the process of taking something away. And that is what creates the resistance and fear. Indigenization is a process that requires learning and unlearning. It is perhaps not even the end goal. And it requires me to remain firmly centered within my own Indigeneity.

Bringing home Indigenization

In the academy I am bombarded constantly by non-Indigenous-centered requests to Indigenize, with expectations of something convenient, colonized and quite different from the Indigenous understandings of Indigenization. Indigenous Peoples, worldviews and knowledge systems are complex, and the complexities were established long before whiteness arrived on this country known by our Peoples as Turtle Island (Maracle 1996). Indigeneity, including Indigenous feminisms and Indigenous research methodologies, has its own identity outside of whiteness. It existed long before Indigenization became "a thing" (Barker 2015; Green 2007; Moreton-Robinson 2002).

Despite my indoctrination into the settler establishment, I have found my way home, peeling back layers of colonization and taking my place among my sisters within the lodge of my ancestors. I have searched for and centered my Indigeneity. I have found the only learning space I know that is "Indigenized" and it is the land where our lodge is. I believe it is from there my research begins. It is not from within the academy. My Indigeneity is the source of my strength.

I conclude with a story about a personal experience: I received word late one winter that my Auntie was gathering us home to her lodge for fasting ceremony. I started preparation almost immediately. Most of those preparations were from within my own mental, physical, emotional and spiritual self, but all were in relation to those around me – my family and community.

I now live hundreds of miles from the territory of my ancestors and have only been away for a few years, but I still miss home tremendously. When I say "home", I realize that in my mind's eye it is the land my people are from and the stories that are borne from it. The Crossing is home. It is the place just on the other side of the South Saskatchewan River before the turn up to where the Battle of Batoche, the Métis last stand, took place. It is the place also known as Gabriel's Crossing, named after one of our Indigenous leaders, the place where the ferry used to cross the river before the bridge was even thought of.

I arrived at The Crossing several days before ceremony was to start. In fact, that first night I was the only one there. In the black of the night I laid on the ground, cradled by Mother Earth, and I greeted the stars, I spoke to the coyotes that were singing in the distance, and I sang to the bears. Over the next couple of days, I connected my spirit to my land and to my ancestors.

Fasters and helpers began arriving, many of whom were women. We all began preparing, individually, but in relation to one another. Sitting on the front porch of my Auntie's summerhouse at the Crossing sipping tea the night before fast, my Auntie stood up, raised her fist in the air and told us, "the most political act of resistance you will ever do is know your ceremonies". And we fasted.

At my Auntie's lodge, many of us are scholars, medical doctors and lawyers, representing six different universities. Many teachings were shared among us over those 10 days. We were our own eco-system. We were our own tribe. We were sovereign. We were not separate from our land, families, communities or scholarly work. I did not have to think about re-centering Indigeneity. We did not need to fight for our place because it surrounded us constantly. There was no resistance at Auntie's.

We nurtured each other for as many days afterwards as we could before we all had to go our separate ways, before we all had to head out into the colonized spaces. I know that I have much more to learn, but what I have learned so far is that I do not need to convince the colonizer of my validity as a way for me to prove my existence.

The biggest threat for the colonizer is the remembering of the colonized. I center my Indigeneity as a 2-Spirit nēhiyaw āpihtākosisān iskwew from mōniyawi-sākahikanihk, Treaty 6 territory, not as an act of decentering whiteness or colonialism but as an act of refusing whiteness and colonialism as the normative default from which all else is borne.

Ekosi – that is all. *Kinanâskomitinawaw.*

8

Reclaiming the first person voice

tebrakunna country and Emma Lee

Identity and myth

It means that there is unfinished business, that we are still being colonized (and know it), and that we are still searching for justice.

Smith 1999, p. 34

In my recent writing I locate myself as a "*trawlwulwuy* woman from *tebrakunna* country, north-east Tasmania, Australia" (*tebrakunna* country & Lee 2017, 2018, 2019). This assertion of who I am, and where I am located, already highlights the tensions and disjunction of being a Black female embodying both a colonizing and relational world of identities (Carlson 2016). Here, my identity is entangled between the local and place-based peoples, cultures, knowledge and practices that belong to a 40,000 year-old history of our *trouwunnan* lands and seas (Cameron 2011) and the name-changing, recent geographies of colonization, such as Tasmania (Melville 2006).

Yet this "I" is also a place where my Black female body is always the "known", the "subject" or the "you" (Chambers & Buzinde 2015; Moreton-Robinson 2011). Colonization has overwhelmed me and contributed to my compliance with, and subjugation to, Western ideologies that even "when we do see ourselves... [we] can barely recognize ourselves through representation" (Smith 1999, p. 35). Therefore, these referents of "I" and "you" can never be fixed or synonymous – they cannot be of the "same content in every context" (Kaplan 1977, p. 521) – as there are structures in play that have pre-determined my position in society. To then refer to an "I" as a self-located place of belief and knowing (Castañeda 1986; Perry 1979) becomes my strength, an action of agency and resistant to substitution.

My statement of my cultural affiliations is of utmost importance to the frame of this essay. Referent points of "I" and "you" are powerful tools of Western privilege: the "you" is a space of Othering and occupying the margins (Said 1978), while to be an "I" expresses faculty and demands a place for voice. For me, the relationship with the academy is one of anxiety and is inextricably linked with the specificities of colonization upon my *trawlwulwuy* person and *tebrakunna* country. My identity as an "I" has been displaced within the world, and the academy, and transformed to a "you".

For my contributions to decolonizing an academic practice of Othering through referents, I draw on the experience of colonization of my peoples, still acutely felt in life and research. In 1803, for *trawlwulwuy*, and other peoples of *trouwunnan*, we became the focus of an accelerated British colonial wave into Australia. The desired goal was not only the usurpation of our lands (Lehman 2006), but also the enactment of war upon our peoples to remove us *in toto* from our sovereign "territories of life" (Brodie 2017; ICCA Consortium 2018, n.p.). The genocide by the British empire was so great, that upon the death of our female countrywoman *Trucanini* in 1876 (Taylor 2012) the decimation of our entire population under the myth of "The Last of the Tasmanians" (Bonwick 1870) was proclaimed to the world.

Our forever "myth-death", once justified as necessary in a time of colonial expansion (Boyce 2008), is now re-packaged and re-told by researchers who still own our histories and reinforce the imperial project by claiming our space (Lee 2020; Smith 1999). The very act, then, of daring to create a first-person authorship out of non-existence indicates the great impact of "I" and "you" referents: I become vitally important in asserting myself because *I* am a *trawlwulwuy* woman from *tebrakunna* country. I exist and the "I" confronts and unsettles the myth that our populations were reduced to naught under British occupation (Madley 2008). The recognition of self as a *trawlwulwuy* Black female body also becomes my authoritative resource for generating agency and demanding rights (De Sousa Santos, Nunes & Meneses 2007). However, despite my awareness of self, this Black female body also has to contend with the knowledge that I too possess a colonized mind (Fanon 2008).

For Frantz Fanon (2008) and James Baldwin (1993) the colonized mind resides within the self, where the constant comparison and measure of self-worth to the colonizer will only ever return feelings of inferiority and self-loathing. In *Decolonising the Mind*, the Gikuyu writer Ngũgĩ wa Thiong'o (1986, p. 16) shows us that colonial power is derived from the domination of the "mental universe of the colonised, the control, through culture, of how people perceived themselves and their relation to the world". Recognizing the colonized mind, then, requires an act of self-awareness. It also requires an agency to begin to repair the unconscious self-harms of being colonized.

I want to begin to articulate what being cognizant of the colonized mind means in the local context of reclaiming myself out of extinction myths. My journey to recognize my colonized mind, and my attempts to shed this skin, is also a close look at how well decolonizing theories and methodologies translate into action. This emic terrain is guided by the experience of learning to write in the first person as an Indigenous researcher, which is characterized here as decolonization work. In developing the strengths of my own referents, *I* also found an unexpected way to advocate for, and connect to, country.

Recognizing the colonized mind and balancing identity tensions

In the 1970s, the era of my birth, global social changes were sweeping into consciousness issues such as women's rights, Indigenous Peoples, anti-war platforms and conservation (Haferkamp & Smelser 1992). In Australia, this was a time of land rights and the establishment of an ongoing protest site, the Aboriginal Tent Embassy, on Parliament lawns and a raft of new, mostly failed, social policies and measures designed by government, without Indigenous input to address our disadvantage (Behrendt 2007; Muldoon & Schaap 2012; Robinson 1994). By this time, almost 100 years have passed since the myth of our non-existence came into being upon *Trucanini*'s death. Since her death, we have been particularly subject to the stripping of Black histories and identities in schools, work, government and communities in Tasmania and Australia and, in my experience, the acculturation has concretized. Yet the 1970s was also a beginning of the long global journey to reclaiming, recovering, revealing and repairing connections to country and culture as Indigenous Peoples (Bell 2014; Nakata 2007). I am of a generation that belongs to both these simultaneous occurrences of recovery and denial, taking strength in developing my cultural life while subject to grave errors of history.

In the gap between "belonging" to a culture being re-energized and "not-belonging" as an extinct person, I now see that I have been subjected to the conditioning of a colonized mind and body. My colonized body begins in the early 1800s, where my many-times grandfather *Mannalargenna* and his daughter, *Woretemoeteyenner*, became subjects of the British Crown. Less than 10 years after first contact, *Woretemoeteyenner* became a mother to *Dalrymple Briggs Johnson*, where the change to Western names is a record of the rapidity in which our culture and lives were no longer our own. *Mannalargenna* and *Woretemoeteyenner* were the last generation to know *tebrakunna* country solely by that name and peopled only by family. Our peoples were wholly displaced from country through disease, massacres and government round-ups, where the remainder of us were removed to the margins on an off-shore island (Plomley 1966). Dispossession and destruction of my *trawlwulwuy* peoples and culture transferred control to the colonizers: my name is now in the English language and my place is now a township rather than *tebrakunna* country as a territory of life.

Some decolonizing texts speak to the ways in which we have had to continually demonstrate our humanity as Indigenous Peoples to gain local and international rights, respect and justice (Césaire 2000; Rigney 2001). In Tasmania, this colonizing demand for justifying our humanness is keenly felt in the face of having to also prove our very *existence*. As an extinct person and *trawlwulwuy* Black female body, the former has always taken precedence over the latter as the characterization of my being. The very existence of my body has had to be defended throughout my life and guarded against accusations of extinction through white annihilation. Our supposed extinction was, and still continues to be, taught, historicized, researched and claimed as fact by the colonizers (Morris 2017; Windschuttle 2002). I hold a clear memory from my mid-teens of a history teacher telling me that I "couldn't be Aboriginal because Governor Arthur was more successful than Hitler in wiping them out".

In recognizing our specific Aboriginal Tasmanian histories, the Ngāti Awa and Ngāti Porou scholar Linda Tuhiwai Smith (whom we honour in our essays) sees more of a multi-car pile-up rather than intersections (Crenshaw 1991) when facing any crowd, let alone a hostile research one, in defending our very humanity. She writes in her seminal text, *Decolonizing Methodologies* (1999, pp. 72–73): "In Tasmania, where experts had already determined that Aborigines were 'extinct', the voices of those who still speak as Aboriginal Tasmanians are interpreted as some political invention of a people who no longer exist and who therefore no longer have claims."

These experts leave trails and waves that continue to rattle me, but also provide the boundaries in which I can advocate for decolonizing change. My Black female body is the contained site where I can exert "control over our resistances" (Smith 1999, p. 38), where I can declare myself. Yet this awareness is still to come, as I have been trained to "write about ourselves as indigenous peoples as if we really were 'out there', the 'Other', with all the baggage that this entails" (Smith 1999, p. 36).

With a body colonized by myth-making and non-being, and our peoples dispossessed and exiled from country, there are few barriers to becoming accustomed to the colonized mind. While I have never acceded to denying my identity, I have previously accepted the rights of the colonizer to question it. This is a colonized mind. The colonizer overlays my truths of existence with their facts to the contrary, such as my history teacher, which requires me to be silent under the weight of those "superior" facts (Latour 2004; Sundberg 2014). As a young woman in an unequal power balance, to pass the schools tests in order to continue with a Western education (the only educational option), I was made mute.

My experience of the colonized mind, as encountered throughout my formal education, had me accepting that white voices, theories, pronouncements and teachings were prominent, correct and unquestioned. Our histories, as oral traditions, stories, activities and things shared among family and country, were kept at home and hardly ever crossed the boundary into formal education. While my *trawlwulwuy* self never doubted these rightful cultural learning moments, the colonized mind justifies and explains these practices from a position of inferiority.

By this, to justify my humanity I give explanations for engaging in a cultural life not from the practices in and of themselves, rather I account for my behaviors from within, and to, a Western framework of reference. I prove my existence through cultural practices that are recognizable to Western gazes (Smith 1999) to disprove extinction. Inferiority feels like having to insert a kernel of doubt within a mainstream victorious narrative of Australian colonial settlement in order to open up the possibilities of cracks within it, rather than speaking from a position of power derived from belonging and existing within my own *tebrakunna* country. In this way I can only exist if I dispute the current views from within, leaving behind my own relational world of Indigeneity as core. White voices have taught me that mine does not count and is secondary at best.

The colonized mind and body, as inferior and silent, also knows that the right to refer to "I" and "we" belongs to the Western academy as a signifier of power. Linda Tuhiwai Smith (1999, p. 35) writes: "I frequently have to orientate myself to a text world in which the centre of academic knowledge is either in Britain, the United States or Western Europe; in which words such as 'we', 'us' 'our', 'I' actually exclude me."

Until I began a PhD in late 2013, and even for a little while longer, I had internalized that Western academic referents of "I" and "our" did not include me. My peoples have always been the "you", and the Other, as our place in conversation or academic paper. Therefore, and at personal pain now, I subjugated myself to an inferior place of uncritical writing using a remote and distant third-person narrative. I personified a colonized mind in my use of "them" and "theirs" and "for Indigenous people" in my early contributions to scholarship (Lee 2015, 2016b). I did this from a place of having no voice, little insight and faint direction into the literature and learning of colonization and decolonization principles and practice.

Yet I consider myself as being born and raised as a cultural woman of country – finding and learning and researching our practices and cultures with family and Elders and the broader communities that comprise us as *trouwunnan*. We are reclaiming ourselves out of truly horrendous circumstances of genocide (Bonyhady & Lehman 2018; Curthoys 2005; Ryan 1996) and our knowledges lost or resting out of sight cannot be repaired in haste. The last 50 years of reclaiming our histories and our place as extant peoples is a practice of cultural resurgence, which Yellowknives Dene scholar Glen Coulthard (2014, p. 179) describes as seeking "to practice decolonial, gender-emancipatory, and economically nonexploitative structures of law and sovereign authority".

Our turn away from the colonized and extinction myth-mind towards a relational world shares in common the mantras that Kahnawake Mohawk and Cherokee theorists Taiaiake Alfred and Jeff Corntassel (2005, p. 613, my emphasis) propose as supporting resurgent cultures: "*land is life*", "*language is power*", "*freedom from fear*" and "*one warrior at a time*". These messages of solidarity and connectedness are tied to real action for rights. They contribute towards an understanding of resurgent possibilities that can occur in the absence, or at the least the lessening, of influence, of the colonized mind (St Denis & Walsh 2016). For me, I have participated in learning cultural activities from Elders, such as the art of shell stringing and sculpting kelp water carriers, and continuing familial cultural practices from childhood, such as caring for living midden sites and sea country. It is this cultural framework of resurgence that I now wish to make central without the need for Western parameters to judge my worth (Evans 2019).

By mid-PhD, my readings of Indigenous methodologies and decolonization theory and practices trickled in and created a shift in my relationship with the world to give priority and precedence to *trawlwulwuy* peoples and *tebrakunna* country. My referents changed and the Western "I" would no longer exclude me but would be reclaimed towards decolonizing my own mind. By this point, in 2015, my life had been a split world of being subject to extinction myths while also being a proud *trawlwulwuy* woman. My mind and body have been colonized and controlled by the dominant Western culture to accept the primacy of their values and histories. This resulting separation of myself from my writing and thinking has further reinforced colonial power. Yet in this unhealthy brew I still know myself as a proud Black female body with a capacity to shift the objects of my captured and bound state. The shifting of colonizing objects, then, begins with recognizing these harms of the colonized mind and developing an agency towards correcting them.

Indigenous methodologies and safe spaces for identity

The work of Unangax woman Eve Tuck with K. Wayne Yang (2012, p. 7) advocates for decolonization strategies that involve the "repatriation of land simultaneous to the recognition of how land and relations to land have always already been differently understood and enacted". For these authors (Tuck and Yang 2012), decolonization is neither metaphor nor synonym and is grounded in truth-telling of Indigenous lives. Decolonization is also the resistance of colonial narratives that make smooth the complexities of dispossession and destruction by focusing on (and forgiving) whiteness rather than centring Indigeneity (Tuck & Yang 2012). For Goenpul scholar Aileen Moreton-Robinson (2015), however, we cannot decolonize until we really understand whiteness and its power structures that manipulate our existence and distort our sovereign rights. Indigeneity and race are tangled up with social constructions of whiteness, therefore we cannot fully know ourselves as contemporary peoples without the critical knowledge of whiteness to unstitch these histories (Kovach 2010b). These ideas are similar to Fanon's (2008) unflinching view of how decolonization is to occur, such as "taking freedom from the master and effecting a violent break" (Karklins 1996, p. 53) through force, and what it accomplishes through a physicality and muscularity of action. To delve here into these critical, social justice and reparative territories to support decolonizing aims is to attack the very heart of colonial control through reclaiming the things that matter – land and power. Decolonization is a tangible movement to destabilize and unsettle dominant social structures in favor of Indigenous rights that the academy should look to uphold.

Readings on Indigenous methodologies have also been important to understand the responsibilities we have in conducting our research, particularly in regard to action-oriented and participatory research. Theories such as Indigenous Standpoint highlight the need for us to center our voices, recover the use of languages and gender roles, and have explicit aims to create Indigenous benefit (Foley 2003; Moreton-Robinson 2013; Rigney 1999). As Datta (2018) found, the cornerstone of Western science methodological practice – the neutral observer role – must be discarded to genuinely engage with Indigenous methodologies and decolonizing practices. Instead, research must become a process that reflects our ways of knowing, the relational characteristics that bind together country, culture, knowledge, practices and peoples, and deliver social justice outcomes and impacts (Datta 2018). In this manner, Indigenous methodologies support decolonizing work by theorizing frameworks for new ways of research that has aims of respectful relationships, real improvements to remove disadvantage and our leadership to drive the process.

To recognize and resist a colonizing mind, these approaches help to reframe how the controls over our worlds operate so that we may consider decolonization as a positive experience for us. By this, decolonization work creates restorative action, an interrogation of power and a positioning of our knowledges and peoples as central to research and practice. These tools have allowed me to engage in cultural resurgence and create a safe space to redefine my referent points. In a 1967 interview with the Martinique grandfather theorist of decolonization Aimé Césaire, the Haitian poet and activist Rene Depestre suggested that it is "equally necessary to decolonize our minds, our inner life, at the same time that we decolonize society" (Césaire 2000, p. 31). Agency generated by seeing our own colonized minds can be actively transformed into statements of decolonization – the "I" becomes inclusive and powerful.

However, many of these writings come from a position of secure identities, whether formal or informal recognition of Indigeneity, and without the burdens of proving group existence. These writings speak to me and spur my own advocacy pathways, but they do not answer questions of how we recover ourselves and our identity out of extinction. How, for example, does the call for land return or Black female leadership in critical thinking sound when my peoples have been held up as a global example of outsized death under colonial greed? Where is the power in rallying calls for restitution when *trawlwulwuy* peoples are confronted by a repetitive cycle of "you can't exist" or "didn't you all get killed off?" The decolonization shout often peters out in the face of such epistemological onslaughts. Hence, for me, there was a safety in distance and a respite from exhaustion to write about myself and other Indigenous Peoples in a third-person narrative.

I am grateful to have found the writings of Ngũgĩ wa Thiong'o (1986) to shed light on understanding the colonized mind as a product of, in our shared cases, the British education system and overwriting English language and his/stories upon our own. This has helped me to reflect on the particular hurts that are a result of other Indigenous Peoples (both from Australia and elsewhere) being surprised at my assertions of Indigeneity, questioning how we survived, repeating facts they too had learned in school and elsewhere: that Aboriginal Tasmanians were extinct. This late-in-life recognition allows me to see that a colonized mind is not singular or random, nor is it solely ours alone (Fanon 2008). The Western education system encourages and continues the structure of colonization upon furthering dispossession of ourselves from our lands and culture by infecting everyone's mind, both white and Black (Battiste 2002; Fanon 2008; Ngũgĩ wa Thiong'o 1986; Wolfe 2006). I can now forgive myself for the inferiority and self-loathing feelings I have experienced upon justifying my existence and Black female body to Indigenous and other people.

Yet these texts still do not address how to recuperate an identity and belonging away from extinction myths, which should count as a pre-condition for even having a referent point. How does one make the leap from not existing to that of action-orientated, reciprocal research? More importantly, how can I undertake decolonizing work without creating further trauma to our *trawlwulwuy* mythologized bodies and families? In suffering the injustice and shame of a global denial of identity, I must tread cautiously to not replicate the patterns of colonization in our *trawlwulwuy* families and *tebrakunna* country. I have a responsibility as a researcher, then, and in light of our special and particular circumstances of colonial harm that consumed our very existence, to first create the safe spaces for recognition to occur (Champagne 2015).

In finding my own safe ground through balancing resurgence activities with awareness of the colonized mind and agency to undertake decolonizing work, I have enjoyed the post-human and more-than-human work of Deborah Rose (1996), Sheridan and Roronhiakewen "He Clears the Sky" Dan Longboat (2006, 2014), Healey and Tagak (2014) and others, such as the collective papers under Bawaka Country authorship (2013, 2014, 2016). These authors show that country has its own agency and epistemologies that open up new forms of research and relationship-building. The ethnographic force and statement of belonging and grounding from Black females such as Indigenous Hawaiian researchers Renee Pulani Louis (2007) and Haunani-Kay Trask (1991) also tease out the local contexts of the intersecting issues of Indigeneity, identity and gender (see also Bravo 2015; Crenshaw 1991; Moreton-Robinson 2013). These authors offered an imagination of identity and referents that are not dependent upon staking a theoretical claim to any particular social outcome, but developing a voice premised upon the strengths and assets of experiencing the Indigenous life, in all its fractured or fully formed glory.

Linda Tuhiwai Smith and others (Smith et al 2016) wrote that the experience of being colonized and our newfound knowledge of these changing times are no less valid as contributions to the substance of Indigenous methodologies, traditional practices and a decolonizing corpus. Therefore, the tensions and complexities of being a colonized person and extinct body and a cultural woman can be recognized as inhabiting the same spheres of concern – that of finding voice and articulating resistance (Dutta 2012). The resurgence of cultural activity, or the returning to country, is integral to my journey of defining a responsible researcher voice for an inclusive "I" as referent and resistance. My connections to country, the process of belonging from kinship and reciprocity, then become the scaffolding and nesting for my decolonizing work that creates no additional harms.

In this manner, by the final PhD stage I was able to create a balance that suited my local context and conditions for coming into being and claim a space within a new referent point. By this, *tebrakunna* country becomes a co-author, following on from Bawaka Country et al (2013), to help guide and anchor my contributions towards decolonizing and ending extinction myths in ways that nurture and recognize *trawlwulwuy* histories and sensitivities. The authorship of my later papers that interrogate whiteness by centering Indigenous ways of knowing and leadership have created an "I" (*tebrakunna* country & Lee 2017, 2019).

I have understood that my colonized mind previously allowed me to accept my lesser, non-being status from others. In finding a pathway towards creating an inclusive "I" and a referent that reflects my deep connections to *tebrakunna* country, I now use country as a co-author to open the spaces for a cultural affiliation and agency to integrate Indigenous methodologies into my decolonizing work. Where other research does not address recuperating identity away from extinction myths, in cloaking myself with country I have begun non-harmful measures into undertaking decolonizing work and finding a safe space away from non-being. This leads me to reflect, in the next section, on where my positioning statement has come from and what it means to my future research behaviors and social outcomes.

Coming into being and belonging to country

While as Indigenous Peoples we have long had to prove our humanity as sentient beings to gain rights, there is a special tension in having to first prove existence at all. This aspect of colonization, the realization of genocide through decimating a population and then claiming a silence or nostalgia or *mea culpa* in the grab for land, power and wealth is seldom viewed through Indigenous and *trawlwulwuy* voices (Lee 2016b; Lehman 2006; Moreton-Robinson 2015; Reynolds 1995; Ross 2017), especially Black female ones. Extinction and coming into being are social and theoretical decolonizing actions that requires new thinking or greater significance within decolonizing research. If restoring peoples' identity and place is not the most important task of decolonizing work, then reparations and power shifts are unlikely to follow as contributing to positive change.

Therefore, my referent and statement of belonging at the beginning of the essay, *I* am "a *trawlwulwuy* woman from *tebrakunna* country, north-east Tasmania, Australia" takes on new meaning. By this, I locate myself not as myth, but as being. I belong to a Peoples and a country; I have a shape and form that is inclusive of the responsibility of a reciprocal researcher and an alertness to my own cultural knowledges. I am aware that the addition of "Tasmania, Australia" speaks to my recognition of being a colonized person. I also understand that the use of the colonizing names "Tasmania, Australia" continues to reinforce whiteness by orientating my country for an international, predominantly Western, readership.

Foremost, though, is the agency that belonging creates. Using country as a co-author, and locating myself through language and kinship, I now possess the means to chip away at the harms that globally embedded myth-making causes. I can contribute to changing our place of extinction to one of vibrant, resurgent and present peoples that can make claim to restorative justice and advantageous impacts through the production of a *trawlwulwuy* voice. In learning to free myself from inferiority while still retaining the strengths from participating in culturally resurgent activities, my decolonization work begins with the centering of our narratives of "always-belonging", rather than justifying a survival on the margins.

While this approach for safe referents may seem far away from the meaty and deliberate decolonizing work to, for example, restructure power and return lands, it does begin to look closely at what is missing from the literature. What can Indigenous methodologies do to heal extinction bodies? What does decolonization work look like for peoples who are non-beings? In revitalizing my identity, I have been concerned with decolonizing myself without the self-loathing or explanations and revelling in the strengths of a power to assert my Black female body as existing. This has been my entry point into decolonization work and the pivot for future efforts. My claim to my Black female body is perhaps what Alfred and Corntassel (2005) mean when they state "one warrior at a time" to recover power and resist colonization as an effort that counts.

A self-knowing buttressed by the supports of theory and practice is behind my statement of belonging. This is an extraordinary gain away from the bulk of nineteenth-century colonial history that has strongly refuted my right to have an identity. Agency, then, begins to look like a freedom to engage and participate in decolonizing work from a different angle, that of the safe spaces to come into being from extinction (*tebrakunna* country & Lee 2019). As Potlotek First Nations woman Marie Battiste (2007, p. 117) states, "[n]o uniform or universal indigenous perspective on indigenous knowledge exists – many do". Our perspective has not only been shaped by the colonized mind of myths, but our continued existence as Aboriginal Tasmanians with knowledges and practices. Our experience in Tasmania is, unfortunately, not unique as a colonizing story of mythical extinctions, as for example Ainu peoples of Japan share similar histories of being denied their very being (Cotterill 2011). However, it is rare that a spectacle to a greed so great becomes a part of popular Western culture, where even Charles Darwin thought to comment on our lamentable existence (Darwin 1839; Debord 2005; Wells 1898). Yet our identity and being can, and will, be recuperated away from these boundaries and towards something that is defined by and for ourselves.

As a *trawlwulwuy* woman from *tebrakunna* country my referent point is vitally important to center my voice and decolonizing work. This work has come from self-determined pathways that, having learnt the conditions of the colonized mind, confront myth-making to unsettle my perception of the world and reinforce my connection to country. There is, however, much required from my actions as a reciprocal researcher to continue to challenge the dominant Western historical view of my non-being. This goes hand-in-hand with seeking a clearer view over extinction and cultural resurgence that can contribute to Indigenous methodologies and decolonizing practices. However, I am still grappling with how to negotiate my statement and position of belonging when writing with multiple and diverse authors.

New voices and co-authorship

Referents can be both liberating and constraining when authorship is shared with country and a voice is developed. In claiming an identity marker of "I" to represent and express myself as a reciprocal researcher to communities and country, I celebrate my power to contribute towards decolonizing the academy. How this approach is sustained and grows is what I am interested in, rather than repeating cultural affiliations in lieu of more action. Decolonizing work for me will always be part of my lifeworld, although I have now lost the fear to make country central in my research.

I am yet to find the space within the academy for genuine mutual benefit in writing with multiple and diverse authors, a place where I do not have to acquiesce to the dominance of Western "I" referents and lose the precious connections with *tebrakunna*. I am vexed by the default setting of Western standards and styles in the co-production of research papers (*tebrakunna* country and Lee & Tran 2016) with people I have built kinship, reciprocity and deep research relationships; people that I like and respect and learn from.

I sting from the "you", with its structures of whiteness, that I consciously adopt and want somehow to turn this into an "ours". It is vitally important that country stays with me in authorship, yet how to avoid reinforcing the primacy of the Western world when whiteness is not the subject of descriptors and nominations of country and culture? Perhaps there is the capacity of country to incorporate new referents that encompass multiple views as a means to decolonize spaces for shared voices (Shultz 2018). Country may be pliant and elastic enough to adopt new languages that do not privilege whiteness and do not detract from working together to decolonize together.

There are recent examples of collective writing that exemplify the critical thinking and reciprocal researcher relationships that speak to seeing ourselves in nurturing ways. The Gay'wu Group of Women (2019) write of Yolŋu histories of North East Arnhem Land as a kinship collective of Indigenous and other Australians that centers women's business and is seamless in author voice. Positionality statements are increasingly being made between author collectives that pay tribute to Elders and communities (Carothers et al 2021), kinship relationships (Jimenez-Luque 2021) and country (Hughes & Barlo 2021; RiverOfLife et al 2020) as central to the work. These new approaches dismantle barriers to ethical knowledge production and begin to heal colonizing harms that have valued sharp distinctions in referents and place.

In this essay I have attempted to show what a colonized mind looks like and how coming into being away from extinction is a slow process of awareness tied to respectful and reciprocal behaviors and careful attention to our methodologies to guide this work. I am still not convinced that the literature has satisfactory answers to recovering from identity loss and cultural resurgence, yet it is these writings that have guided my advocacy. I believe, however, that there is great potential for Indigenous methodologies to assist in new forms of research and shared referents that deconstruct whiteness and provide a cultural safety to experiment with new knowledges. In creating a first person authorship out of non-existence suggests that the impact of 'I' and 'you' referents is vitally important in locating the self and place as a means of decolonization. It is this journey to understand the colonized mind through connections to country that has been the surprise. I have felt a deeper kinship with *tebrakunna* country through the act of signifying our relationship as co-authors to produce a grounded statement of belonging. Decolonization does not need to be a traumatic process to occur, but rather a generous position of belonging.

Part Five

Seeing Ourselves

9

Resist and assert – Indigenous work in GLAM

Lauren Booker (Garigal)

Introduction

Since 1788, collecting institutions have been implicated in the colonial project of Australia and, still today, institutional collections contain masses of Aboriginal and Torres Strait Islander[1] cultural material, information and knowledges. Many of these collections were formed from the exotification, surveillance, assimilation and attempted genocide of Aboriginal and Torres Strait Islander Peoples under the guise of anthropological research and government "protection" policies. Collecting institutions are inclusive of galleries, libraries, archives and museums (GLAM) across both public and private sectors. These include any galleries, libraries, archives and museums embedded in the tertiary education sector, such as a university-based archive or discipline specific museum. Collecting institutions are complicit in, and responsible for, many colonial and assimilatory acts of surveillance, misrepresentation and removal of Aboriginal and Torres Strait Islander Ancestors and cultural and intellectual property.

These contested sites of collection, research and display have long been critiqued and resisted by communities, artists, scholars and GLAM workers, who face the ongoing repercussions of collecting institution practice both old and new. In Henriette Fourmile's "Who Owns the Past? Aborigines as Captives of the Archive" (1989), she says: "To Aboriginal people, the key to our historical

---

[1] The term Aboriginal and Torres Strait Islander refers to First Nations/Indigenous Nations within Australia and the Torres Strait Islands, to whom the collections, actions and practitioners discussed in this essay are connected. The term Indigenous is also used interchangeably with Aboriginal and Torres Strait Islander Peoples. I want to recognize that there are varied preferences for terminology – Indigenous and Aboriginal and Torres Strait Islander are two that refer to the many nations across the continent and the surrounding seas.

and cultural resources and therefore to our cultural and historical identities is firmly clasped in a white hand".

Fourmile identifies the power and power imbalance held in collecting institutions. To this day, radical divesting of that power and transformative change across collecting institutions is yet to be seen (Thorpe 2019). As Indigenous GLAM workers, scholars, artists and activists raise awareness of the complicity of collecting institutions in the ongoing colonial project, what was once an undisturbed site of privilege and fictional neutrality is now being prised open and laid out for questioning. In recent years there have been international movements such as Decolonize this Place, Museum Detox, Museums Are Not Neutral and Rhodes Must Fall, led by the voices of Black, Indigenous and People of Color organizers formulating numerous ways to disrupt the violent colonial narratives and practices of collecting and research institutions. In Australia, Aboriginal and Torres Strait Islander Peoples and allies have been pushing back against the colonial project of collecting institutions through scholarship, arts practice and policy advocacy. Aboriginal and Torres Strait Islander resistance and critique in relation to collecting institutions is far from a new practice. I pay my respects to those people who have laid the path and those who continue to surge forward that have enabled my reflection to take place.

This essay aims to question the application of decolonizing methodologies to collecting institutions in Australia, by illuminating coloniality within the GLAM sector, and identifying Indigenous-led resistance work being done in those spaces. It pays homage to those individuals and communities that work to resist and redefine these spaces formed by colonialism and collecting. This is by no means an exhaustive review of coloniality in collecting institutions, nor of the resistance work taking place: it is rather a very small portion.

There are many threads that are still being woven or that I do not mention, and I draw attention to the issues of academic writing forever having gaps and exclusions. I extend this essay as a personal response to the consideration of decolonization as I navigate colonial structures within and around me. I will draw upon my personal experiences as an archivist and researcher, in a body born of colonization, within the academic and collecting institution sector. As I investigate the viability of applying decolonization praxis to collecting institutions, I cannot surely say that decolonization of collecting institutions is possible. I ask myself – can there be transformative change driven from within collecting institutions and is decolonization the right term for this radical change?

Many policies and guidelines have been enacted at both government and collecting institution sector level, recognizing complicity in traumatic colonial histories that continue to negatively affect Aboriginal and Torres Strait Islander Peoples today (ATSILIRN 2012; HREOC 1997; ICA 2019; Janke 2018). There has been, and continues to be, significant work in recognizing these policies and guidelines, as well as enabling restitutions, reparations and repatriations in Australia. However, many structural changes still need application and advocating for. In this essay, I would like to specifically consider and highlight Indigenous resistance to the continuing colonialism of collecting institutions, and the work done to apply and advocate for structural change. I see Indigenous resistance across collecting institutions presenting in radical and beautiful ways, in quiet and sorrowful ways, but most importantly in self-determined ways of enacting agency of voice, body, past and future.

GLAM, memory institutions, collecting institutions

I recognize the historical inter-institutional nuances that blur when discussing galleries, libraries, archives and museums as a combined whole. The merging, intersecting and boundary drawing of galleries, libraries, archives and museums into a singular talking point (the "GLAM sector" or collecting institutions) has undulated between support and critique over time (VanderBerg 2012). Galleries, libraries, archives and museums are also sometimes referred to as "Memory Institutions", defining the four institutions as places of personal and collective heritage preservation that speak to national identity and shared narratives (Robinson 2012). In this essay, collecting institutions are purposefully combined into a singular topic of discussion as sites that directly affect Aboriginal and Torres Strait Islander Peoples, through issues of power and control (Fourmile 1989; Russell 2001), and tools of colonial propaganda and silence (Dodson 1994; Harkin 2019). However, it is important to recognize each of these institutions – galleries, libraries, archives and museums – as having distinct disciplines and histories that inform them. Therefore, when viewing the Indigenous-led work and resistance that takes place in each of these four types of institution, there will be different policies, pressures and practices to navigate. This essay experiments with discussing these institutions as a combined whole, in order to consider them as a sum of their foundational colonial parts and ideals. I do this to illuminate the institutional connections to their shared function in the colonial project. Referring to function over form (collecting institutions, rather than

GLAM), and colonial and imperial intent over notions of neutrality (collecting institutions, rather than memory institutions), assists in recognizing that under all the sector rhetoric there remain interconnected collections, structures and functions that need to be considered. In positioning collecting institutions as a sum of intentions and actions that often conflate colonization with a concise and reconciled national identity, I show that the intentions of the institute are less important than the structural damage they can enact. Collecting institutions are not neutral windows into colonial power of the past; rather they maintain colonial power that can still be exercised in the present. Before I begin to discuss movements of resistance against the colonialism of collecting institutions, there is a need to identify where and how colonialism resides in these structures.

Colonialism and the collecting institution

Colonial collecting institutions aim to strengthen colonial power and identity by creating and controlling Eurocentric ideals of Indigenous inferiority to bolster white supremacy (McKemmish et al 2011; Russell 2001). Australian and international collecting institutions have amassed monolithic collections focused on Aboriginal and Torres Strait Islander Peoples (Cooper 1989) and are based on ideals that exclude Aboriginal and Torres Strait Islander agency and voice (Russell 2001).

As purveyors of status quo with claims and agendas of neutrality, collecting institutions are tools of colonial power assertion, othering and silencing. These functions are so deeply entrenched in the historical structure of the collecting institution that the problematization of coloniality in collecting institutions often splits sector opinion, with some critical of the changing paradigm (Hunt 2019; ICOM 2004). The changing paradigm aims to identify coloniality in collecting institutions, problematize it and strategize ways to resist and renew institutional forms and functions (Kassim 2019; Sentance 2018). By imperial and colonial design, the collecting institution is a repository of representations of people, place and knowledge – that at its origin sought to center whiteness, often in line with supremacist intentions to prove whiteness as superior.

In Australia, collecting institutions have attempted to define Indigenous Peoples by distinguishing difference and inferiority to the settler-colonial project. Many nations across the continent were often homogenized into a pan-Indigenous Other, relegating dynamic peoples, places and knowledges into the constantly diminishing past (Russell 2001). Lynette Russell (2001, p. 3) identifies this as the "homogeneity paradigm" of settler-colonial representations of the "sameness" of Aboriginal and Torres Strait Islander Peoples, aiming to proliferate obsolescence.

Many collections that currently exist outside of Australia were aimed at favoring the settler-colonial state to export a state-determined representation of Aboriginal and Torres Strait Islander Peoples as a past that has been superseded. Aboriginal and Torres Strait Islander Peoples have worked tirelessly in innovative ways to advocate for Ancestors and cultural materials held overseas to return to communities and Country; from accessing collections to forming foundations of new artists work in both revitalization and institutional critique (for example the work of Mutti Mutti/Yorta Yorta/Boon Wurrung/Wemba Wemba artist Maree Clarke, Waanyi multimedia artist Judy Watson and Yuwaalaraay artist and designer Lucy Simpson), to advocating through writing and curatorial practices (Andrews 2017; Gumbula 2009; Moulton 2018). The ongoing institutional control of Aboriginal and Torres Strait Islander Ancestral remains, cultural material and records is a traumatic and paternalistic dislocation from Country and community that is directly connected to the colonial foundations of the institution.

If colonialism is both the cause, and the ongoing effect, of the collecting institutional paradigm, decolonization must be an action resisting that which is colonial, but also enabling the figuration of something new. Decolonization is not just critical awareness of the colonial structure; rather, it needs to also be a proactive "divesting of colonial power" (Smith 2012, p. 101). For the collecting institution sector to consider its ability for "decolonization", there needs to be consideration of how land, identity and power, as foundational tenets of colonialism, are engaged with. In the settler-colonial state where the physical institutional structure is relatively immovable, and with the onset of the digital "GLAM" space becoming the new normal, how can colonial paradigms of land, identity and power be movable?

The connection of land dispossession to collecting institutions

The invasion and violent colonization of Australia and the surrounding seas, motivated and supported by legal fictions and racial supremacism, disregarded the sovereignty of over 500 Aboriginal and Torres Strait Islanders nations (Behrendt 2010). Professor Aileen Moreton-Robinson (2015, p. xi), Goenpul woman from the Quandamooka First Nation, asserts that this understanding of Australia as uninhabited and, subsequently, a possession of the Crown was established through the "possessive logic of patriarchal white sovereignty", which continues to pervasively dictate the relationship between Indigenous Peoples and the nation state. Collecting institutions have played a key role in the act of possessing and transferring ownership of everything that could be collected and re-categorized: cultural materials, language, Ancestors and records pertaining to families and individuals. Galleries, libraries, archives and museums have held the legislated power to determine definition and display of collections and proliferate negative representations of Aboriginal and Torres Strait Islander Peoples whilst built on unceded lands (Russell 2001).

In the nineteenth and twentieth century, Australia implemented multiple violent, paternalistic and eugenics informed policies intended to dispossess and assimilate Aboriginal and Torres Strait Islander Peoples (HREOC 1997). These policies were applied by state governments and included forcible removal of Indigenous children from families, the forced relocation of many people from their Country to reserves and missions or to other Peoples Country, and restrictions regarding cultural practices and languages (HREOC 1997). Connections to Country include language, stories, knowledge, cultural materials made from the land, and the ability to be physically present on that land with kin. The interruption and oppression of Indigenous self-determination via legal fictions, exploitation and genocidal government policies were not only documented by collecting institutions in Australia, but also sustained and supported by collecting institutions as sites of surveillance, regulation and national identity (Harkin 2019).

To aid in the settler-colonial project in Australia, collecting institutions have either benefited from and/or directly worked for discriminatory government policies, amassing collections about Aboriginal and Torres Strait Islander Peoples that exclude self-determined authorship (Russell 2005). For example, state archives amassed collections created under state government's "protection" policies – such as the Aborigines Welfare Board (Harkin 2019). The Bringing Them Home report highlighted the importance of access to government and non-government records for Stolen Generations survivors and their families, drawing public attention to the ongoing trauma and barriers presented by archives and recordkeeping for Aboriginal and Torres Strait Islander Peoples (HREOC 1997). Museums across the country have relied on researchers and collectors, both academic and amateur, to build their collections and have engaged in the international trade of Ancestral remains for study and display (Turnbull 2017). Libraries and archives have substantial collections of linguistic documents containing Indigenous languages. They have become important repositories for Indigenous language revitalization projects (Thorpe & Galassi 2014) in returning documentation to communities to assist in repairing what successive government policies attempted to destroy.

Collecting institutions across Australia are implicated in national histories of racism and social injustice through the collections they hold and the collecting practices that built them. The disconnection of Peoples' power to self-determine their own identity and representation is aided by long histories of collecting institutions making decisions without Aboriginal and Torres Strait Islander Peoples driving those decisions. The conversation of decolonization in the collecting institution sector is one that directly relates to Indigenous self-determination regarding all decisions made in connection to Country and identity; and Country and identity are present in all collections.

Decolonization in the collecting institution requires the re-centering of land/Country and a total divestment from state power towards Indigenous self-determination. The requests for repatriation of Ancestral remains and cultural materials to communities and Country, for example, are not only about reparations; they are also an assertion of self-determination in the colonial collecting paradigm (Fforde 2002). Furthermore, they are enacting Indigenous connection to Country. The call for decolonization of collecting institutions is complex; however, at its core it is a recognition of the colonial power held by collecting institutions, its disruption and the re-centering of Aboriginal and Torres Strait Islander self-determination of identity and Country.

Decolonizing methodologies and the collecting institution

Decolonization ... is now recognised as a long-term process involving the bureaucratic, cultural, linguistic and psychological divesting of colonial power.

Smith 2012, p. 101

Linda Tuhiwai Smith's foundational text, *Decolonizing Methodologies* (2012), stated that decolonization is a necessary continual resistance of colonial power and practical assertion of Indigenous sovereignty. Smith (2012) recognizes decolonization working on two fronts – state focused resistance and assertions of Indigenous sovereignty. Decolonization has become increasingly referred to as a goal for the collecting institution sector, and it is a key focus that often features in the titles of Australian collecting institution sector conferences, symposiums, seminars, papers and tertiary classes. However, this raises questions on how many of these discussions on decolonization and the collecting institution sector are actually organizing state focused resistance and assertions of Indigenous sovereignty, and how much just remains metaphorical, as Tuck and Yang (2012) notably warned against.

Perhaps, the conceptualization of decolonization within the collecting institution sector sits in parallel with the conceptualization of social justice as "always a process [that] can never fully be achieved" (Duff et al 2013, pp. 324–325). However, with this in mind we can turn to Tuck and Yang (2012) and their clear position that "Decolonization is not a metaphor". There should be careful consideration of delineating between what is a decolonization conversation and what is a social justice conversation (Tuck & Yang 2012). Tuck and Yang (2012) aim to turn statements into action, where decolonization is about the fruitful return of Indigenous lands and recognition of sovereignty, rather than the conversations over semantics or impacts.

I suggest that a key component to the potential involvement of collecting institutions in engaging with conversations around decolonizing is to focus on providing radical transparency around institutional parameters of what can and cannot be achieved in regards to divestment from colonial and state power. The collecting institution itself may support a specific community or individual's decolonization aims and practices, but the deeply embedded foundations of colonial power make me question if decolonization as applied to the institution itself is an achievable goal. Many of the actions that could be labeled as destabilizing colonial power in a collecting institution would actually fall under the *minimum standards* of Indigenous rights as laid out in United Nations Declaration of the Rights of Indigenous Peoples (UNDRIP).

As a site and tool of colonialism, collecting institutions will never be able to fully engage in decolonization efforts without radical reconsideration of governance, form and function. This is not to say that collecting institutions cannot continue to have these aspirations, and more importantly, support the rights and goals of Aboriginal and Torres Strait Islander Peoples, whether that is decolonization, treaty, reparation, repatriation or Indigenous Cultural and Intellectual Property (ICIP) rights. Ho-Chunk Nation scholar Dr Amy Lonetree asserts that to engage a museum in the decolonization process is to recognize the museum as "a means for repairing colonization's harm" (2012, p. 171). Furthermore, Lonetree (2012, p. 27) sees the potential for transformation of museums into "sites of conscience" by recognizing the specific harm and ongoing grief perpetrated by museums' colonial paradigm and engaging in decolonizing methodologies to support the healing practices of Indigenous communities. New means and methods of supporting healing goals may be found by engaging in the truth-telling of institutional involvement in colonial and assimilatory histories, as well as continuing to support the Indigenous voices that are resisting and asserting sovereignty.

Self-determination and the collecting institution

Decolonization practices and principles are global in nature but are ultimately undertaken at the local level. For example, UNDRIP is a guiding document that recognizes how collecting institutions have contributed to the oppression of Indigenous self-determination internationally, whilst needing specific enactment locally. UNDRIP has set a global mandate for the understanding and support of Indigenous Peoples' self-determination in the access, care and control of their own cultural knowledge, heritage and intellectual property. Australia was one of four countries to delay ratification of UNDRIP until 2009; however, since then many institutional policies, protocols and guidelines have utilized the UNDRIP as the basis for commitments to rights-based practice. Key to UNDRIP is the mandate for Indigenous self-determination to all areas of life – political, cultural and social (UNDRIP 2007).

Specifically, in relation to collecting institutions, Article 11, Article 12 and Article 31 reference the right of Indigenous Peoples to self-determination over access, protection, maintenance, development and control of materials and knowledges held in collecting institutions, as well as repatriation of stolen Ancestors:

Article 11
Indigenous peoples have the right to practise and revitalize their cultural traditions and customs. This includes the right to maintain, protect and develop the past, present and future manifestations of their cultures, such as archaeological and historical sites, artefacts, designs, ceremonies, technologies and visual and performing arts and literature.

Article 12
Indigenous peoples have the right to manifest, practise, develop and teach their spiritual and religious traditions, customs and ceremonies; the right to maintain, protect, and have access in privacy to their religious and cultural sites; the right to the use and control of their ceremonial objects; and the right to the repatriation of their human remains.

Article 31

Indigenous peoples have the right to maintain, control, protect and develop their cultural heritage, traditional knowledge and traditional cultural expressions, as well as the manifestations of their sciences, technologies and cultures, including human and genetic resources, seeds, medicines, knowledge of the properties of fauna and flora, oral traditions, literatures, designs, sports and traditional games and visual and performing arts. They also have the right to maintain, control, protect and develop their intellectual property over such cultural heritage, traditional knowledge, and traditional cultural expressions.

UNDRIP 2007

There are a growing number of projects, policies and programs across Australia that reflect the collecting institution and research sector's recognition of specific Indigenous communities' rights and needs surrounding access, care and control of collections as asserted by UNDRIP. Collaborative initiatives between communities and the collecting institution sector are beginning to consider what is needed to facilitate the divestment of decision-making power from institutional control. Some examples of this collaborative work include: the support of community specific access conditions for digital archives (Christen, Merrill & Wynne 2017); digital returns and localization of collections (Ormond-Parker & Sloggett 2012); repatriation of Ancestral remains from museums (Poll 2015; Fforde, McKeown & Keeler 2020); and access to records for people affected by past government policies that, for example, removed language from people and children from families (Thorpe & Galassi 2014).

Guidelines and policy advocacy that aim to intervene with business-as-usual have begun to set precedents in how collecting institutions must consider ICIP, Free Prior and Informed Consent and repatriation. These include *First Peoples: A Roadmap for Enhancing Indigenous Engagement in Museums and Galleries* (Janke 2018) and the movements of ICIP rights and Indigenous Data Sovereignty. On paper, it seems like momentum is building for collecting institutions to directly take responsibility for colonial and assimilatory complicity and to address the requests and rights of Aboriginal and Torres Strait Islander Peoples. However, this momentum remains at the will of the institutions themselves and would have to take place while the Australian Government continues to ignore refusals and block requests from Aboriginal and Torres Strait Islander communities (Davis 2018). It would have to take place whilst there continues, for example, to be the poisoning of water in the NT by fracking (Hoosan 2018), the planning and implementation of sacred site destruction for the building of highways and the mining of Country (Djab Wurrung Heritage Protection Embassy 2020; Wahlquist 2020); and the continued brutal injustice of Aboriginal deaths in custody (McQuire 2020). The collecting institution sector has a long way to go in seeing the interconnectedness of their form and function and the daily violence of the settler-colonial state, and perhaps this may be something that is never arrived at fully. Furthermore, this cannot be the role of Aboriginal and Torres Strait Islander GLAM sector workers alone to take responsibility for shouldering all the advocacy work whilst also engaging in their work and community roles.

New fields of critical thinking regarding the effects of colonization are also contributing to responses to international and sector mandates, such as Wiradjuri Professor Juanita Sherwood's work detailing the ongoing effect of colonization on Aboriginal and Torres Strait Islander Peoples' health and wellbeing. Sherwood insists that in order to provide appropriate health-care for Indigenous patients, health professionals must have detailed knowledge of both experiences and intergenerational trauma felt by Indigenous Peoples in settler-colonial societies (Sherwood 2013). In line with this thinking, collecting institutions need to broaden their consideration of restitution and reparation beyond the scope of their collections, and look to the health of people as a key component of supporting and delivering on the rights of Indigenous Peoples. Australian collecting institutions need to be further interrogated for their impact on Aboriginal and Torres Strait Islander communities' (inclusive of Aboriginal and Torres Strait Islander GLAM workers) health and wellbeing. There continues to be strong Indigenous voices advocating for and implementing Indigenous-led initiatives across collecting institutions. If decolonization is the divestment of colonial power, then the collecting institution sector needs to be radically transparent about the ways in which colonial power can be divested from in a sector that greatly relies on state support and legislated ownership of collection materials. Furthermore, if decolonization is being raised as a priority for a collecting institution, questions must be raised around who is driving this and how this aligns with communities' needs and goals. Going back to UNDRIP (2007), in which every article raised is only the *minimum* standard for Indigenous Peoples' rights internationally:

Article 43
The rights recognized herein constitute the minimum standards for the survival, dignity and well-being of the Indigenous peoples of the world.

Indigenous resistance and the collecting institution

Over the last two decades, Aboriginal and Torres Strait Islander artists and sector workers have been engaging with the colonial foundations of collecting institutions through interaction with, and disruption of, the colonial narratives of collections. The list of Aboriginal and Torres Strait Islander artists who critique, examine, engage and resist the collecting institution sector in the content of their work is long and ever growing, including the "Sovereign Acts" series by The Unbound Collective, and the "Spirit of Things: The Sound of Objects" by Nardi Simpson and Kaleena Briggs. These artists, and many more not written here, are part of an international movement of First Nations Peoples from seas and lands globally, that address the collecting institution sector in their arts practice and work.

Two particular examples of artist works, those by Wiradjuri/Kamilaroi artist Jonathan Jones and Narungga activist-poet Natalie Harkin, expose and disrupt the colonial narratives of collecting institutions through direct intersection with collections and collecting practices. As discussed by Noongar writer Cassie Lynch (2017, n.p.), Aboriginal and Torres Strait Islander artists' works are "epistemological disruptions" that can not only counter but rise above the "assumed certainties" in the colonization narrative. Importantly, the works of Jones and Harkin sit in displays of Indigenous sovereignty; of identity; of dynamism, of resilience; of un-apologetic truth-telling.

In Jones' 2016 sculptural installation project "barrangal dyara (skin and bones)" for Kaldor Public Art Projects, 15,000 gypsum shields were created in multiple styles from across the southeast of Australia. These shields were laid out over the original site of the Garden Palace, in the now Royal Botanical Gardens in Sydney, an exhibition hall that burnt down in 1882 which contained Ancestral remains and cultural materials from southeast Aboriginal communities. The shields outlined the forgotten presence of the Garden Palace across 20,000 square meters, with kangaroo grass planted within what was the giant of the colonial collecting institutions in Australia.

"barrangal dyara (skin and bones)" was a response to the immense loss of Ancestral remains and specifically southeast Aboriginal cultural materials and knowledges held in the Garden Palace, and more broadly during the violence of the colonial and assimilation eras (Kaldor Public Art Projects n.d.). Jones described "barrangal dyara (skin and bones)" as an act of mourning and remembering Ancestors and Ancestral knowledge: "peeling the layers of skin back off this site and revealing these bones in the landscape" (Jones quoted in Sebag-Montefiore 2016, n.p.). That which has been buried and silenced in the

Australian narrative regarding Aboriginal and Torres Strait Islander Peoples in relation to collecting institutions, is being brought forward for the public to consider their forgetfulness. In the opening of Natalie Harkin's "Archival Poetics" (Colonial Archive, Archival-Poetics 1) there is a prelude and a warning, notifying all to witness that which will be brought to light:

ATTENTION:
RECORD KEEPERS OF THE STATE
WE HAVE YOU UNDER SURVEILLANCE
WE HAVE YOU UNDER SURVEILLANCE

Harkin 2019, p. 7

"Archival Poetics" is structured in three parts to interrogate the archive; bringing forth its structure of racist and gendered violence, and how the experience of the state archive is woven into the personal. Harkin combines personal and institutional archival materials and intimate memories to identify the silence in the record and challenge the official historical narrative with a response. Nathan "Mudyi" Sentance, Wiradjuri man, librarian and museum educator, describes "Archival Poetics" as Harkin exercising a right of reply, highlighting its significance as: "assert[ing] the power that we First Nations people hold and have always held – a power that exists outside of colonial systems" (Sentance 2019, n.p.). This goes back to Smith's (2012, p. 101) description of decolonization of a "divestment of colonial power". "Archival Poetics" critically interrogates the colonial archive and the ongoing effects of what the archive both presents and represents; uncovering how the colonial archive as a site and a structure simultaneously holds truths and untruths, presence and absence. This is further explored by the work of The Unbound Collective, of which Harkin is a collaborator alongside Faye Rosas Blanch, Simone Ulalka Tur and Ali Gumillya Baker, in their "Sovereign Acts" series. Harkin (2017) takes up her responsibility and sovereignty as a Nurungga woman, by disrupting the officiated narrative whilst determining and weaving her own archive and story – for the past and future.

Both Jones' and Harkin's works present methods of truth-telling that challenge ownership and the authority of colonial narratives, while asserting Indigenous self-determination over knowledges, histories and identities. The receptiveness of some Australian collecting institutions to engage with the truth-telling that Indigenous artists and GLAM sector workers bring to these spaces seems to be at a time when momentum is building towards institutional responsibility for institutional coloniality.

However, as discussed earlier, when one zooms out to look at the broader situation in Australia regarding Indigenous rights being upheld, this feeling of momentum seems uncertain. The more time I spend working in or around collecting institutions, the more I see institutional and government receptiveness as less and less important in the collecting institution sector. Jonathan Jones discusses this in his article "Lighting the Fire: Cultural Renaissance in the South-East", where he highlights that: "*In recent times we have experienced a return to traditional practices in south-east Australia.... The rapid emergence of these projects, often around kitchen tables, schoolrooms and campfires, away from galleries and museums, is by nature intimate and remains largely undocumented*" (Jones 2014, p. 35, my emphasis). Aboriginal and Torres Strait Islander artists are continuously highlighting the ongoing coloniality of collecting institutions and pushing back in resistance. They are not waiting for permission to enact Indigenous agency in the historical narrative and future direction of collections and institutional (mis)representations. I say this not to detract from the hugely significant work of policy change, but rather to highlight the daily work of revitalizing, reclaiming or resisting that Indigenous Peoples are doing regardless of collecting institutional support.

In the final part of "Archival-Poetics (Blood Memory, Archival-Poetics 3)", we are brought back to the beginning, with another warning – that in these archival interactions, Indigenous Peoples are not guaranteed closure or easy endings (Harkin 2019). Harkin (2019) reminds us to breathe when we can and prepare for this possibility. "Archival-Poetics", however, is also a love letter, dedicated to family and Grandmothers past, present and to come (Harkin 2019). It is in this act of responsibility of love and care in truth-telling that both Jones' and Harkin's work pushes outside of the colonial paradigm, as observed by Henrietta Fourmile that Aboriginal Peoples are "captives of the archive" (Fourmile 1989). "Archival-Poetics" and "barrangal dyara (skin and bones)" enact a responsibility to Country and kin in reconnecting stories, languages and knowledges that have been removed from place, People and practice. The resistance and disruption of the trauma, homogenization and decontextualization that collecting institutions proliferate against Indigenous Peoples are something that can only be realized with Indigenous People leading the work.

An assumed certainty of the colonization narrative was that there would be an eventual destruction of Aboriginal and Torres Strait Islander Country and identity. Many collecting institutions had expectations that the collections they held were to be remnants and artifacts of complete cultural loss (Russell 2001). This, however, was and is not the case. Some of these same collections are now being returned to Country and community, and others are being accessed for revitalization, reuse and resistance work (Andrews 2017; Jones 2014). In my opinion, this is where collecting institutions can focus their reparative action: through truth-telling and supporting the rights and goals of Indigenous Peoples, whether working internal or external to the institution, to determine the futures of collections. The question of decolonization as applied to the collecting institution must not descend into metaphor (Tuck & Yang 2012). Foundational elements of the collecting institution, in both form and function, are immutable characteristics of colonialism. It is important that the collecting institution sector becomes more reflexive and transparent regarding what transformative change can and cannot be done by a key site and tool of colonialism. Collecting institutions can be facilitators and supporters of an Indigenous-led decolonization aim and decolonizing methodologies; however, there needs to be critical engagement and disruption of any action that works to benefit institutional power rather than support Aboriginal and Torres Strait Islander sovereignty. Collecting institutions are intrinsically linked to Country and identity – not only in their placement on unceded land or in their institutional histories, but also in the collections and stories that they hold. For Aboriginal and Torres Strait Islander Peoples, what is held in the collections' stores and stacks tells of Country, Ancestors, identity and future. As Yolngu elder and scholar, Dr Gumbula (2009, p. 1) said:

Everything is telling us who we are.

10

What form can an atonement take?

Pauliina Feodoroff (skolt sámi)

Like a small pulse. That was what my body felt before I saw what I was sensing.

In the summer of 2012, equipped with newly bought digital cameras Snowchange Cooperative had sponsored for our small group of skolt sámi fishermen, as we had wished, for monitoring the changes in our land, I was walking with my father to our family's fishing cabin by the River Njâuddam.[1]

The small hut was the very first of many houses my father built as an 18-year-old boy – every skolt sámi woman was expected to be able at least to knit a pair of socks and mittens to keep her family warm, and a basic requirement for manhood was the ability to build a house with a stove – for a place chosen by his step-grandfather,
who also decided the places for all of his family line: a sign of vitality too few possessed at that time. It was his wife, my great-grandmother, who spent all her summers fishing there, being born to the shores of Barents Sea and always longing to be by water, while he was serving as a guide and cook for groups of geologists, who were prospecting the very same nickel vein that had brought our people here by force.

First summers by the River Njâuddam my great-grandmother lived in a turf hut, then in the houses her husband and her sons and grandsons started to build, little by little introducing ourselves to the river our tribe has always lived with, but not our family.

The hut has become the center for us to fish, to berry-pick, to tell stories, to reroot.

---

[1] Näätämöjoki in Finnish, Neiden elva in Norwegian.

It was only in 1949 our people were settled here, to the Njâuddam siida winter pasture areas, being forcibly evacuated from our traditional territories that Finland lost to the Soviet Union, Norway having taken her share already almost 100 years earlier.

My father's life, as well as my own, has been a long line of careful steps, trying to form a new relationship to an area where our ancestors were not born, nor died, while still being a part of the people that have been here since the end of the last ice age.

I walk with him, because he is the one who teaches us to fish in the family. It is most of the times a journey with his brothers, uncles, male friends. Being with the land is being with the men.

I've brought this UN university project (Arctic Council 2016; Mustonen 2013; Mustonen & Feodoroff 2018) – local observations of climate change – to our community, due to my small asset of academic connections, but also constantly hearing short stories, sentences from my relatives about the thunder storm in the middle of winter, strangely behaving ice, new winds rising in the darkest time of the year when it should be still. Not being a reindeer herder, a hunter or a fisher myself but a theater director of all trades, it is the men, and my father, that I go to ask for permission and guidance for the work I have started without having any expertise for it, only the need for acting.

The men discuss my proposal, take their time.

"Stock us with cameras," they say, "and we will show you what we see happening when going around, instead of trying to explain. But what do you do with that what we will show you?", they ask.

"I show the evidence to the scientists," I reply.

"But they cannot stop the change, can they?", they challenge.

"I don't think so," I answer.

"So, what is the use for this work then, other than us getting new cameras?", they comment wryly. "Then that is the use," I conclude, and try to keep the spirits up for both sides.

Our team, being uncertain what is expected from us, and the scientists, who I try to convince that we all are on the same page and things are rolling, fearing them leaving us for a more aware sámi community, and starting the collaboration there. Who would then pay for the cameras I've already promised?

So we walk, and I start interviewing my father. I ask questions, the kind of questions I would presume climate scientists would be interested in the hearing answers to:

Have you monitored changes in the river flow? Do you see changes in snow? Are there changes in animal stocks? I know I irritate him talking too much in the forest, speaking in a way that makes him uncertain about his own knowledge. The language is wrong, but I do not have a better one in stock either.

I ask about the river, the lake, the forest and the weather at the same time, in the same sentence, without really comprehending or documenting what he tries to answer.
In later years, he has these talks on his own with scientists and both sides end up being happy. I am both relieved and envious about the straight-forwardness he seems to reach with outsiders.

We are crossing the last lake in our journey to our cabin, when I feel a small change in temperature and, before the reason gets in the way, I let my body locate the source of something vibrating. At the bow of our boat where my rucksack is sits a big, shining bug that I have never seen before. I ask my father about it and he says he doesn't know. I take a photo with our brand-new camera and my whole body is filled with uncertainty, the source of which I do not recognize.

———

The bug was identified by Snowchange to be a scarabaeiod beetle (*Potosia cuprea*), verifying that southern species are indeed on the move to the north, and both the observation (Pecl et al 2017) and the methodology-visual histories (Mustonen 2015) were later represented in different scientific publications, gaining more credibility inside and outside of our team. We started to be referred to as *co-researchers* and the work shifted from monitoring to restoring. Science is being written, traditional knowledge is mentioned often, photos of our team are nowadays taken, and I am said to be leading the work. Still, why is my every step so shaky and doubt in my body endless, when the men around me seem to just do their work?

——

What do the women—?

I read.

Whether
this world was born out of the egg of a bluebill, the magnificent waterfowl, or the Big Bang, it was the name Skäävsuâll, or Skäädsuâll, my people's ancestors gave her.

Skääv or skääd, depending on which school of thought of the skolt sámi language you prefer, even though,
we do not know any longer the meaning of the word, but suâll means an island: the logical question that follows, is what then surrounds the island, and what is the shore we are looking at the sky from?

My people's ancestors perceived the genders of different waters, based on the ability – or inability – to act as cradles of life, to spawn. In this skääv or skääd island, always paying special attention to water, it is the element connecting us to the spheres above us, identifying the male and the female lakes, rivers and ponds. And the name of the foremother, the grandmother of all waters, was given to the sea, where all life has been created.

Till this day, I have not heard,
or read from any written materials, studying the heritage of my people, a creation story for a human being.
Obviously, this doesn't necessarily mean that there is no such thing.

But it could also mean that there is no separate creation story for a human being.

And maybe so, in our endemic world, there is no separate human being, yet.

The creation stories that my ancestors told are all about the alliances between places, animals and families – how those commitments were born.

How time, animals and families began to interact, collaborate, how every now and then something usually went wrong, and after the erratic behavior, mostly from the side of the man, the interaction continued, the wrongdoer transformed into a steep or a cape and the harmony hereby restored. The erratic, or dangerous behavior that could interfere with the dynamics of the interaction, petrified. It froze the unwanted motion into stone.

Our ancestors left their marks on the land by turning into soil, generation after generation.

We do not have a creation story for the following term either: land rights.

But we do have a myriad of different practices, policies, systems of how the alliances between the families, animals and places were governed and managed and living, understanding how those unwritten, physical conventions that lasted for millennia are manifested, for example, in place names our ancestors left behind, covering all of the area where our cultural inhabitancy has taken place. That is what I conclude by listening to the men of my family and I try to make it visible for others to see.

All the work that I do is basically concentrating on documenting, verifying and promoting witness statements, or testimonies from the people – my people – who still got to live within the fully functioning siida: the endemic self-governing system of the sámi. And it has been the skolt sámi that were the last of all sámi siidas to lose their sovereignty in 1944. And even after the forced evacuation the Second World War set upon us, rudiments of that traditional law are still in practice, especially in the systems governing fishing. I learn.

Where does following the fishing lead you then?

To the alliances between spawning waters – fish that will come back to spawn only if the water is nurtured and respected by not interfering with her life – and the families, who each have a duty as a guardian of their own lake or river.

The Act of telling a world to be
The Act of saying aloud
The world is spoken out to be
So say it.

If I say aloud my family is a guardian of this river, will we become one?
And whose voice it is the land reacts to?
What voice does the land listen to?
What words or way of speaking makes her want to throw me out?
With what words will she pull me closer and let me be with her, let me stay?

I listen to the men and filter through years of discussions something I *feel* to be most relevant:

The grandfather lake Sevetti that does not tolerate any noise and hardly stands humans at all.
The Sei´ttjäu´rr that does not want to have anything to do with a certain family.
The Äjjsuâll that is only for the men.
And the similar, less phallic small islands, that are only for women.
Not mixing this knowledge was the source of good and balanced living. *Was?*

Is this documentation following a romantic dream, an idea about life of harmony, or a path away from the ecological destruction we all are living in now? When our physical reality is being altered,
modified
or destroyed every day,

our perceptions and knowledges about the world start to
alter, modify
and destruct.

It is not certain anymore do I exist.
If I exist,
do you share the same reality with me?
Is there a reality?

Is that just a conceptual relic, as any kind of absolute, whether it would be a law or a Truth? Have these alterations altered the ecosystems so much that what used to be the natural law or nature's law that does not exist anymore, and therefore my conscience doesn't exist as a part of nature either?

Is there a reason to ask about fishing when our relationship with the salmon has changed so much during the last 40 years and our traditional practices being overrun? Would that be just an imitation of a cultural practice, now empty for us, or is there still a relevance that can be turned back to?

———

I am documenting. "For what?", asks our team and I avoid answering.

I come from a culture in which there is no traditional word for Art per se, but rather a central, essentialist concept of Beauty, which pierces every spheres of life as a guideline, and a law system: everything must be done beautifully. Beauty is what you do and how you do it, your whole life and existence as an expression of beauty and balance, the imperative of beauty in your everyday life.

Balance in co-existing and not wasting anything are the central elements of what is beautiful.

One of the most beautiful objects that I have ever seen is a vase, sewn from four tiny legs of a reindeer calf, her nails still attached, forming the base of the vase and the upper part from the tibia, still under the incredibly thin skin. The reindeer doe had a miscarriage and the calf was born dead: way too early but still nearly fully developed. Just in a miniature scale.

It was Tsetseg's reindeer, who had such a difficult time having her does breed, since for some unknown reason, practically all of the calves died inside of their mothers' bellies in north-Mongolia. Tsetseg is living in a fully nomadic society, a dukkha herself, and we met her in her summer lands.

She had found the small one dead, mourned her and admired the red color of the undeveloped fur, which starts to darken immediately after the calf is born. Tsetseg wanted to make something out of it. Since everything else was so petite and soft, she used hard parts: the legs, sewing the vase. Surreal, balanced design: exposing to the human eye something that is not yours to be seen – a shadow of the calf before she got to be a calf in Tsetseg's tent, in which the vase was the only object that was served solely by existing.

"Maybe someday I will collect some flowers to it," Tsetseg explained. "Otherwise I remember the calf this way."

To her I had traveled to see with my own eyes if it was true what my father told about his childhood. If such alliances existed and can still exist. Between families, areas and animals. Since I never witnessed that. Just ruins.

And I needed a place to hide while trying to figure it out. I disappeared into Art, the Western haven for freedom.

The habit of using euphemisms "I'm from theater," "I make documentaries," "I mess with many things," when someone asks "what do you do?", I have abandoned during the last years: I have started to call myself an artist too.

In the hierarchy of Knowledges, the Art Knowledge does not have a particularly high status compared to, for example, natural sciences, but it is characteristic for Art Knowledge not to give a damn about statuses, or hierarchies. Rather it might deny their existence and imagine a new world order instead.

Originating also from a culture of people that has been for centuries in the very bottom of all hierarchies, including our knowledge. The superior comes from the source that also trained and recognized me to be an artist. I have more influence as a sámi on my own issues that way. And I take the space where I can find it. But where is the land in ideas? My work is my tool to spend time with the river, to defend our people's right to be with her, to protect her. I end up writing and talking about her, looking through a lens. Is this really the way to come closer?

Since a worldview that cannot be rooted into practices, into living bodies, hanging in air, and is a cause of distraction and unclear focus.

And it is meaningless, or to be more precise, unsafe, to speak about the endemic qualities of communicating with the nature, the land, if we don't address the mechanisms that have for a long period of time interfered with that communication, to the point of extinction.

In this time of ecological and existential crisis, you cannot cherry-pick Indigenous cosmological practices in a philosophical, artistic or theoretical way: if we are to go there, we have to undo the damage as well that has been made to those practices, and mostly, the lands that are the source of all knowledge. But who do I do it with then, and how?

———

I read.

We are still facing and living with the consequences of the state foundation masoned in 1648, as the brilliant south sámi lawyer, Doctor of Law, Mattias Åhrén (2016, p. 10) eloquently writes:

> The Peace of Westphalia cemented the realm of the kingdoms in Europe, and offered the idea of certain stability in the relations between the "nations" of the region. At Westphalia, European sovereigns agreed that order was to be guaranteed by the sovereigns themselves. Implicit in this notion was that the right of the sovereigns to provide order was inherent.

Another powerful sámi man that I listen to, the mastermind of the *Girjás versus Sweden* case (Hofverberg 2020) who won in court rights to hunt and fish, knew his sovereignty.
To what extent our endemic ways of organizing, our traditional laws, thus, the alliances between places, animals and families are legal subjects? And legal subjects they must become, if they wish to have a say.

The eradication of the alliances between families, animals and areas is deeply rooted in our current juridical system, the Finnish constitution,
and,
what eventually is a quality in sensitivity perceiving all around you – the past and the current happenings, but also what is about to come – will be a marginal curiosity reserved only for art and research, rather than being the central principle guiding the everyday life of a society, or a civilization.

———

I listen, I read, I try to understand.

I am so really tired all the time.

I turn down jobs and halt projects, but it doesn't help. Finally, I am not capable of doing anything. At this point it is not a matter of choice. I can't function even if I try.

My body starts to fall apart. I've always had asthma, but now I can't breathe anywhere. Then my back breaks so I can't walk. When laying in a hospital bed, pumped with morphine and the room literally spinning around, unable to control any parts of my body, I realize I have not been feeling basically anything for a long, long time. Finally, the doctor I speak to diagnoses me with a severe depression, and some weeks later I am in a hospital, constantly monitored due to high risk for suicide.

My lust for living is all gone, and I have no capacity to find it again on my own. What has happened to me to get me this down – or have I been here all along, without realizing it earlier?

I sit with Finnish therapists who are asking me questions about my childhood, family and things that had happened recently. "Nothing special has happened to me," I say, "it has happened to us," in the middle of giving long lectures about my people's history in order to be understood at least a bit.

Why is the only thing circling in my mind death?

I sit with my therapists; they ask something about me, and I speak about my people. Because my people's history is my family's history. We are so few, so everyone is linked by blood. My therapists are asking what I am avoiding when I am not talking about myself, I only speak about the sámi.

I try to reflect if I am a person. Is there such a "me", a living creature, capable of happiness and continuation, without my collective? Without capable family, clan, which is my people? If I am the only one jumping out from the sinking boat and surviving, who am I then? An individual without her own people? That cannot exist?

You have chosen not to kill yourself; you have chosen not to drink; something is driving you, say my therapists. What?
I ran away from death, I answer.

Do you want to discuss death?

In my family, in my tribe: death of sisters and a brother, death of healthy genes, death of a generation of young men who killed themselves after the massive land losses. All family, all kin. Death of my own family areas, now all waste lands of nickel smelter – an area of total destruction – death of those structures that connected us with our lands. No more going to summer places in Holmengrå, as Norwegians call it now. No more passing our sacred sites. Death of all my elders. Death of traditional law.

The forests stay silent. The ancestors stay silent.

It is thought that people would be more noble in the time of crisis. I disagree. The people who have lost everything will be lowest of the low among the others. Until they manage to sustain a stable footing again. As individuals, and if lucky enough, as a collective as well. And if the latter is successful, the culture will continue.

"Why is it so painful for you to pass your culture – which you hold so dear – to your own daughters?", ask my therapists. Because it is not enough if I alone decide that this language, this culture will continue. If no-one else shares that determination with me.

My mother is a Finn, coming from a culture that assimilates my people. Both worlds are within me. And I am demanding my father to raise me up to be a sámi woman, whether he likes it or not.

My siblings didn't have määccuǩ, our traditional costumes, when we were kids. I started to sew my own as a teenager. And when I got parts of sámi costume for my father, he answered that he never wanted them in the first place, never wanted to be a part of these people and everything, that I just had to bury the whole idea of cultural resurrection and survival. Cultural survival is not only deciding that we will speak the languages and maintain the livelihoods. It is about reversing, undoing a process. Almost like going back in time and changing the future. And when doing so, you will end up dealing with much pain and untold, unwitnessed acts of violence both in personal and collective levels that are still being denied. Instead of sharing those experiences with their families and children, my father's generation chose – unknowingly or knowingly – to deny us, who were trying to go back to our very own, not to go there at all. And even when being angry and hurt, a part of me understood, all along, that he chose that because he wanted us to be safe.

The biggest obstacles not only to language revitalization but also to land rights recognition, voicing our histories and being an active political participator are psychological, we conclude with my friends.

I learn the word *decolonize* from Jenni, who had read this incredible book written by a Māori woman named Linda (Smith 1999). "You should check this out," she says, her eyes burning.
To get my father to speak sámi to me I have to become a detective and create a "profile" about his "case" – to find out what had happened. To his parents, to reconstruct their lives, their parents' lives, as long back as I could go, and similar time, reconstruct the society they were living in. Inspecting its changes. Its deaths. Its losses.

And telling all this back to my father.

And only after that, during long years of difficult conversations, he opens his mouth and tells about his childhood. In residential school. So many of our relatives died in there. Mostly mentally. Some also physically.

That is still not an acknowledged part of Finland's history. People are still saying it did not happen. As the confiscation of all my grandmother's family's property by the Finnish state did not happen. Neither the hunting nor killing of her family members by the Finnish army.

My people have written land rights documents from the sixteenth century. My people have the last existing and partly functioning siida council, which is included in the Finnish constitution. But the survival of those two is referred to as an example of Finnish tolerance and good will towards us, rather than an expression of potency of our own.

I remember and forget all this, depending on the day. Remember and forget. And try to keep going.

——

If there is such thing as a general sámi world, I would dare to suggest that it is characteristically permeable, flexible. It bends. I am not aware of that many historical or current forms of open, hostile resistance against the sovereignty of national states.

The great-grandmother of my friend Tiina refused to recognize the new borderline drawn through Suo´nn´jel in 1922,[2] and despite the protests of her alarmed son, declared that the lake the border penetrated belonged to her family and she had every right to do as she has always done: fish for her family. So, the son needed to get his head straight and listen to what his mother says, instead of believing the foolishness of people that don't know the area at all and sit on the boat and row so she could set her nets as usual. That boat trip ended with border patrol opening fire, the grandmother being hit by the bullet and the profound understanding that times and borderlines had changed, and what she thought to be her world was no longer to be approached and lived in.

Skolt sámi borderlines were living, flexible, constantly renegotiated.

And new governing structures that were cemented in a short period of time, functioning from a top-down principle, drove people who considered themselves as self-governing, into despair and madness.

The massive land theft, and the replacement of a fully functioning system that included the whole sphere of life into the decision-making, was justified with a skolt sámi Settlement Act (NOR) that frames us as objects of charity. Writing our people's existence out of the Finnish history. This catapulted a rough cycle of violence in skolt sámi communities, where the aggression has turned totally inwards. One ran into a lake to drown, another shot himself, another hanged herself, who threw her baby into a fireplace and ran away. Blows were given but not to the conqueror, instead to ourselves.

The cultural continuation of siidas, that is rooted in the creation stories from a time when the balance of land, animals and families was obviously imperative for survival. What is the mind, from whose context we are making decisions about the water and land use management, about the last pockets of ecosystems that are not yet fully exploited? It seems that quite many of the sámi women of

---

[2]   Treaty of Tartu, signed between the Soviet Union and Finland.

my generation – born at the junction of collapsing traditions and approaching modernity – have ended up working with defending our waters and lands, everyone at their own scale, guided by the pain we feel in our bodies.

In other words, our bodies are the indicators for environmental changes, first ones to alarm something is going on.

The restoration work in River Njâuddam is based on the observations made by traditional fishermen and reindeer herders about man-made changes to the river basin. Those findings, combined with research, provide us concepts and a shared language for articulating something that the waters of our bodies have known and pointed out long before that: changes in temperature, pain and its passing, different forms of waves and termal penetrations are uneasily communicated knowledge that women in particular seem to be more likely to receive from their environments. And the awareness rising from this realization is that the work done for land protection is no longer a choice, but a bodily commitment. This raises questions about what or who controls the body, especially in a time of broken traditions. Land and water want to prosper and bloom, just as peoples and its members do. The man-made natural damages that are unprocessed, both in thought and reality, cause pain both in body and mind, sickness, and eventually fading, withering, dying away.

The revolution of landing into your own body. Accepting the physical shape and tone you are in this physical world. Because it is your current form of existing.

I am convinced that the most profound and dominant force in us is our sexual energy. It is the receptor that ties us not only to other people but the places – lands, waters. Skies. It is the channel that allows the other forces to pass us, trespass us, connect us and reload and repair us. It is the channel of strong knowledge; you feel to know more. Maybe due to these qualities, it has always been an essential tool for colonization to restrict the colonized from their core power. By stigmatizing and denying most of the expressions of sexual energy.

——

I study death.

Finnish professor of ethnology, Nils Storå writes in 1971 about the *Burial Customs of the Skolt Lapps*. "We call ourselves sämmlaz," I mutter while reading.

> In attempting to obtain a picture of early burial customs among the Lapps and other northern hunting and fishing peoples, interesting parallels are provided by hunting rites. Taking care of and preserving the bones ensured the continuation of the species.

A new animal grew from the bones of the dead one.

—The skeleton was thrown back into the water so that a new fish would be born of it. From the bones of a human body a new person would be born the same way.

—It is natural that each family should have its own burial ground within the boundaries of its own lands.

—Islands, clearly demarcated and remote from human habitation or migration routes, offered special advantages as shrines, too.

> The knowledge about my people's conceptions about death, resurrection, cycles of life and the customary law governing and ensuring the new arrival of the salmon,
> the deer,
> the reindeer,
> the bear,
> the trout,
> the dipper,
> the grayling,
> the Domna,
> the Fekla,
> the Kiureli,
> the Pimen,
> the Vasko,
> the Ee´led and the Vassi,
> among others,
>
> has been made accessible to other peoples (and finally, to me) by literally
> opening the graves – both
> above and under the ground,
> digging up the bones,
> making inventories of the bones,
> examining the bones

and interviewing the living relatives of the deceased, the relatives who were only having their other foot in the grave during the time of interviews.

Most of the interviews for the study have been made in the Njâuddam siida – the self-governing unit meaning both the people and the area – which in the 1970s was already totally taken over first by the Finns, the Kvens and then the Norwegians.

The relatives interviewed seem to be having consensus that their world does not resurrect and rebirth anymore, so it is all the same to share the information outside the kin and to stop the cycle there.

There are several different categories of ownership in (Indigenous) Traditional Knowledge, points out my friend Tero Mustonen from Snowchange.
There are knowledges that are owned by the people, such as a language, for example.

Some knowledges are owned by a family, such as certain macro-vocabularies to family areas. And there are knowledges owned by individual persons, such as certain *events and responsibilities* concerning the family area. The latter category can be such that the transmission of that particular knowledge is done only once and to a certain family member – from a mother to an (eldest) daughter, from a father to an (eldest) son.

I am searching transmissions from the books and archives. It is not enough for me what the men in my family tell, when we discuss our basic concepts of what is a human being and what is a human being's place in the world.

Our cosmology has been successful in its main core until last century: protecting our lands and waters. The other cosmology that has overrun and replaced us has not done the same. I want the men *and* the women to have those discussions with us, their children.

"And why does it look like the cosmology does not matter?", asks Asta Baltto, one of the most respected sámi scholars. She has spoken about the ways how the sámi decorated and dressed in especially bright and beautiful colors for moving to the summer lands from winter pastures so "that the reindeer would have more joy of watching us".

And how do we integrate our cosmology to the management of natural resources?

"The land heals a human being/ I feel the joy of the land in my body/ she feels the joy of the land in her body while she collects the rubbish away," speaks Baltto, and I shiver, listening to a sámi woman, giving a glimpse of something most hidden and precise in her words.

The term decolonization has been, rightfully, criticized because it sets the colonization in the middle of our focus.

It is self-evident that we must know our history and especially what has happened, but the focus needs to be shifted to the very question: what do we want now? What do we do now? With our damaged selves, I learn by listening to the discussions other Indigenous thinkers have among each other.

We live in the middle of highly human-altered environments and realities.
The atom has been split,
the DNA has been modified,
the Earth has been drilled almost to the core just to see what is in there,
geoengineering aka modification of the climate such as solar radiation management, which seek to reflect the sunlight by example, using stratospheric sulfate aerosols, have all already taken place,
among so many other processes.

Is there a reason to decorate ourselves for the reindeer anymore?

When the laws that ensure the eternal cycle – everything comes always back – is broken and the bones are not left to be reborn,
instead stored in research chambers, the solution is not to forget and abandon the knowledge *why* have we been doing it like this for millennia and *what is the reason* behind it (trying to unlearn seeing our ancestors as more childish and uneducated than us), bone by bone, letting everything go back to the continuation so that the deceased can be reborn, the damage is undone, I know. My mind starts to know. But my body doesn't follow the thought, yet.

And the very same way the reindeer have always been watching us, the colonized have always been watching the colonizer and asking, analyzing why this is happening.

This is where I am at:
my family is a second-generation immigrant on other skolt sámi group's lands.

And we are facing a real harsh reality: we have nowhere else to go. Mining both side of the borders, Norway and Russia, and nobody wants us, as a collective. So, we have no other choice than to try to form a living relationship with these old new lands as soon as possible – or perish. And gather the crucial bits and pieces for survival from all possible sources, including scientific texts. As a part of that process, we have started to re-establish the skolt siida self-governance in a practical manner: bringing back traditional water management practices to River Njâuddam as a climate change adaptation strategy.

Over the past seven years our team, consisting of reindeer herders, fishermen, scientists and, yes, artists, have gathered traditional knowledge and observations on how land is changing in a changing climate. Combined with weather diaries, catch diaries, interviews, temperature diaries and measurements of the heavy metals in water, we have focused on observations about the introduction of foreign species to the area, analyzing the status of known spawning sites and place names as a source of valuable information.

Special interest has been rested on site-specific macro-vocabularies and traditional law practices on the river. Based on the observations and analytical work, both from the traditional and scientific knowledges point of view, the first physical watershed restorations began two years ago.

We are currently restoring the watershed areas, where the past land use, such as logging and burning the land, man-made water flow alterations and construction of roads and bridges, has led to a loss of spawning sites for salmon, trout and other fishes. By reintroducing old spawning sites, we are giving the salmon and their relatives more possibilities for survival with extreme heat waves. In the years 2013, 2014 and 2019, parts of the river shed, in Vainosjoki, dried totally.

Especially this kind of record-high temperatures, such as we are witnessing now, that vaporizes the water way too high to be raining down far away from its natural cycle, drought that follows in autumn and introduction of new algae might be called the new normal.

Diatoms are a major group of algae, specifically microalgae, found in the oceans, waterways and soils of the world, and based on the samples taken from the River Vainos on 3 August 2018, now also covering the River Njâuddam watershed area.

The freshwater mussel has disappeared from the river nearly totally.

July, 2012, the picture taken in Lake Opukas (Figures 1 and 2), the Owl Lake, was then the northernmost observation on *Potosia cuprea*, the Scarabaeoid beetle. More newcomers are on the way.

The same summer this observation was made, we also gave back the bones to the river with my father. He told that he has learned that, among everything else he knows about fishing, from his grandmother. "It has always been the female that lead," he says. "The reindeer, the people, always the older female." I continue to listen to the men, and have started to try to speak with them too. I've noticed it interests my father what I share with him; it expands his knowledge too.

We can only undo the man-made damages. The river needs to find her own way to cope with changing climate. We just must not interfere with her in this extremely demanding process.

The collective memory on how the siida system really functioned is just a stone cast away with the skolt sámi. Few people, who were born to its absolute power, are still alive. The memory has not yet morphed into texts, recordings, archive materials. It is, yes, scattered, hidden, deep frozen when it had to, due to the active banning. But it is still a functioning work memory, too little used, but still functioning, when left to function.

So, what form can an atonement take?

Despite the continuous +22°C temperature of River Vainos in the Njâuddam riveshed, the almost year-old graylings come eagerly to greet us, the restoration workers,
who are hopelessly 20 years too late with our work. They nip my hands, swim on my lap in small groups, still seeking for a contact while I lay my camera under the water, wishing to hear more about their life.

The colonial processes imposed to those young graylings and their habitats are my kind's doing: humankind. Realizing that, my self-image bends, reshapes and at least the possibility for a new alliance, new continuation with balanced relationships with the grayling is born.

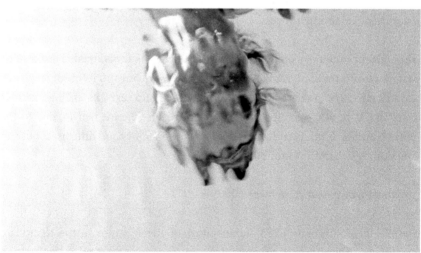

Figures 1 and 2 Rewilding efforts with graylings, collaboration with Risto Semenoff, Jouko Moshnikoff, Vladimir Feodoroff, Juha Feodoroff, Tero Mustonen, Janne Raassina, Pauliina Feodoroff, Stina Aletta Aikio, Petteri Feodoroff, Markku Porsanger and our forever remembered Teijo Feodoroff, Illep Jefremoff and Jouni Moshnikoff. (Photograph: Pauliina Feodoroff)

Review: weaving stories and data to decolonize methodologies

Distinguished Professor Maggie Walter (*palawa*)

This edited collection, developed and written by a global group of all Indigenous female scholars, is a tribute to the ground-breaking work of Professor Linda Tuhiwai Smith, especially her radical and formative text, *Decolonizing Methodologies: Research and Indigenous Peoples*. Each author, through their individual scholarly voice and from different Indigenous worldviews, reflects how their journey through research and academia has been shaped and influenced by Tuhiwai Smith's inspirational work. In doing so, all the essays mirror how *Decolonizing Methodologies* finally broke open the Western paradigm of methodology. This cracking of the status quo demonstrated not only the poverty of what had been the traditional trope of research about Indigenous Peoples, but also what Indigenous research, particularly Indigenous research by Indigenous researchers, could be.

There remains stubborn patches of resistance to the decolonizing and the Indigenizing of methodology. This resistance, however, is largely limited to non-Indigenous researchers whose dominance of the field was challenged by this new way of understanding the research process. Tuhiwai Smith's book forever disrupted the old model by rebutting and refuting the power relationship of the Indigene as the fitting object of the non-Indigenous research gaze. Indigenous researchers, globally, enthusiastically threw off the damaging methodological shackles that constrained how, why and what we could research and how we could be researchers. We also gleefully began to challenge the long pattern of chastisement from grant reviewers, journals editors and institutions that our research and scholarship did not follow the traditional Western models of research about Indigenous Peoples, nor was it as rigorous, robust or valid as that which did. It was and it is.

This edited collection definitely, and defiantly, rejects the Western paradigm of Indigenous research. The result is a divergent, yet coherent, set of scholarly essays that all decolonize methodology but also reflect a wide gamut of Indigenous scholarly views from different Indigenous shores. In this final chapter, it is my role to consider each of these in turn, as well as draw together some thoughts on what they bring collectively to our understanding of the many ways that a decolonizing Indigenous methodological approach adds to the richness of our scholarly understanding of Indigenous lived realities.

This book is also somewhat prescient. As I write this chapter in September 2020, the hashtag *#BecauseofLindaTuhiwaiSmith* is trending globally. Twitter users are being asked to share how the academic work of world-renowned Indigenous educator Professor Linda Tuhiwai Smith has impacted them. Within three days the hashtag had been used more than 3800 times and was the number one trending hashtag for a short period during September (Gabel 2020). The hashtag has globally prompted many scholars, not only just Indigenous scholars, to take the time to reflect on how their own scholarship, research and careers had been impacted by the work of Professor Tuhiwai Smith. The resultant tweets reflect both a looking back on the impact Tuhiwai Smith, her scholarship and advocacy have had on individuals, as well as a looking forward on how her work has changed the way in which they live and the work that they do now and into future. They include, from Māori and other Indigenous scholars:

> I will be doing some deep reflecting about what kind of legacy I want to leave in my role as Māori public servant, and as mama, for our mokopuna.

> She helped me to see that the answers and the future is in our hands. We just need to free our minds from the colonial misinformation and trauma, and look within ourselves, to our culture, to our values, our korero, our waiata! Keir a Tatou!
>   Wearing Purple in solidarity and memory of the historical sacrifice of Indigenous ancestors.

Referring to Tuhiwai Smith's book, another writes:

> This is the key academic textbook I have read since joining (a university) and I regularly return to in my academic work – it has been instrumental in setting me on a journey of self-discovery as a European researcher in Aotearoa.

Even the Royal Society Te Aparangi adds a tweet:

The final 150th Te Takararigi book is Professor Linda Tuhiwai Smith's landmark publication *Decolonizing Methodologies*. This revolutionary text continues to resonate powerfully with indigenous scholars and indigenous communities.

It is fitting, before I address my task of reviewing the essays in this collection, to reflect on the impact of Tuhiwai Smith's scholarship on my own journey. I am *palawa*, an Aboriginal woman from *lutruwita*/Tasmania who, like so many Indigenous scholars, came late to academia. Leaving school early meant I had to take the long trail through an undergraduate degree, part-time and by distance, and then to an honor's year – all the while being in paid employment as well as raising small children. I finally started my PhD at the age of 42. I read *Decolonizing Methodologies* soon after I began my first tenured academic position, and like all those writing in this book, it completely changed how I understood Indigenous research, both my own and that of others. All the research and writing I have done over the 20 odd years since has reflected this altered mindset and way of seeing the research world. Until that time, I had not really thought about methodology (as opposed to research method) and, once I did, I could not help but see the research process from this new vantage point. What also became immediately obvious was not just how restricted and restricting the standard trope of Western Indigenous research methodologies were, but of their hegemonic power. This hegemony was maintained, unquestioned, by Western researchers mostly, with the power of the model upheld by a reluctance to discuss or think about methodology at all. I noted, and have been noting since, that most Western researchers never discuss their epistemological or ontological approach to why they are asking the research questions that they are, why they are choosing to research this particular topic, or why they are researching topics in a particular way. Instead the focus is all on the method: why and how they are using qualitative in-depth interviews, for example.

More critically, they *never, never,* discuss their own socio-cultural and racial positioning as it relates to their research, something Indigenous researchers have always done. Indeed, I have observed that even many ally non-Indigenous researchers, even writing in Indigenous focused books, often struggle hugely with the task of including such positioning alongside their Indigenous co-authors. It is not that they do not want to do it, it is just that as a member of the dominant group (within academia and without), despite their commitment to Indigenous rights, they are complete novices in self socio-cultural and racial examination. But imagine how much better all research would be, not just

Indigenous research, if all researchers reflected on their own epistemological and ontological stance as a standard part of their scholarship.

Volume essays

In the following section I overview each of the book's essays. My purpose is not to summarize or repeat what each author has written. Rather, my purpose is to highlight the key decolonizing message of each essay and to demonstrate how they link together and to the decolonizing framework of Tuhiwai Smith's paradigm setting scholarship.

The first Part of the volume, "Country and Connection", begins with Karen Fisher's essay "Decolonizing rivers in Aotearoa New Zealand" (Essay 1) and uses Māori knowledges to decolonize environmental governance. This essay emphasizes the interconnectedness and complexity of natural and social systems, which underpin the centrality of relationality and reciprocity between humans and non-humans in Te Ao Māori, or the Māori worldview. Comparing Indigenous ontology with the nature/culture divide that characterizes Western knowledge systems, the essay highlights the damage wrought through colonization of Māori spaces and places, reshaping the environment to the detriment of all. Focusing on rivers as "sites of ontological inconsistency" (p. 20) the author applies a scholarly lens to the rigidity of the focus on ownership and rights within colonizing settler water management. Bringing her personal experience, as an academic and a member of Ngāti Maniapoto, the author details the long, but Māori knowledge-centered, process of recognition of the Waipā River. "By centering a *taniwha* into all considerations ... and the relationship between Waiwaia, the Waipā and Ngāti Maniapoto, the river became more than a physical object or entity to be carved up into discrete resource units to be managed" (p. 29). As the essay concludes, it is not simply a matter of what is done but how it is done. The benefits of decolonizing river management outweigh the needs of settler institutions, for rivers and for people.

Essay 2 by Jennifer Evans (*Dharug* woman living on, and with connections to, *palawa* country), "Can men weave baskets in Queer country?", explores the decolonization of the concept and reality of Country. Through the related application of critical and political theory to Country (queer theory, query ecology, eco-feminism and nature conservation), Evans asks: "[i]f country is non-gendered, and has its own agency, what boundaries apply to gendered cultural practices including *nokegerrer?*" (p. 33). Country, the essay argues, has been gendered through the eyes of the colonizer and the traditional Western androcentric view; however, making space for *palawa* realities allows the possibility that *terri* (baskets) have agency themselves, that they are not empty. Visualizing her methodology as a form of weaving, the author casts the four clubs of theory onto Country, seeing where they fall. Through this decolonizing theoretical act, none is a good fit, but all add something to the puzzle. Country, the essay concludes, is open to possibilities. Country can be queered and it has the agency to invite Queer connections and relations. Rather than arriving at a definitive answer, Country is positioned as allowing our bodies and Dreaming to be sites of social change that disrupt the colonized power systems that dictate cultural practices: a place where men could seek to weave baskets.

In the second Part, "Violence and Safety", Essay 3, "Black panopticon: who wins with lateral violence?" by Jacinta Vanderfeen (*trawlwulwuy*), explores lateral violence, where the phenomenon in need of decolonization is Indigenous identity. Pointing to the co-occurrence of the physical assaults of colonization with the assaults on the minds of the colonized survivors, the essay reminds us that being the object of surveillance across multiple dimensions always results in being subject to multiple oppressions. Drawing on Foucault's use of Bentham's term for ideal prison architecture, the panopticon, as a way of illustrating the power relationships implicit in discipline, control and surveillance, the author builds the case for a black panopticon. Using her own people of *lutruwita* Tasmania, and the structural violence of identity politics, as the lived example, she highlights how the black panopticon makes Indigenous Peoples both our own prisoners and our own keepers, reinforcing the structures of colonization. Lateral violence, she argues, is the core means of discipline under the Black panopticon and the perfect tool for keeping *palawa* colonized. Through the Black panopticon, *palawa* control *palawa*, mirroring the same patterns of Indigenous identity denial that were used by the colonizer to declare the *palawa* Peoples extinct in 1876. Decolonizing identity would expose this identity lateral violence, common to many colonized Indigenous Peoples, as a colonizing, not Indigenous, tool of control.

In the same vein, Essay 4, "Blak & Salty: reflections on violence and racism" by Donna Moodie, Kelly Menzel, Liz Cameron and Nikki Moodie, looks at the decolonization of Indigenous spaces in institutions. Reflecting the experience of four Indigenous academic women (a Gomeroi mother and daughter, a Ngadjuri and a Dharug woman) the essay asks first, how can Indigenous women do Indigenous research in the White Australian academy? The second aligned question is how can this work better support the creation of safe cultural spaces in the academy? Citing Tuhiwai Smith's thoughts on the implications of Indigenous governance of Indigenous education, the authors juxtapose the realities of universities as Indigenous spaces and as on-going sites of settler-colonial racism and violence. The authors note that contestability within Indigenous spaces can extend into lateral violence, whereby internalized racism leads to harmful, undermining practices aimed at some by other group members. Such practices are especially prevalent when Aboriginal people are achieving, rather than being in need of "help". Set out as the individual experiences of these four academics, the essay positions universities as sites of articulation of Indigenous identities, Indigenous strengthening and the resurgence of Indigenous knowledge. All authors have experienced culturally unsafe practices within universities, being treated differently because of their Aboriginality and having obligations imposed that did not apply to their non-Indigenous colleagues. All have also observed or experienced what they describe as "mobbing" (p. 80), whereby Indigenous staff are exposed to vindictive and disruptive attacks, by both Indigenous and non-Indigenous colleagues. The authors conclude that Indigenous women's role in universities is to combat racism in all its forms, and to "create spaces and practices in the academy that have a high degree of cultural fidelity" (p. 85).

In the third Part, "Wisdom and Knowledge", the personal facet of Indigenous scholarship is at the heart of these essays. Decolonizing is a process, not a state, and it is this aspect, the journey of decolonizing the self, that is the topic of Essay 5 by Kelly Ratana. Positioning Indigenous researchers as a bridge between decolonizing theories and decolonizing practice, this role becomes multidimensional. Building the essay across a series of the self as "bridge", through our approach to our work, through time, that journey (as it is for all Indigenous scholars) is one of intense learnings, but also uncertainties: being "comfortable with being uncomfortable" (p. 92). The essay details the tensions struggled with, "both seen and unseen" (p. 90), between her place in Te Ao Māori and the Western scientific academy. Part of that journey and its inherent tensions is of being an academic in a system where Indigenous methodologies and the ideas that sit under them are almost entirely absent, yet still understanding and living via our research the validity of Indigenous knowledges. The author also details here the experience of being a decolonizing bridge between accepting and supporting the potential value of Western science to our communities, while keeping in mind that we must always still ask the epistemological questions of "whose science?" and "why this science?", creating the opportunity for our communities to access "all the available knowledge and tools to achieve their research aspirations" (p. 101).

In Essay 6, "A spoke in the wheel: Ancestral women's legacies", by Angela Burt (*palawa*), epistemology is the subject of decolonization. Told through her own history, as a *palawa* woman and framed around the writings of her great aunt, Auntie Molly Mallett, a renowned *palawa* leader and educator, the author argues that the decolonization of epistemological norms requires Indigenous Peoples to be able to tell our own histories and stipulate our own knowledges. For the *palawa*, and many, many other Indigenous Peoples, stories of our colonization provide a fertile topic of scholarship. These histories, most of which only depict Indigenous Peoples as existing through colonization, as though this is the event that defines us, can be empathetic and careful. But they remain, despite such empathy and care, as history from the colonial and colonizer lens, while our stories and knowledges are excluded within them. While our bodies are there, our voices are not. The essay demonstrates via the scholarship and writings of Auntie Molly of her own life story, inclusive of her childhood experience and memories of herself and her community being subjected to personal and invasive research from anthropologists, that telling our history is the only way we can be known: to ourselves and to others. As Auntie Molly wrote, "Can't people see that the written history is not true . . . I think we have enough educated Tasmanian Aboriginal people . . . to put a spoke in some of the wheels and write the truth about us" (Mallett 2001, p. 46). It falls to all of us to continue Auntie Molly's legacy, and the legacy of Tuhiwai Smith to continue to disrupt the colonized epistemological trope of what can be known, how it can be known, who is a knower and whose knowledge prevails.

The decolonizing focus of Essay 7 by Lori Campbell, "Indigeneity, Indigenous feminisms and Indigenization", introduces us to the fourth Part, "De/colonizing Minds", and refers to the global movement to Indigenize institutions, particularly universities, in Anglo-colonized nation states. Drawing on her experience in the

Canadian nation-state, and her own deep, personal reflection of Indigenization, the name argues that the Indigenous-centered concept of Indigenization has itself now been "stolen, interpreted, translated and repurposed into a colonized idea of what Indigenization should be" (p. 124). This co-option of the term, and concept and discussion of how Indigenous people might successfully navigate this process, are the essay's focus. Situating herself, first as one of the many First Nations children taken by the state from their parents in the modern era, the author details her initial embrace of feminism and then her rejection of a feminism that "ignored and erased" (p. 125) her Indigeneity. Discovering Indigenous feminisms recovered her engagement, but also led to a broader exploration of allyship, with the work of non-Indigenous feminists in the field. Citing the work of Flowers (2015), the author questions whether many non-Indigenous scholars derive personal benefit from their "witnessing" (p. 127) of Indigenous recountings of colonization's depredations. Settlers, she argues, do not need to be allies to have good relations with Indigenous women, nor can they claim Indigeneity by association. Using the widely adopted Castellano (2014, n.p.) definition of Indigenization as "that every subject at every level is examined to consider how and to what extent current content and pedagogy reflect the presence of Indigenous peoples and the valid contribution of Indigenous knowledge", the author explores how the concept is being strategically adopted at Canadian universities. The reality, the essay contends, is that many are happy to promote courses on Indigenous knowledge. But there is far less willingness to position Indigenous knowledges as equal to White knowledge, or to allow Indigeneity within the university outside of the confines of named courses, or to examine universities' own complicity in colonialism. Returning to her own experience, she relates how she is now constantly bombarded by non-Indigenous center requests to Indigenize, with expectations of something convenient, colonized and quite different from Indigenous understandings of Indigeneity. From this perspective, Indigenization can itself be a weapon of embedding colonization.

Essay 8, from *tebrakunna* country and Emma Lee, "Reclaiming the first person voice", decolonizes the embedded academic practices of othering through how referents are deployed. Writing from the position of a *trawlwulwuy* woman from Country, the authors address the use of the referent point of "I" and "you" as powerful tools of Western privilege, where Indigenous peoples are permanently positioned, as you, they and them; the perpetual other. This is an even more fraught positioning where, as in the authors' case, the Peoples being othered have also been deemed "extinct" by colonial powers. In Tasmania, the colonized demand of the other to demonstrate their humanness is always accompanied by the preceding need to prove their very existence. As *tebrakunna* country and Lee write, the very act of "creating a first-person authorship out of non-existence suggests that the impact of 'I' and 'you' referents is vitally important in locating the self and place as a means of decolonization" (p. 150). It also allows the scholarly transition from not existing to being an action-orientated, reciprocal researcher. With Country as a co-author, these connections to Country and belonging from kinship and reciprocity become the scaffolding for decolonizing work. In conclusion, the author argues that a critical decolonizing act of the academy is to redefine how referent points are used when Indigenous authors write with non-Indigenous authors. The simple reversal of who is "I" and who is "you" decolonizes the foundations of collaborative work.

In the final Part, "Seeing Ourselves", Essay 9, "Resist and assert – Indigenous work in GLAM" by Lauren Booker, queries the decolonizing process in galleries, archives, libraries and museums (GLAM). Framed around the exhausting Indigenous labor of "pushing back" against the assumed right of colonial framed institutions to collect, keep and categorize Indigenous knowledges and Peoples, Booker applies the decolonizing lens to institutional processes and practices, illuminating how coloniality is still the underpinning rationale on how and why they collect. Booker draws on her personal experience as an archivist and researcher to documents how these institutions remain both windows into colonial power and simultaneously tools of colonial power. Despite the regular discussion of decolonizing at GLAM seminars and conferences, the essay points to difference between the rhetoric and reality in the sector, where the Aboriginal and Torres Strait Islander voice is still actively excluded even as these institutions proclaim their decolonizing ambitions. The key question of this essay is how can collecting institutions support a decolonizing agenda? Using Articles, 11, 12 and 31 of the United Nations Declaration of the Rights of Indigenous Peoples (UNDRIP), Booker reasserts Indigenous Peoples' rights to control over access, maintenance and use of materials and knowledges held in GLAM institutions. Decolonizing such institutions will require a radical reimagining of the responsibilities and obligations of institutions to both the Indigenous collections that they hold and to the Peoples to whom those collections belong.

Essay 10 by Pauliina Feodoroff (skolt sámi), "What form can an atonement take?", takes the concept of decolonization into the actualization space. What is it that decolonization needs to do to be decolonization? A poetic contribution that, after Fisher's essay, also includes a river, the River Njâuddam, the essay is a chronicle of ecological destruction and the physical and existential threats that the destruction creates. But it also about much more. The story told, with beauty and with depth, is deeply personal as it catalogues the struggle to hold onto our Indigenous identity in the face of colonization and the price of that struggle. It is about denial, about loss, about theft, about forced change, about violence, the common realities of colonized Peoples across the world. The essay also embraces the commonly felt uncertainty as we try to make sense of our ontological position. The term decolonization, the author notes, "has been, rightfully, criticized because it sets the colonization in the middle of our focus" (p. 185). The fundamental but critical truth that the colonizer needs to engage with is that decolonization is not a mindset alone; it needs to be accompanied by action. Just as the damage of colonization is physical as well as psychological, the damage needs to be undone to the land, to the natural systems, to the rivers, to the animals, to the Peoples and to the generations. There can be no decolonization without an atonement.

Decolonizing and Indigenizing data

It is now time for my small contribution. My topic is Indigenous data and how such data sit at the center of the colonization processes and structures, then and now. Indigenous data are information about Indigenous Peoples that relate to or impact Indigenous Peoples' lives. More broadly, the term "Indigenous data" refers to information or knowledge in any format, inclusive of statistics that are about Indigenous Peoples and that impact Indigenous lives at the collective and/ or individual level (Walter et al 2018; Walter & Russo Carroll 2020). Three prominent categories fit within this definition of Indigenous data. These are: data related to Indigenous resources, environments, lands, geological or water information; data about Indigenous Peoples or populations, inclusive of demographic or social data such as legal, health and education; and data from Indigenous Peoples such as traditional knowledge or cultural data, archives, oral literature or community stories.

My quantitative background leads me to concentrate on the second category – data about us – and my scholarship and Indigenous data advocacy work revolves around these types of data. It is important to note that Tuhiwai Smith's groundbreaking 1999 publication *Decolonizing Methodologies* did not specify a particular research method as synonymous with Indigenous research. However, for a variety of reasons, including the (often valid) suspicion that many Indigenous Peoples have towards statistics, most Indigenous scholarship on decolonizing research has tended to be aligned with qualitative research (see Kovach 2009; Walter & Suina 2019; S. Wilson 2008). In the following section I discuss Indigenous data in terms of both decolonization and Indigenization, different but both critical processes to turning Indigenous data from a tool of the colonizer to a tool for Indigenous Peoples.

Decolonizing Indigenous data

Decolonization of data is the process that needs to be applied to the existing processes and practices of Indigenous data. These data, both now and in the past, have been a primary tool of colonization (Walter & Andersen 2013). Data are political and data are powerful. In Australia, for example, Aboriginal and Torres Strait Islander Peoples were specifically excluded from being counted in the national census by the 1901 Australian Constitution. This exclusion did not, however, stop the counting of Indigenous Peoples in Australia, where Aboriginal and Torres Strait Islander populations have been heavily surveilled by the colonial and later nation-state since colonization. Rather, the purpose was to exclude these populations from the numerical portrait of Australia as a country, as if by such exclusion the nation-state could pretend that these populations did not exist; they were part of the unspoken, and unspeakable, past.

With this constitutional clause overturned by referendum in 1967, the inclusion of Indigenous populations in the 1971 Census of Population and Housing made some change. But while this inclusion meant that Aboriginal and Torres Strait Islander People were now visible in population counts, the way we were and are counted reinforced our colonized position (Chesterman & Gallagin 1997). In a pattern that is similar across the Anglo-colonized world, the data that are collected about our populations concentrate, to the virtual exclusion of all other data, on statistical tallies of Indigenous disparity, deprivation, disadvantage, dysfunction and difference: what I have labeled "5 D Data" (Walter 2016, p. 80). Those of us working in this space sometimes joke to ourselves that these counts are only undertaken to check that colonization is still working – still the poorest, tick; still the sickest, tick; still the least educated, tick; still the most incarcerated, tick.

It is these data that need to be decolonized. The focus needs to be altered so that these data are presented in context. The data need to do more than just (repeatedly) focus on the "what". Why, for example, are Indigenous Peoples always the sickest, poorest, most incarcerated and least educated? The answer, then and now, is that colonization, as a structure and a process, sits behind these devastating statistical pictures. And if the "why" is never asked in these official statistics, then they will just continue to be part of the colonizing process, positioning Indigenous populations within the nation-state as hopeless, helpless and complicit in their disadvantage and marginalization (Walter & Russo Carroll 2020).

Indigenizing Indigenous data

Decolonizing these data, however, is not enough. The use of data as a tool of colonization has meant that the only data that are produced are based around what the colonizing nation-state wants to know about its Indigenous sub-populations. There is almost no overlap between what the nation-state wants to know and what Indigenous Peoples themselves want and need to know. Indigenous data should reflect Indigenous priorities, values, culture, lifeworlds and diversity. Indigenizing the data, therefore, means collecting Indigenous data that reflect Indigenous lifeworlds. By this, I mean data that allow us to reflect, and measure as needed, the realities of Indigenous Peoples' lives. For example, how do urban communities function? How is the Indigenous lifecourse negotiated within households, communities and the wider nation-state? These and many, many other questions cannot be answered by current data. We also need data that is at the level that our First Nations and communities need. Yet most current Indigenous data is at the national or state level. Such data are unusable by communities and nations. Indigenous defined data priorities and needs are also missing from existing data and the data infrastructure of the nation-state, in Australia at least, seems incapable of understanding Indigenous data needs. This is primarily a function of official statistics agencies being unable to conceptualize Indigenous data outside of the needs of the nation-state. But we need data for our nations also, for First Nation rebuilding and redevelopment (Kukutai & Cormack 2020).

Indigenous data sovereignty

The key to decolonizing and Indigenizing Indigenous data is Indigenous data sovereignty. Indigenous data sovereignty centers on Indigenous collective rights to data about our peoples, territories, lifeways and natural resources and is supported by Indigenous Peoples' inherent rights of self-determination and governance over their communities, Country and resources as described in the United Nations Declaration on the Rights of Indigenous Peoples (UNDRIP) (Taylor & Kukutai 2015). The concept is defined as the right of Indigenous Peoples to determine the means of collection, access, analysis, interpretation, management, dissemination and reuse of data pertaining to the Indigenous Peoples from whom it has been derived, or to whom it relates (Kukutai & Taylor 2016; Snipp 2016). Data sovereignty is practiced through Indigenous data governance, which assert Indigenous interests and Indigenous decision-making across the data ecosystem; from data conception to control of access and usage of data. Indigenous decision-making is a prerequisite for both the decolonization and Indigenization of data. As such, I am a founding member of the Australian Maiam nayri Wingara Indigenous Data Sovereignty Collective and also a founding member of the Global Indigenous Data Alliance, a "network of networks" that brings together Indigenous data sovereignty networks from around the globe.

Conclusion

Reading through this collection of essays, the first thing that strikes is the strength of the Indigenous voices in each of the essays and the frequent use of Indigenous scholarship. Strong Indigenous scholarly voices are the essential ingredient in decolonizing research and academia. Critically, the use of this scholarship to support, inspire and evidence the on-going production of more scholarship is a necessary aspect of decolonizing research. Scholarly knowledge is built, one piece of scholarly writing at a time, and we all need to know and cite the literature in our field. Yet, in the field of Indigenous research, especially in my nation-state, Australia, it is still not unusual to read a reference list that does not cite Indigenous scholarly literature at all. I am not sure if this is because many of the non-Indigenous researchers in the field do not understand the ontological frame of their Indigenous colleagues, or if Indigenous scholarship is still viewed as niche – nice to have but a sidebar to the serious work going on in the halls of the academy. Mostly, it is left up to Indigenous framed books, such as this one, to lead the way in citing our scholars and scholarship.

All essays are also personal journeys. This again is a key aspect of decolonizing. Research and scholarly writing are personal. To pretend otherwise is a colonizing fiction. But it is not work for the faint-hearted. Putting ourselves into our work is dangerous and it takes bravery to reject the comfortable pretense that the scholarship is not shaped, formed and framed by the ontological, axiological and epistemological positioning of the scholar. The personal journey is also a timely reminder that although each Indigenous Peoples have their own story of colonization to tell, colonization is both structure and a process. As per Wolfe (2006), colonization processes, then and now, bring predictable ways of dispossessing and oppressing those whose lands and identity they covet. Each, in its own way, embodies one of the key messages of Tuhiwai Smith's *Decolonizing Methodologies* that, as Indigenous researchers and Indigenous scholars, we will and must always go into spaces and places where we struggle with the near absolute dominance of the Western way of seeing the world, and our Indigenous place within it. We must forge ahead, in our scholarly challenge, in our Indigenous framed approach to research in spite of our fear.

Speaking to this reality, the book also includes a dedication to all Indigenous and First Nations women and their contributions to creating a better, fairer world for our children and communities. There is also a specific acknowledgement to two authors who were unable to participate in the volume. For one author, this was because of pressure to *not* write her essay because of the risk to her career. As the acknowledgement notes, this reinforces the core reality, as faced by Tuhiwai Smith, and the many Indigenous female scholars before and following her work, that to challenge colonial power is dangerous work. The danger can be even more pronounced when we speak from positions of strength, such as from an accomplished academic format, because then we cannot be so easily dismissed as inferior or lacking. When our challenge has a chance of succeeding in changing mindsets and practices we become serious threats and face serious risks. It is up to those of us who are heading towards the end of our careers, who are secure in our employment and our scholarly standing, to take the most risks, to draw the most fire, and in doing so, protect our more vulnerable sisters (as in career and other mainstream opportunities).

This set of essays has traversed a broad terrain around the concept and the practice of decolonizing methodologies. In doing so, many have also outlined key aspects of Indigenizing methodologies. As per my own short contribution, decolonizing and Indigenizing are part of the same methodological spectrum. We cannot Indigenize without decolonizing, and decolonizing on its own is not enough – it requires the careful attention and inclusion of Indigenous scholars.

This volume has done something remarkable in giving back to Indigenous women their rights to research and reclaim their space as a collective and as a restitution towards women's governance and business. These women have made it their task to honor Tuhiwai Smith's body of work that, 20 years ago, set the foundational questions of what is important to Indigenous Peoples in research. For other Indigenous women, this book should provide an avenue of confidence that their stories and scholarship are important and should be published as legitimate research.

For those for whom this volume is their first foray into decolonizing and Indigenizing methodologies, I recommend that you read widely and read specifically the work of Indigenous scholars in the field, established and emerging, to inform new ways of engaging with diverse knowledge. For those who are familiar with the concept and its practical aspects, my advice is the same – continue to dig deep into the literature and find something new in Indigenous concepts or ways of thinking. These essays are as rich in tone as they are in substance, which assists to return to them again and again as multiple understandings are gained from reflecting on their messages. However, there is still a large gap between the articulation of the concepts and their practical implementation into our institutions and social systems. We all have a role to play and this volume will become part of our guidebooks into respectful scholarship with, of, for and from Indigenous Peoples.

Wulika.

References

ABC (2016) "Aboriginality Test Changes Will 'Swamp the Community with White People', Tasmanian Aboriginal Centre Fears" 22 January 2016, *ABC Premium News*, viewed 1 November 2019, https://www.abc.net.au/news/2016-01-22/concerns-for-tasmanian-aboriginality-test-changes/7106664

Aboriginal and Torres Strait Islanders Library and Information Resource Network (ATSILIRN) (2012) *ATSILIRN Protocols Brochure*, viewed 18 October 2020, http://aiatsis.gov.au/atsilirn/docs/ProtocolBrochure2012.pdf

Acker, J. (2006) "Inequality Regimes, Gender, Class and Race in Organisations", *Gender and Society*, Vol. 20, No. 4, pp. 441–464.

Adams, T.E. & Holman Jones, S. (2008) "Autoethnography Is Queer", in N.K. Denzin, Y.S. Lincoln & L.T. Smith (eds), *Handbook of Critical and Indigenous Methodologies*, SAGE Publications, Thousand Oaks, CA, pp. 373–390.

Åhrén, M. (2016) *Indigenous Peoples' Status in the International Legal System*, Oxford University Press, Oxford.

Alaimo, S. (2010) "Eluding Capture: The Science, Culture, and Pleasure of 'Queer' Animals", in C. Mortimer-Sandilands & B. Erickson (eds), *Queer Ecologies: Sex, Nature, Politics, Desire*, Indiana University Press, Bloomington, IN, pp. 51–72.

Alexander, B.K. (2008) "Queer(y)ing the Postcolonial Through the West(ern)", in N.K. Denzin, Y.S. Lincoln & L.T. Smith (eds), *Handbook of Critical and Indigenous Methodologies*, SAGE Publications, Thousand Oaks, CA, pp. 101–134.

Alford, K. & James, R. (2007) *Pathways and Barriers: Indigenous Schooling and Vocational Education and Training Participation in the Goulburn Valley Region*, National Centre for Vocational Education Research, Adelaide.

Alfred. T. & Corntassel, J. (2005) "Being Indigenous: Resurgences against Contemporary Colonialism", *Government and Opposition*, Vol. 40, No. 4, pp. 597–614.

Allen, C. (2012) *Trans-Indigenous Methodologies for Global Native Literary Studies*, University of Minnesota Press, Minneapolis.

Altman, J.C., Biddle, N. & Hunter, B.H. (2009) "Prospects for 'Closing the Gap' in Socioeconomic Outcomes for Indigenous Australians?", *Australian Economic History Review*, Vol. 49, No. 3, pp. 225–251.

Anderson, W. (2008) *The Cultivation of Whiteness, Health and Racial Destiny in Australia*, Basic Books, New York.

Andrews, J. (2017) "Indigenous Perspectives on Museum Collections", *Artlink*, Vol. 37, No. 2 June, pp. 88–91.

Anzaldúa, G. (2012) *Borderlands/La frontera: The New Mestiza*, Aunt Lute Books, San Francisco.

Applebaum, B. (2010) *Being White, Being Good: White Complicity, White Moral Responsibility, and Social Justice Pedagogy*, Lexington Books, Lanham, MD.

Archibald, L. (2006) *Final Report of the Aboriginal Healing Foundation, Volume III: Promising Healing Practices in Aboriginal Communities*, Aboriginal Healing Foundation, viewed 21 October 2019, http://www.ahf.ca/downloads/final-report-vol-3.pdf

Archibald Q'um Q'um Xiiem, J., Bol Jun Lee-Morgan, J. & De Santolo, J. (2019) *Decolonizing Research Indigenous Storywork as Methodology*, Zed Books, London.

Ardill, A. (2013) "Australian Sovereignty, Indigenous Standpoint Theory and Feminist Standpoint Theory: First Peoples' Sovereignties Matter", *Griffith Law Review*, Vol. 22, No. 2, pp. 315–343.

Arnold, J. (2018) "Canadian and Australian First Nations: Decolonizing Knowledge", *International Journal of Critical Indigenous Studies*, Vol. 11, No. 1, pp. 1–18.

Arvin, M., Tuck E. & Morrill, A. (2013) "Decolonizing Feminism: Challenging Connections Between Settler Colonialism and Heteropatriarchy", *Feminist Formations*, Vol. 25, No. 1, pp. 8–34.

Ashmore, P. (2015) "Towards a Sociogeomorphology of Rivers", *Geomorphology*, Vol. 251, pp. 149–156.

Asmar, C., Page, S. & Radloff, A. (2011) "Dispelling Myths: Indigenous Students' Engagement with University", AUSSE Research Briefing Vol. 10, *Australian Council for Education Research*, Camberwell, viewed 17 October 2019, http://research.acer.edu.au/ausse/2/

Assante, E. (2005) "Negotiating Identity: Aboriginal Women and the Politics of Self-Government", *The Canadian Journal of Native Studies*, Vol. 25, No. 4, pp. 1–34.

Australian Bureau of Statistics [ABS] (2011) "Australian Social Trends: Education and Indigenous Wellbeing", cat. no. 4102.0, ABS, viewed 17 October 2019, https://www.abs.gov.au/AUSSTATS/abs@.nsf/Lookup/4102.0Main+Features50Mar+2011

Australian Bureau of Statistics [ABS] (2018) "Prisoners in Australia: Aboriginal and Torres Strait Islander Prisoner Characteristics", cat. no. 4517.0, ABS, viewed 17 October 2019, https://www.abs.gov.au/ausstats/abs@.nsf/Lookup/by%20Subject/4517.0~2018~Main%20Features~Aboriginal%20and%20Torres%20Strait%20Islander%20prisoner%20characteristics%20~13

Australian Human Rights Commission (AHRC) (2007) *Social Justice Report 2007 – Chapter 3: The Northern Territory "Emergency Response" Intervention*, viewed 15 May 2020, https://humanrights.gov.au/our-work/social-justice-report-2007-chapter-3-northern-territory-emergency-response-intervention

Australian Institute of Aboriginal and Torres Strait Islander Studies (AIATSIS) (2018) *Guidelines for Ethical Research in Australian Indigenous Studies*, viewed 21 October 2019, http://aiatsis.gov.au/sites /default/files/docs/research-and-guides/ethics/GERAIS.pdf

Backhouse, J. (1838) *Extracts from the Letters of James Backhouse: Whilst Engaged in a Religious Visit to Van Diemen's Land, New South Wales, and South Africa, Accompanied by George Washington Walker*, Harvey and Darton, London.

Bacon, J. (2019) "Settler Colonialism as Eco-social Structure and the Production of Colonial Ecological Violence", *Environmental Sociology*, Vol. 5, No. 1, pp. 59–69.

Bailey, K. (2020) "Indigenous Students: Resilient and Empowered in the Midst of Racism and Lateral Violence", *Ethnic and Racial Studies*, Vol. 43, No. 6, pp. 1032–1051.

Baldwin, J. (1993) *The Fire Next Time*, First Vintage International Press, New York.

Ballance, P. (2009) *New Zealand Geology: An Illustrated Guide*, Second Edition, Geoscience Society of New Zealand, Auckland.

Bamblett, L. (2013) *Our Stories Are Our Survival*, Aboriginal Studies Press, Canberra.

Barker, J. (ed) (2015) *Indigenous Feminisms in Oxford Handbook of Indigenous People's Politics*, Oxford University Press, viewed 4 November 2018, http://www.oxfordhandbooks.com/view/10.1093/oxfordhb/9780195386653.001.0001/oxfordhb-9780195386653-e-007

Barker, J. (2017) *Critically Sovereign: Indigenous Gender, Sexuality and Feminist Studies*, Duke University Press, Durham, North Carolina.

Barnes, H.M. (2000) "Kaupapa Māori: Explaining the Ordinary", *Pacific Health Dialog*, Vol. 7, No. 1, pp. 13–16.

Baskin, C. (2016) *Strong Helpers' Teachings: The Value of Indigenous Knowledges in the Helping Professions*, Second Edition, Canadian Scholars' Press, Toronto, Canada.

Battiste, M. (2000) *Reclaiming Indigenous Voice and Vision*, UBC Press, Vancouver.

Battiste, M. (2002) *Indigenous Knowledge and Pedagogy in First Nations Education: A Literature Review with Recommendations*. Government of Canada, Department of Indian and Northern Affairs (INAC), Ottawa, Canada.

Battiste, M. (2007) "Research Ethics for Protecting Indigenous Knowledge and Heritage: Institutional and Researcher Responsibilities", in N.K. Denzin (ed), *Ethical Futures in Qualitative Research: Decolonizing the Politics of Knowledge*, Left Coast Press, California, pp. 111–132.

Battiste, M., Bell, L. & Findlay, L.M. (2002) "An Interview with Linda Tuhiwai Te Rina Smith", *Canadian Journal of Native Education*, Vol. 26, No. 2, pp. 169–201.

Baudin, N. ([1802]1974) *Journal of Nicolas Baudin 1800 to 1803*, Libraries Board of South Australia, Adelaide, p. 345.

Baudrillard, J. (2001) *Jean Baudrillard: Selected Writings*, Stanford University Press, Stanford.

Bawaka Country, Suchet-Pearson, S., Wright, S., Lloyd, K. & Burarrwanga, L. (2013) "Caring *as* Country: Towards an Ontology of Co-becoming in Natural Resource Management", *Asia Pacific Viewpoint*, Vol. 54, No. 2, pp. 185–197.

Bawaka Country, Wright, S., Suchet-Pearson, S., Lloyd, K., Burarrwanga, L., Ganambarr, R., Ganambarr-Stubs, M., Ganambarr, B. & Maymuru, D. (2014)

"Working With and Learning From Country: Decentring Human Authority", *Cultural Geographies*, Vol. 22, No. 2, pp. 269–283.

Bawaka Country, Wright, S., Suchet-Pearson, S., Lloyd, K., Burarrwanga, L., Ganambarr, R., Ganambarr-Stubs, M., Ganambarr, B. & Maymuru, D. (2016) "Co-becoming Bawaka: Towards a Relational Understanding of Place/Space", *Progress in Human Geography*, Vol. 40, No. 4, pp. 455–475.

Behrendt, L. (2007) "The 1967 Referendum: 40 Years On", *Australian Indigenous Law Review*, Vol. 11, pp. 12–16.

Behrendt, L., Larkin, S., Griew, R. & Kelly, P. (2012) *Review of Higher Education Access and Outcomes for Aboriginal and Torres Strait Islander People: Final Report*, Australian Government, Canberra.

Bell, A. (2014) *Relating Indigenous and Settler Identities: Beyond Domination*, Palgrave Macmillan, London.

Bennett, B. (2014) "How Do Light-Skinned Aboriginal Australians Experience Racism?", *Alternative*, Vol. 10, No. 2, pp. 180–192.

Berk, C. (2017) "Palawa Kani and the Value of Language in Aboriginal Tasmania", *Oceania*, Vol. 87, No. 1, pp. 2–20.

Berry, K.A., Jackson, S., Saito, L. & Forline, L. (2018) "Reconceptualising Water Quality Governance to Incorporate Knowledge and Values: Case Studies from Australian and Brazilian Indigenous Communities", *Water Alternatives*, Vol. 11, No. 1, pp. 40–60.

Bessarab, D. & Ng'andu, B. (2010) "Yarning About Yarning as a Legitimate Method in Indigenous Research", *International Journal of Critical Indigenous Studies*, Vol. 3, No. 1, pp. 37–50.

Bignall, S., Hemming, S. & Rigney, D. (2016) "Three Ecosophies for the Anthropocene: Environmental Governance, Continental Posthumanism and Indigenous Expressivism", *Deleuze Studies*, Edinburgh University Press, Vol. 10, No. 4, pp. 455–478.

Birdsell, B. (1939) "Australian Daily Field Journal 1938–1939", *Harvard and Adelaide Universities Expedition*, Vol. 3, No. 3, pp. 1–26.

Bishop, R. (1999) "Collaborative Storytelling: Meeting Indigenous Peoples' Desires for Self-Determination in Research", paper presented to *The World Indigenous People's Conference: Education*, Albuquerque, New Mexico, 15–22 June 1996, viewed 14 April 2020, https://files.eric.ed.gov/fulltext/ED467396.pdf

Bishop, R. (2005) "Freeing Ourselves From Neo-colonial Domination in Research", in N.K. Denzin & Y.S. Lincoln (eds), *The Handbook of Qualitative Research*, Third Edition, Sage, Thousand Oaks, CA, pp. 109–138.

Blair, N. (2019) "Lilyology as a Transformative Framework for Decolonizing Ethical Spaces Within the Academy", in J. Archibald Q'um Q'um Xiiem, J. Lee-Morgan & J. De Santolo (eds), *Decolonizing Research Indigenous Storywork as Methodology*, Zed Books, London, pp. 203–223.

BlaQ, BlaQ Aboriginal Corporation (2021) *Blaq Mail, Tropical Fuits*, Blaq Aboriginal Corporation, Redfern Sydney, viewed 15 March 2021, https://www.blaq.org.au/media

Blaser, M. (2013) "Ontological Conflicts and the Stories of Peoples in Spite of Europe: Toward a Conversation on Political Ontology", *Current Anthropology*, Vol. 54, No. 5, pp. 547–568.

Blaser, M. (2014) "Ontology and Indigeneity: On the Political Ontology of Heterogeneous Assemblages", *Cultural Geographies*, Vol. 21, No. 1, pp. 49–58.

Blue, B. (2018) "What's Wrong with Healthy Rivers? Promise and Practice in the Search for a Guiding Ideal for Freshwater Management", *Progress in Physical Geography*, Vol. 42, No. 4, pp. 462–477.

Blue, B. & Brierley, G. (2016) "But What Do You Measure?' Prospects for a Constructive Critical Physical Geography", *Area*, Vol. 48, No. 2, pp. 190–197.

Bodkin-Andrews, G. & Carlson, B. (2016) "The Legacy of Racism and Indigenous Australian Identity Within Education", *Race Ethnicity and Education*, Vol. 19, No. 4, pp. 784–807.

Bond, C. (2006) "The Abuse of Aboriginal Women Via Racialized and Gendered Discourses", *Black Nations Rising*, Vol. 4, pp. 8–9.

Bonilla-Silva, E. (2009) "When Whites Love a Black Leader: Race Matters in Obamerica", *Journal of African American Studies*, Vol. 13, No. 2, pp.176–183.

Bonwick, J. (1870) *The Last of the Tasmanians*, Sampson Low & Marston, London.

Bonyhady, T. & Lehman, G. (2018) *The National Picture: The Art of Tasmania's Black War*, National Gallery of Australia, Canberra, ACT.

Bourdieu, P. (1986) "The Forms of Capital", in J. Richardson (ed), *Handbook of Theory and Research for the Sociology of Education*, Greenwood Press, Connecticut, pp. 241–256.

Boyce, J. (2008) *Van Diemen's Land*, Black Inc., Melbourne.

Bozovic, M. (1995) "An Utterly Dark Spot", in J. Bentham, *The Panopticon Writings*, Verso, London, pp. 1–28.

Branch, S., Ramsey, S. & Barker, M. (2012) "Workplace Bullying, Mobbing and General Harassment: A Review", *International Journal of Management Reviews*, Vol. 15, No. 3, pp. 280–299.

Bravo, K.E. (2015) "Black Female 'Things' in International Law: A Meditation on Saartjie Baartman and Truganini", in J.I. Leavitt (ed), *Black Women and International Law: Deliberate Interactions, Movements, and Actions*, Cambridge University Press, New York, pp. 289–326.

Breen, S. & Summers, D. (2006) *Aboriginal Connections with Launceston Places*, Launceston City Council, Launceston, Tasmania.

Brierley, G., Tadaki, M., Hikuroa, D., Blue, B., Šunde, C., Tunnicliffe, J. & Salmond, A. (2019) "A Geomorphic Perspective on the Rights of the River in Aotearoa New Zealand", *River Research and Applications*, Vol. 35, No. 10, pp. 1640–1651.

Brodie, N.D. (2017) *The Vandemonian War: The Secret History of Britain's Tasmanian Invasion*, Hardie Grant Books, Richmond, Victoria.

Brown, K. (2018) *Stoking the Fire Nationhood in Cherokee Writing, 1907–1970*, University of Oklahoma Press, Norman.

Brown, V., Harris, J.S. & Russell, J. (eds) (2010) *Tackling Wicked Problems through the Transdisciplinary Imagination*, Earthscan, Abingdon, Oxon.

Browning, D. (2018) "When Mardi Gras Is Over, Indigenous LGBTI People Still Walk a Difficult Path", *ABC News*, 2 March, viewed 13 March 2019, https://www.abc.net.au/news/2018-03-02/after-mardi-gras-indigenous-lgbti-people-walk-a-lonely-road/9502268

Bunda, T. (2007) "The Sovereign Aboriginal Woman", in A. Moreton-Robinson (ed), *Sovereign Subjects: Indigenous Sovereignty Matters*, Allen & Unwin, pp. 75–80.

Burin, M. (2016) "Sistergirls and Brotherboys Unite to Strengthen Spirits", *ABC News*, 21 November, viewed 13 March 2019, https://www.abc.net.au/news/2016-11-21/sistergirls-and-brotherboys-unite-to-strengthen-spirits/8040928

Burton, L. & Cocklin, C. (1996) "Water Resource Management and Environmental Policy Reform in New Zealand: Regionalism, Allocation, and Indigenous Relations", *Colorado Journal of International Environmental Law and Policy*, Vol. 7, No. 1, pp. 75–106.

Calder, I.R. (2005) *The Blue Revolution: Land Use and Integrated Water Resources Management*, Earthscan, London.

Cameron, P. (1994) "Pallawah Women: Their Historical Contribution to Our Survival, *yah taweh tiwah warraweh – mena pallawah trouwerner lowanna* (Greetings from the Ancestors – I am an Aboriginal Tasmanian Woman), Part I: A Matriarchal Heritage", in P. Brock (ed), *Women, Rites and Sites*, AIATSIS, Canberra, pp. 65–67.

Cameron, P. (2011) *Grease and Ochre: The Blending of Two Cultures at the Colonial Sea Frontier*, Fullers Bookshop, Launceston, Tasmania.

Cameron, P. (2016) *Grease and Ochre: The Blending of Two Cultures at the Colonial Sea Frontier*, University of Tasmania, Community, Place & Heritage Research Unit, Riawunna, Hobart, Tasmania.

Cameron, P. & Miller, L. (2011) "Reclaiming History for Indigenous Governance: Tasmanian Stories", in S. Maddison & M. Brigg (eds), *Unsettling the Settler State: Creativity and Resistance in Indigenous Settler-State Governance*, Federation Press, New South Wales, pp. 32–50.

Cameron, P. & Miller, L. (2016) "Reclaiming History for Aboriginal Governance: Tasmanian Stories", *Journal of Australian Indigenous Issues*, Vol. 19, No. 1–2, pp. 32–50.

Campbell, M. (1973) *Halfbreed*, University of Nebraska Press, Lincoln, Nebraska.

Cannella, G. & Manuelito, G. (2008) "Feminisms from Unthought Locations: Indigenous Worldviews, Marginalized Feminisms, and Revisioning an Anticolonial Social Science", in N.K. Denzin, Y.S. Lincoln & L.T. Smith (eds), *Handbook of Critical and Indigenous Methodologies*, SAGE Publications, Thousand Oaks, CA, pp. 45–60.

Canon, M. (2018) "Teaching and Learning Reparative Education in Settler Colonial and Post-TRC Canada", *Canadian Journal of Native Education* [Special Issue: Indigenization, Decolonization, and Reconciliation: Critical Considerations and

Cross-Disciplinary Approaches in Post-Secondary Classrooms], Vol. 40, No. 1, pp. 164–181.

Cariño, J. (2005) "Indigenous Peoples' Right to Free, Prior, Informed Consent: Reflections on Concepts and Practice", *Arizona Journal of International & Comparative Law*, Vol. 22, No. 1, pp. 19–39.

Carlson, B. (2016) *The Politics of Identity Who Counts as Aboriginal Today*, Aboriginal Studies Press, Canberra.

Carothers, C., J. Black, S. J. Langdon, R. Donkersloot, D. Ringer, J. Coleman, E. R. Gavenus, W. Justin, M. Williams, F. Christiansen, C. Stevens, B. Woods, S. Clark, P. M. Clay, L. Mack, J. Raymond-Yakoubian, A. Akall'eq Sanders, B. L. Stevens & Whiting. A. (2021) "Indigenous Peoples and Salmon Stewardship: A Critical Relationship", *Ecology and Society*, Vol. 26, No. 1, pp. 16–38.

Castañeda, H-N. (1986) "Practical Reason: Reasons for Doing and Intentional Action", *Theoría: Revista de Teoria, Historia y Fundamentos de la Ciencia*, Vol. 2, No. 1, pp. 69–96.

Castellano, M.B. (2014) "Indigenizing Education", *Education Canada Magazine*, viewed 23 October 2020, https://www.edcan.ca/articles/indigenizing-education/

Catton, P. (2009) "Is Mātauranga Māori Science?" *New Zealand Science Teacher*, Vol. 120, pp. 36–38.

Césaire, A. (2000) *Discourse on Colonialism*. Trans. by J. Pinkham, Monthly Review Press, New York.

Chambers, D. & Buzinde, C. (2015) "Tourism and Decolonisation: Locating Research and Self", *Annals of Tourism Research*, Vol. 51, pp. 1–16.

Champagne, D. (2015) "Centering Indigenous Nations Within Indigenous Methodologies", *Wicazo Sa Review*, Vol. 30, No. 1, pp. 57–81.

Chandler, D. & Reid, J. (2018) "'Being in Being': Contesting the Ontopolitics of Indigeneity", *The European Legacy*, Vol. 23, No. 3, pp. 251–268.

Chesterman, J. & Galligan, B. (1997) *Citizens Without Rights, Aborigines and Australian Citizenship*, Cambridge University Press, Cambridge.

Chilisa, B. & Tsheko, G. (2014) "Mixed Methods in Indigenous Research: Building Relationships for Sustainable Intervention Outcomes", *Journal of Mixed Methods Research*, Vol. 8, No. 3, pp. 222–233.

Chisholm, J. (2018) "Muxe, Two-Spirits, and the Myth of Indigenous Transgender Acceptance", *International Journal of Critical Indigenous Studies*, Vol. 11, No. 1, pp. 1–15.

Christen, K., Merrill, A. & Wynne, M. (2017) "A Community of Relations: Mukurtu Hubs and Spokes", *D-Lib Magazine*, Vol. 23, No. 5/6 (online journal), viewed 18 October 2020, http://www.dlib.org/dlib/may17/christen/05christen.html

Clark, M. (2015) "Indigenous Subjectivity in Australia: Are We Queer?", *Journal of Global Indigeneity*, Vol. 1, No. 1, pp. 1–5.

Clark, Y. & Augoustinos, M. (2015) "What's in a Name? Lateral violence Within the Aboriginal Community in Adelaide, South Australia", *The Australian Community Psychologist*, Vol. 27, No. 2, pp 19–34.

Clark, Y., Augoustinos, M. & Malin, M. (2016) "Lateral Violence Within the Aboriginal Community in Adelaide: 'It Affects Our Identity and Wellbeing'", *Journal of Indigenous Wellbeing Te Mauri – Pimatisiwin*, Vol. 1, Issue 1, pp. 43–52.

Clark, Y., Augoustinos, M. & Malin, M. (2017) "Evaluation of the Preventing Lateral Violence Workshop in Adelaide, South Australia: Phase Two Qualitative Aspect", *Journal of Indigenous Wellbeing*, Vol. 2, No. 3, pp. 54–66.

Cockerill, J. (2018) "Hauntology on Country", *Overland*, 22 March, viewed 13 March 2019, https://overland.org.au/2018/03/hauntology-on-country/

Colchester, M. (2004) "Conservation Policy and Indigenous Peoples", *Cultural Survival Quarterly*, Cambridge, Vol. 28, No. 1, pp. 17.

Collins, P.H. (1991) "Learning from the Outsider Within: the Sociological Significance of Black Feminist Thought", in M.M. Fonow & J.A. Cook (eds), *Beyond Methodology, Feminist Research Lived Research*, Indiana University Press, Bloomington, pp. 35–59.

Collins, P.H. (2000) *Black Feminist Thought: Knowledge, Consciousness, and the Politics of Empowerment*, Routledge, New York.

Cooper, C. (1989) *Aboriginal and Torres Strait Islander Collections in Overseas Museums*, Aboriginal Studies Press, Canberra, Australia.

Cotterill, S. (2011) "Ainu Success: The Political and Cultural Achievements of Japan's Indigenous Minority", *The Asia-Pacific Journal*, Vol. 9, No. 12, pp. 1–27.

Coulthard, G. (2007) "Subjects of Empire: Indigenous Peoples and the Politics of Recognition in Colonial Contexts", *Contemporary Political Theory*, Vol. 6, pp. 437–460.

Coulthard, G.S. (2014) *Red Skin, White Masks: Rejecting the Colonial Politics of Recognition*, University of Minnesota Press, Minneapolis.

Craven, R. (2005) "Turning Points in Indigenous Education: New Findings That Can Really Make a Difference and Implications for the Next Generation of Indigenous Education Research", *paper presented to the Australian Association for Research in Education Annual Conference*, Parramatta, 27 November–1 December. Viewed 17 October 2019, https://www.aare.edu.au/data/publications/2005/cra05318.pdf

Crenshaw, K. (1991) "Mapping the Margins: Intersectionality, Identity Politics, and Violence Against Women of Color", *Theorizing Feminisms*, Vol 43, No. 6. pp. 159–173.

Crothers, C. (2014) "Decolonizing Methodologies: Research and Indigenous Peoples", *Ethnic and Racial Studies*, Vol. 37, No. 5, pp. 878–880.

Curry, P. (2008) "Nature Post-Nature", *New Formations*, Vol. 26, pp. 51–64.

Curthoys, A. (2005) "Raphaël Lemkin's 'Tasmania': An Introduction", *Patterns of Prejudice*, Vol. 39, No. 2, pp. 162–169.

Daniel, B.J. (2005) "Researching African Canadian Women Indigenous Knowledges and the Politics of Representation", in G.J. Sefa Dei & G. Singh Johal (eds), *Critical Issues in Anti-Racist Research Methodologies*, Peter Lang, New York, pp. 53–78.

Danjoo Koorliny Social Impact (2019) *Social Impact Magazine*, Season: Makuru, Issue 1, Centre for Social Impact, University of Western Australia.

D'Arcy, J. (2007) "'The Same but Different': Aborigines, Eugenics, and the Harvard-Adelaide Universities' Anthropological Expedition to Cape Barren Island Reserve January 1939", *Tasmanian Historical Studies*, Vol. 12, No. 1, pp. 59–90.

Darwin, C. (1839) *Narrative of the Surveying Voyages of His Majesty's Ships Adventure and Beagle Between the Years 1826 and 1836. . . . Journal and Remarks. 1832–1836*, Henry Colburn, London, viewed 1 April 2019, http://darwinonline.org.uk/content/fr ameset?pageseq=1&itemID=F10.3&viewtype=text

Datta, R. (2018) "Decolonizing Methodologies: A Transformation from Science-Oriented Researcher to Relational/ Participant-Oriented Researcher", *American Indian Culture and Research Journal*, Vol. 42, No. 1, pp. 115–130.

Davenport, N., Schwartz, R.D. & Elliott, G.P. (2002) *Mobbing: Emotional Abuse in the American Workplace*, Civil Society Publishing, Ames.

Davis, F. (2009) "Calculating Colour: Whiteness, Anthropological Research and the Cummeragunja Aboriginal Reserve, May and June 1938", in J. Carey & C. McLisky (eds), *Creating White Australia*, Sydney University Press, Sydney, pp. 103–120.

Davis, M. (2018) "The Long Road to Uluru: Walking Together: Truth Before Justice", *Griffith Review*, Vol. 60, No. 13–32, pp. 41–45.

Davis, M.D. & Threlfall, J. (2006) "Integrated Water Resource Management in New Zealand: Legislative Framework and Implementation", *Journal of Contemporary Water Research and Education*, Vol. 135, No. 1, pp. 86–99.

de La Cadena, M. (2010) "Indigenous Cosmopolitics in the Andes: Conceptual Reflections Beyond 'Politics'", *Cultural Anthropology*, Vol. 25, No. 2, pp. 234–370.

de Leeuw, S. & Hunt, S. (2018) "Unsettling Decolonizing Geographies", *Geography Compass*, Vol. 12, pp. 1–14.

De Sousa Santos, B., Nunes J.A. & Meneses, M.P. (2007) "Opening up the Canon of Knowledge and Recognition of Difference" in B. De Sousa Santos (ed), *Another Knowledge Is Possible: Beyond Northern Epistemologies*, Verso, London, pp. xx–lxii.

Dean, A. (2018) "The Growing Over-Representation of Aboriginal and Torres Strait Islander Children in Care", *Child Family Community Australia*, 7 May, viewed 17 October 2017, https://aifs.gov.au/cfca/2018/05/07/growing-over-representation-aboriginal-and-torres-strait-islander-children-care

Debord, G. (2005) *Society of the Spectacle*. New Unauthorised Trans. M. Knabb. Rebel Press, London.

Deloria, J.V. (2003) *God Is Red: A Native View of Religion*, 30th Anniversary Edition, Fulcrum Publishing, Golden.

Denenberg, R. & Braverman, M. (2001) *The Violence Prone Workplace: A New Approach to Dealing with Hostile, Threatening, and Uncivil Behavior*, Cornell University Press, Ithaca.

Denholm, M. (2015) "Brawl Over 'Wannabe' and "Tick-a-Box-Aborigines", *The Australian*, 16 February, viewed 12 November 2019, https://www.theaustralian.com. au/nation/brawl-over-wannabe-and-tickabox-aborigines/news-story/ d4a8a3a47cf478d08a17b7c466d09e66

Denzin, N.K. (2005) "Emancipatory Discourses and the Ethics and Politics of Interpretation", in N.K. Denzin & Lincoln Y.S. (eds), The SAGE Handbook of Qualitative Research, SAGE, Thousand Oaks, California, pp. 933–958.

Denzin, N.K. & Lincoln, Y.S. (2008) "Preface", in N.K. Denzin, Y.S. Lincoln & L. Tuhiwai Smith (eds), *Handbook of Critical and Indigenous Methodologies*, SAGE, Los Angeles, pp. ix–xv.

Denzin, N.K. & Salvo, J. (eds) (2020) *New Directions in Theorizing Qualitative Research: Indigenous Research*, Myers Education Press, Gorham, Maine.

Denzin, N.K., Lincoln, Y.S. & Smith, L.T. (eds) (2008) *Handbook of Critical and Indigenous Methodologies*, SAGE, Los Angeles.

Djab Wurrung Heritage Protection Embassy (2020) *Djab Wurrung Heritage Protection Embassy*, viewed 18 October 2020, https://dwembassy.com/

Dodson, M. (1994) "The End in the Beginning", in M. Grossman (ed), *Blacklines: Contemporary Critical Writing by Indigenous Australians*, Melbourne University Press, Melbourne, Australia, pp. 25–42.

Dodson, P. & Cronin, D. (2011) "An Australian Dialogue: Decolonising the Country", in S. Maddison (ed), *Unsettling the Settler State: Creativity and Resistance in Indigenous Settler-State Governance*, Federation Press, Annandale, NSW, pp. 189–205.

Dowie, M. (2009) *Conservation Refugees the Hundred-Year Conflict Between Global Conservation and Native Peoples*, The MIT Press, Cambridge.

Doyle, K., Cleary, M., Blanchard, D. & Hungerford, C. (2017) "The Yerin Dilly Bag Model of Indigenist Health Research", *Qualitative Health Research*, Vol. 27, No. 9, pp. 1288–1301.

Driskill, Qwo-Li (2010) "Doubleweaving Two-Spirit Critiques", *GLQ: A Journal of Lesbian and Gay Studies*, Duke University Press, Druham, NC, pp. 69–92.

Dudgeon, P. (2017) "Mothers of Sin: Indigenous Women's Perceptions of Their Own Identity and Gender", in P. Dudgeon, J. Herbert, J. Milroy & D. Oxenham (eds), *Us Women, Our Ways, Our World*, Magabala Books Aboriginal Corporation, Broome, Western Australia, pp. 106–128.

Dudgeon, P., Garvey, D. & Pickett, H. (2000) "Violence Turned Inwards", in P. Dudgeon, D. Garvey & H. Pickett (eds) *Working with Indigenous Australians: A Handbook for Psychologists*, Gunada Press, Perth.

Duff, W., Flinn, A., Suurtamm, K. & Wallace, D. (2013) "Social Justice Impact of Archives: A Preliminary Investigation", *Archival Science*, Vol. 13, pp. 317–348.

Dutta, M.J. (2012) *Voices of Resistance: Communication and Social Change*, Purdue University Press, Indiana.

Elliott, E. (2018) "Riawanna Centre Hosts Basket Weaving Workshop", *The Advocate*, 30 July, viewed 13 March 2019, https://www.theadvocate.com.au/story/5554563/craft-woven-with-culture/

Evans, J. (2016) "Valuing the Tarkine: A Systematic Quantification of Optimal Land Use and Potential Conflict Compromise", PhD thesis, University of Tasmania.

Evans, J. (2018) "Giving Voice to the Sacred Black Female Body in *takayna* Country" in J. Liljeblad & B. Verschuuren (eds), *Indigenous Perspectives on Sacred Natural Sites:*

Culture, Governance and Conservation, Routledge, Abingdon, Oxon, New York, pp. 1–13.

Evans, J. (2019) "Giving Voice to the Sacred Black Female Body in *takayna* Country", in J. Liljeblad & B. Verschuuren (eds), *Indigenous Perspectives on Sacred Natural Sites Culture, Governance and Conservation*, Routledge, London, pp. 17–31.

Evans, J., Kirkpatrick, J.B. & Bridle, K.L. (2018) "A Reciprocal Triangulation Process for Identifying and Mapping Potential Land Use Conflict", *Environmental Management*, Vol. 62, No. 12, pp. 777–791.

Evans, M., Miller, A., Hutchinson, P.J. & Dingwall, C. (2014) "Decolonizing Research Practice: Indigenous Methodologies, Aboriginal Methods, and Knowledge/ Knowing", in P. Leavy (ed), *The Oxford Handbook of Qualitative Research*, Oxford University Press, Oxford.

Everett, J. (2017) *The First Tasmanians: Our Story* [Exhibition], Queen Victoria Museum and Art Gallery, Royal Park, Launceston, Tasmania, viewed 13 March 2019.

Falkenmark, M. (2004) "Towards Integrated Catchment Management: Opening the Paradigm Locks Between Hydrology, Ecology and Policy-making", *International Journal of Water Resources Development*, Vol. 20, No. 3, pp. 275–281.

Fanon, F. (2008) *Black Skin, White Masks*, Pluto Press, London.

Felton, H. (1989) *Living with the Land: Aborigines in Tasmania*, Department of Education and the Arts, Tasmania.

Fforde, C. (2002) "Collection, Repatriation and Identity", in C. Fforde, J. Hubert & P. Turnbull (eds), *The Dead and Their Possessions: Repatriation in Principle, Policy, and Practice*, Routledge, London, pp. 25–46.

Fforde, C., McKeown, C., & Keeler, H. (2020) *The Routledge Companion to Indigenous Repatriation: Return, Reconcile, Renew*, Routledge, London.

Fforde, C., Bamblett, L., Lovett, R., Gorringe, S. & Fogarty, B. (2013) "Discourse, Deficit and Identity: Aboriginality, the Race Paradigm and the Language of Representation in Contemporary Australia", *Media International Australia*, No. 149, pp. 162–173.

Finley, C. (2011) "Decolonizing the Queer Native Body (and Recovering the Native Bull-Dyke): Bringing 'Sexy Back' and Out of Native Studies' Closet" in Q. Driskill, C. Finley, B. Gilley & S. Morgensen (eds), *Queer Indigenous Studies Critical Interventions in Theory, Politics, and Literature*, University of Arizona Press, Tucson, pp. 31–42.

Flanagan, R. (2002) "The Lost Tribe", *The Guardian*, 14 October 2002, viewed 20 April 2020, http://www.guardian.co.uk/world/2002/oct/14/australia.features11

Flowers, R. (2015) "Refusal to Forgive: Indigenous Women's Love and Rage", *Decolonization: Indigeneity, Education, & Society*, Vol. 4, No. 2, pp. 32–49.

Foley, D. (2003) "Indigenous Epistemology and Indigenous Standpoint Theory", *Social Alternatives*, Vol. 22, No. 1, pp. 44–52.

Fotopoulou, A. (2012) "Intersectionality Queer Studies and Hybridity: Methodological Frameworks for Social Research", *Journal of International Women's Studies*, Vol. 13, No. 2, pp. 19–32.

Foucault, M. (1972) *The Archaeology of Knowledge; and the Discourse on Language*, Trans. by A. Sheridan Smith, Pantheon Books, New York.

Foucault, M. (1979) *Discipline and Punish: The Birth of a Prison*, Random House, New York.

Foucault, M. (1980) *Power/Knowledge: Selected Interviews and Other Writings 1972–1977*, Harvester Wheatsheaf, New York.

Foucault, M. (1998) *The Will to Knowledge: The History of Sexuality (Vol. 1)*, Penguin Books, London.

Foucault, M. (2006) *Psychiatric Power: Lectures at the Collège de France 1973–1974*, J. Lagrange (ed), Palgrave MacMillan, New York.

Fourmile, H. (1989) "Who Owns the Past?: Aborigines as Captives of the Archives", *Aboriginal History*, Vol. 13, pp. 1–8.

Fox, C.A., Reo, N.J., Turner, D.A., Cook, J., Dituri, F., Ressell, B., Jenkins, J., Johnson, A., Rakena, T.M., Riley, C., Turner, A., Williams, J. & Wilson, M. (2017) "'The River Is Us; The River Is in Our Veins': Re-defining River Restoration in Three Indigenous Communities", *Sustainability Science*, Vol. 12, pp. 521–533.

Frankenberg, R. (1993) *White Women, Race Matters: The Social Construction of Whiteness*, University of Minnesota Press, Minneapolis.

Fredericks, B. & White, N. (2018) "Using Bridges Made by Others as Scaffolding and Establishing Footings for Those That Follow: Indigenous Women in the Academy", *Australian Journal of Education*, Vol. 62, No. 3, pp. 243–255.

Friberg, N., Angelopoulos, N., Buijes, A., Cowx, I., Kail, J., Moe, T., Moir, H., O'Hare, M.T., Verdonschot, P.F.M. & Wolter, C. (2016) "Effective River Restoration in the 21st Century: From Trial and Error to Novel Evidence-Based Approaches", *Advances in Ecological Research*, Vol. 55, pp. 535–611.

Fricker, M. (2013) "Epistemic Justice as a Condition of Political Freedom?", *Synthese*, Vol. 190, pp. 131–133.

Frogley, A. (2011) "I'm Not a Racist, But... Report on Cultural Respect, Racial Discrimination, Lateral Violence & Related Policy at Australia's Universities", National Indigenous Unit of the National Tertiary Education Union, *ISSUU*, viewed 20 September 2019, http://issuu.com/nteu/docs/im_not_a_racist_but

Frogley, A. (2018) "I'm Still Not a Racist, But...", *Advocate: Journal of the National Tertiary Education Union*, Vol. 3, p. 20.

Frost, A. (2009) "Fibre Across Time: A History of Tasmanian Aboriginal Women's Fibre Work", in Tasmanian Museum and Art Gallery, *tayenebe Tasmanian Aboriginal Women's Fibre Work*, Tasmanian Museum and Art Gallery, Hobart, pp. 3–38.

Fryirs, K. & Brierley, G. (2013) *Geomorphic Analysis of River Systems: An Approach to Reading the Landscape*, Wiley-Blackwell Publishing, UK.

Gabel, J. (2020) "Thousands Use Twitter Hashtag to Show Impact of Indigenous Scholar", 12 September 2020, *NZ Herald*, viewed on 12 September 2020, https://www.nzherald.co.nz/nz/education/thousands-use-twitter-hashtag-to-show-impact-of-indigenous-scholar/EBZ76SMSWJNS7RZ5S6TGR75SOQ/

Galič, M., Timan, T. & Koops, B. (2016) "Beyond: An Overview of Surveillance Theories from the Panopticon to Participation", *Philosophy & Technology*, March 2017, Vol. 30, No. 1, pp. 9–37.

Ganesharajah, C. (2009) *Indigenous Health and Wellbeing: The Importance of Country, Native Title Research Report No. 1/2009 April 2009*, Native Title Research Unit, Australian Institute of Aboriginal and Torres Strait Islander Studies, Canberra, ACT.

Garland, D. (1995) "Panopticon Days: Surveillance and Society", *Criminal Justice Matters*, Vol. 20, No. 1, p. 3–4.

Garnett, S.T., Burgess, N.D., Fa, J.E. . . . Leiper, I. (2018) "A Spatial Overview of the Global Importance of Indigenous Lands for Conservation", *Nature Sustainability*, Vol. 1, pp. 369–374.

Gay'wu Group of Women (2019) *Songspirals: Sharing Women's Wisdom of Country Through Songlines*, Allen & Unwin, Sydney.

Gooda, M. (2011a) *Aboriginal and Torres Strait Islander Social Justice Commissioner, Social Justice Report 2010*, Australian Human Rights Commission, Canberra, ACT.

Gooda, M. (2011b) *2011 Social Justice Report*, Australian Human Rights Commission, Sydney.

Google Scholar (2020) Google, Mountain View, California, viewed 18 June 2020, https://scholar.google.com.au/scholar?hl=en&as_sdt=0%2C5&q=Decolonizing+met hodologies%3A+research+and+Indigenous+peoples&btnG=

Gorringe, J. (2009) "Twining Culture", in Tasmanian Museum and Art Gallery, *tayenebe Tasmanian Aboriginal Women's Fibre Work*, Tasmanian Museum and Art Gallery, Hobart, pp. 39–41.

Gough, J. (2009) "Fibre Across Time: A History of Tasmanian Aboriginal Women's Fibre Work", in Tasmanian Museum and Art Gallery, *tayenebe Tasmanian Aboriginal Women's Fibre Work*, Tasmanian Museum and Art Gallery, Hobart, pp. 3–38.

Graham, M. (2009) "Understanding Human Agency in Terms of Place: A Proposed Aboriginal Research Methodology", *PAN: Philosophy Activism Nature*, No. 3, pp. 71–78.

Gramsci, A. (1971) *Selections from the Prison Notebooks*, International Publishers, New York.

Green, J. (ed) (2007) *Making Space for Indigenous Feminism*, Fernwood Publishing, Winnipeg.

Greeno, L. (2009) "*tayenebe*: Weaving Our Stories", in Tasmanian Museum and Art Gallery, *tayenebe Tasmanian Aboriginal Women's Fibre Work*, Tasmanian Museum and Art Gallery, Hobart, pp. 43–57.

Greeno, L. & Gough, J. (2014) "Honouring the Past/Making a Future, the Tasmanian Aboriginal Shell Necklace Tradition", in J. Gough & L. Greeno, *Lola Greeno: Cultural Jewels*, Object: Australian Design Centre, Darlinghurst, NSW, pp. 79–88.

Greensmith, C. & Giwa, S. (2013) "Challenging Settler Colonialism in Contemporary Queer Politics: Settler Homonationalism, Pride Toronto, and Two-Spirit

Subjectivities", *American Indian Culture and Research Journal*, Vol. 37, No. 2, pp. 129–148.

Grieves, M. (2009) *Aboriginal Spirituality: Aboriginal Philosophy the Basis of Aboriginal Social and Emotional Wellbeing*, Cooperative Research Centre for Aboriginal Health, Casuarina, Australia.

Gumbula, J. (2009) *Makarr-Garma: Aboriginal Collections From a Yolngu Perspective*, Macleay Museum, University of Sydney.

Habibis, D. & Walter, M. (2009) *Social Inequality in Australia: Discourses, Realities & Futures*, Oxford University Press, Victoria.

Haferkamp, H. & Smelser, N.J. (eds) (1992) *Social Change and Modernity*, University of California Press, Berkeley.

Hall, T. (2000) "Decolonizing Methodologies: Research and Indigenous Peoples by Linda Tuhiwai Smith", *Contemporary Sociology*, Vol. 29, No. 3, pp. 567–568.

Hallinan, C.J, Bruce, T. & Burke, M. (2005) "Fresh Prince of Colonial Dome: Indigenous Players in the AFL", *Football Studies*, Vol. 8, pp. 68–78.

Halperin, D.M. (2003) "The Normalization of Queer Theory", *Journal of Homosexuality*, Vol. 45, No. 2–4, pp. 339–343.

Haraway, D. (2003) *The Haraway Reader*, Routledge, New York.

Harkin, N. (2017) "On Responsibility", *Overland Journal*, Vol. 226 Autumn, viewed 18 October 2020, https://overland.org.au/previous-issues/issue-226/column-natalie-harkin/

Harkin, N. (2019) *Archival-Poetics*, Vagabond Press, Sydney.

Harmsworth, G., Awatere, S. & Robb, M. (2016) "Indigenous Māori Values and Perspectives to Inform Freshwater Management in Aotearoa-New Zealand", *Ecology and Society*, Vol. 21, No. 4, p. 9 (online journal).

Harris, M., Carlson, B. & Poata-Smith, E. (2013) "Indigenous Identities and the Politics of Authenticity", in M. Harris, M. Nakata & B. Carlson (eds), *The Politics of Identity: Emerging Indigeneity*, Sydney: University of Technology, Sydney E-Press, pp. 1–9.

Harrison, N. (2011) *Teaching and Learning in Aboriginal Education*, Second Edition, Oxford University Press, Melbourne.

Hasluck, P. (1961) *The Policy of Assimilation*, Decisions of Commonwealth and State Ministers at the Native Welfare Conference, Canberra, viewed 10 October 2019, https://aiatsis.gov.au/sites/default/files/catalogue_resources/18801.pdf

Healey, G. & Tagak, A. (2014) "'PILIRIQATIGIINNIQ Working in a Collaborative Way for the Common Good': A Perspective on the Space Where Health Research Methodology and Inuit Epistemology Come Together", *International Journal of Critical Indigenous Studies*, Vol. 7, No. 1, pp. 1–14.

Hikuroa, D. (2017) "Mātauranga Māori – the ūkaipō of Knowledge in New Zealand", *Journal of the Royal Society of New Zealand*, Vol. 47, No 1, pp. 5–10.

Hill, R. (2011) "Sediment Management in the Waikato Region, New Zealand", *Journal of Hydrology*, Vol. 50, No. 1, pp. 227–240.

Hird, M.J. (2004) "Naturally Queer", *Feminist Theory*, Vol. 5, No. 1, pp. 85–89.

Hodgman, W. (2016) "The Premier's 2016 Australia Day Address", Tasmanian
Government, viewed 4 April 2019, http://www.premier.tas.gov.au/speeches/
will_hodgman_speeches/the_premiers_2016_australia_day_address

Hofverberg, E. (2020) "Sweden: Supreme Court Recognizes Sami Indigenous Group's
Exclusive Right to Confer Hunting and Fishing Rights in Sami Area", *Global Legal
Monitor*, 14 February 2020, viewed 10 October 2020, https://www.loc.gov/law/
foreign-news/article/sweden-supreme-court-recognizes-sami-indigenous-groups-
exclusive-right-to-confer-hunting-and-fishing-rights-in-sami-area/

hooks, b. (1984) *Feminist Theory from Margin to Center*, South End Press, Boston.

Hoosan, G. (2018) "Gadrian Hoosan: When Water is Death", *Indigenous X*, viewed
18 October 2020, https://indigenousx.com.au/gadrian-hoosan-when-water-is-death/

Huggins, J. (1998) *Sister Girl: The Writings of Aboriginal Activist and Historian Jackie
Huggins*, University of Queensland Press, St Lucia, QLD.

Hughes, M. & Barlo, S. (2021) "Yarning With Country: An Indigenist Research
Methodology", *Qualitative Inquiry*, Vol. 27, No. 3–4, pp. 353–363.

Human Rights and Equal Opportunity Commission [HREOC] (1997) *Bringing Them
Home Report, National Inquiry into the Separation of Aboriginal and Torres Strait
Islander Children from their Families*, Australian Government Publishing Service,
Canberra.

Hunt, L. (2016) "Changes to Tasmania's Aboriginal Identity Test Labelled Outrageous",
ABC News, 1 July 2016, viewed 14 October 2019, https://www.abc.net.au/news/2016-
07-01/changes-to-aboriginal-identity-test-labelled-outrageous/7561128

Hunt, T. (2019) "Should Museums Return Their Colonial Artefacts?", 29 June 2019, *The
Guardian*, viewed 18 October 2020, https://www.theguardian.com/culture/2019/
jun/29/should-museums-return-their-colonial-artefacts

ICCA Consortium (2018) "Territories and Areas Conserved by Indigenous Peoples and
Local Communities", *ICCA Consortium*, viewed 30 March 2019, https://www.
iccaconsortium.org/index.php/discover/

International Council on Archives (ICA) (2019) *Tandanya – Adelaide Declaration*,
viewed 18 October 2020, https://www.archivists.org.au/documents/item/1545

International Council of Museums (ICOM) (2004) "Declaration on the Importance and
Value of Universal Museums", *ICOM News*, Vol. 1, viewed 18 October 2020, http://
archives.icom.museum/pdf/E_news2004/p4_2004-1.pdf

Jackson, S. (2018) "Water and Indigenous Rights: Mechanisms and Pathways of
Recognition, Representation, and Redistribution", *WIREs Water*, Vol. 5, No. 6,
p. e1314 (online journal).

Jaimes Guerrero, M.A. (2003) "Patriarchal Colonialism and Indigenism: Implications for
Native Feminist Spirituality and Native Womanism", *Hypatia – Journal of Feminist
Philosophy*, Vol. 18, No. 2, pp. 58–69.

Jaimes Guerrero, M.A. (2004) "Biocolonialism and Isolates of Historic Interest", in
M. Riley (ed), *Indigenous Intellectual Property Rights: Legal Obstacles and Innovative
Solutions*, Altama Press, Walnut Creek, pp. 251–277.

James, D. (2015) "Tjukurpa Time", in J. McGrath & M. Jebb (eds), *Long History, Deep Time: Deepening the Histories of Place*, ANU Press and Aboriginal History, Canberra, ACT, pp. 33–46.

Janke, T. (2018) *First Peoples: A Roadmap for Enhancing Indigenous Engagement in Museums and Galleries*, Australian Museums and Galleries Association, Canberra.

Jeffery, D. & Nelson, J. (2009) "'The More Things Change. . .: The Endurance of Culturalism' in Social Work and Healthcare", in C. Schick & J. McNinch (eds) *"I Thought Pocahontas Was a Movie": Using Critical Discourse Analysis to Understand Race and Sex as Social Constructs*, CPRC Press, Regina, pp. 91–109.

Jimienez-Luque, A. (2021) "Decolonial Leadership for Cultural Resistance and Social Change: Challenging the Social Order through the Struggle of Identity", *Leadership*, Vol. 17, No. 2, pp. 154–172.

Jimmy, R., Allen, W. & Anderson, V. (2015) "Kindred Practice: Experiences of a Research Group Working Towards Decolonization and Indigenization in the Everyday", *Education Matters: The Journal of Teaching and Learning*, Vol. 3, No. 1, viewed 23 October 2020, https://journalhosting.ucalgary.ca/index.php/em/article/view/62926/Kindred%20Practice

Johnson, E.P. & Hendersen, M.G. (2005) *Black Queer Studies a Critical Anthology*, Duke University Press, Durham, NC.

Jones, C. (2016) *New Treaty, New Tradition: Reconciling New Zealand and Maori Law*, University of British Columbia Press, Toronto.

Jones, J. (2014) "Lighting Fire and the Return of the Boomerang Cultural Renaissance in the South-East", *Artlink*, Vol. 34, No. 2, June, pp. 35–38.

Jørgensen, M. (2010) "The Terms of Debate: The Negotiation of the Legitimacy of a Marginalised Perspective", *Social Epistemology*, Vol. 24, No. 4, pp. 313–330.

Kaldor Public Art Projects (n.d.) *Project 32: Jonathan Jones. Project Summary*, viewed 18 October 2020, http://kaldorartprojects.org.au/project-32-jonathan-jones

Kaplan, D. (1977) "Demonstratives", Reprinted in J. Almog, J. Perry, & H. Wettstein (eds), (1989) *Themes from Kaplan*, Oxford University Press, Oxford, pp. 481–563.

Karklins, A.C. (1996) *Albert Camus, Frantz Fanon, and French Algeria: The Colonial Experience and the Philosophy of Revolt*, MA Thesis, University of Montana.

Kassim, S. (2019) "The Museum is the Master's House: An Open Letter to Tristram Hunt", *Medium*, viewed 18 October 2020, https://medium.com/@sumayakassim/the-museum-is-the-masters-house-an-open-letter-to-tristram-hunt-e72d75a891c8

Kerry, S. (2014) "Sistergirls/Brotherboys: The Status of Indigenous Transgender Australians", *International Journal of Transgenderism*, Vol. 15, No. 3–4, pp. 173–186.

Kerry, S. (2017) *Trans Dilemmas Living in Australia's Remote Areas in Aboriginal Communities*, Routledge, London.

Kessaris, T. (2006) "About Being Mununga (Whitefulla): Making Covert Group Racism Visible", *Journal of Community & Applied Social Psychology*, Vol. 16, No. 5, pp. 347–362.

Kincheloe, J.L. & Steinberg, S. (2008) "Indigenous Knowledges in Education: Complexities, Dangers, and Profound Benefits", in N.K. Denzin, Y.S. Lincoln & L.T. Smith (eds) *Handbook of Critical and Indigenous Methodologies*, SAGE, Los Angeles, pp. 135–156.

Kingsley, J.T., Townsend, M. & Hendersen-Wilson, C. (2013) "Exploring Aboriginal People's Connection to Country to Strengthen Human-nature Theoretical Perspectives", *Ecological Health: Society, Ecology and Health*, Emerald Group Publishing, Bingley, UK.

Kinnane, S. (2002) "Recurring Visions of Australindia", in A. Gaynor, M. Trinca & A. Haebich (eds), *Country: Visions of Land and People in Western Australia*, Western Australian Museum, Perth, WA, pp. 21–23.

Kleiner, R. (2009) "Norfolk Island Plaiters", *2899 Magazine: Norfolk Island Lifestyle Magazine*, Vol. 2, Issues 1, pp. 19–25.

Koch, T. (2011) "Call to Target 'Lateral Violence'", *The Australian*, 6 March, viewed 25 March 2019, https://login.ezproxy.utas.edu.au/login?url=http://search.ebscohost.com/login.aspx?direct=true&db=rps&AN=201106031006323213&site=eds-live

Kong, T.S., Mahoney, D. & Plummer, K. (2002) "Queering the Interview", in J.F. Gubrium & J.A. Holstein (eds), *Handbook of Interview Research*, Sage, Thousand Oaks, pp. 239–258.

Kovach, M. (2009) *Indigenous Methodologies*, University of Toronto Press, Toronto, Canada.

Kovach, M. (2010a) "Conversational Method in Indigenous Research", *First Peoples Child & Family Review*, Vol. 5, No. 1, pp. 40–48.

Kovach, M. (2010b) *Indigenous Methodologies: Characteristics, Conversations, and Contexts*, University of Toronto Press, Toronto.

Kovach, M. (2011) *Indigenous Methodologies and Modified Grounded Theory Method*, PowerPoint slides, Summer Institute in Program Evaluation Winnipeg, Manitoba, 13 July, viewed 17 October 2019, http://www.thesummerinstitute.ca/wp-content/uploads/Indigenous-Methodologies.pdf

Kubota, R. (2019) "Confronting Epistemological Racism, Decolonizing Scholarly Knowledge: Race and Gender in Applied Linguistics", *Applied Linguistics*, Vol. 41, No. 5, pp. 712–732.

Kukutai, T. & Cormack, D. (2020) "'Pushing the Space': Data Sovereignty and Self-Determination in Aotearoa NZ", in M. Walter, T. Kukutai, S. Russo Carroll & D. Lonebear-Rodriguez (eds) *Indigenous Data Sovereignty and Policy*, Routledge, London, pp. 20–35.

Kunnie, J. & Goduka, N. (eds) (2006) *Indigenous Peoples' Wisdom and Power Affirming Our Knowledge Through Narratives*, Ashgate Publishing, Hampshire, UK.

Kusch, L. (2019) "'It's Hopeless': Prof Who Called for U of M Leadership Overhaul Resigns", *Winnipeg Free Press* 5 February 2019, viewed 23 October 2020, https://www.winnipegfreepress.com/local/Prof-who-called-for-U-of-M-leadership-overhaul-resigns-505387991.html#:~:text=Dr.,18

Kynard, C. (2015) "Teaching While Black: Witnessing and Countering Disciplinary Whiteness, Racial Violence, and University Race-Management", *LICS Literacy in Composition Studies*, Vol. 3, No. 1, pp. 1–20.

Lambie, J. (2016) Additional Comments from Senator Jacqui Lambie, Commonwealth Funding of Indigenous Tasmania, Senate Committee Findings, Parliament of Australia, Parliamentary Business, 28 November, viewed 12 May 2020, https://www. aph.gov.au/Parliamentary_Business/Committees/Senate/Finance_and_Public_ Administration/IndigenousTasmanians/Report/d01

Lambert-Pennington, K. (2012) "'Real Blackfellas': Constructions and Meanings of Urban Indigenous Identity", *Transforming Anthropology*, Vol. 20, No. 2, pp. 131–145.

Langton, M. (2002) "The Edge of the Sacred, the Edge of Death: Sensual Inscriptions", in B. David & W. Meredith (eds), *Inscribed Landscapes: Marking and Making Place*, University of Hawaii Press, Hawaii, pp. 253–269.

Langton, M. (2003) "The 'Wild', the Market and the Native: Indigenous People Face New Forms of Global Colonization", in W.M. Adams & M. Mulligan (eds), *Decolonizing Nature Strategies for Conservation in a Post-Colonial Era*, Earthscan Publications, London, pp. 52–107.

Langton, M. (2008) "The End to Big-Men Politics", *Griffith Review*, No. 2, pp. 11–38.

Latour, B. (1993) *We Have Never Been Modern*, Harvard University Press, Cambridge.

Latour, B. (2004) "Why Has Critique Run Out of Steam? From Matters of Fact to Matters of Concern", *Critical Inquiry*, Winter 2004, University of Chicago Press, pp. 225–248.

Lavallee, L. (2019) "Recommendations and Thoughts Regarding Indigenous Governance and Matter in Academia and UofM", *Indigenous Resurgence and Insurgence*, viewed 23 October 2020, https://lynnflavallee.home.blog/2019/01/03/recommendations-and-thoughts-regarding-indigenious-governance-and-matters-in-academia-and-uofm/

Lave, R., Wilson, M.W., Barron, E.S., Biermann, C., Carey, M.A., Duvall, C.S., Johnson, L., Lane, K.M., McClintock, N., Munroe, D., Pain, R., Proctor, J., Rhoads, B.L., Robertson, M.M., Rossi, J., Sayre, N.F., Simon, G., Tadaki, M. & Van Dyke, C. (2014) "Intervention: Critical Physical Geography", *Canadian Geographer*, Vol. 58, No. 1, pp. 1–10.

Law, J. & Lien, M.E. (2013) "Slippery: Field Notes in Empirical Ontology", *Social Studies of Science*, Vol. 43, No. 3, pp. 363–378.

Lee, E. (2015) "Green Glitter Hides Cultural Truth", *The Mercury*, 24 January, viewed 15 March 2018, http://www.themercury.com.au/news/opinion/saturday-soapbox-green-glitter-hides-cultural-truth/news-story/cda2398165796569f570e402a729801a

Lee, E. (2016a) "Protected Areas, Country and Value: The Nature-Culture Tyranny of the IUCN's Protected Area Guidelines for Indigenous Australians", *Antipode*, Vol. 48, No. 2, pp. 355–374.

Lee, E. (2016b) "Aboriginal Cultural Heritage Protection in Tasmania: The Failure of Rights, the Restorative Potential of Historical Resilience", in P.F. McGrath (ed), *The*

Right to Protect Sites: Indigenous Cultural Heritage Management in the Era of Native Title, AIATSIS Research Publications, Canberra, pp. 315–341.

Lee, E. (2017) "Establishing Joint Management Processes and Models for Tasmania's Protected Areas", PhD thesis, University of Tasmania.

Lee, E. (2019) "We 'Love-Bombed' the Tasmanian Government to Win Indigenous Rights", *ABC News*, 13 June 2019, viewed 12 May 2020, https://www.abc.net.au/news/2019-06-13/winning-indigenous-aboriginal-rights-in-tasmania/11202128

Lee, E. (2020) "A Long Journey Home", Inside Story, viewed 8 April 2021, https://insidestory.org.au/the-long-journey-home/

Lee, R. & Brotheridge, C. (2006) "When Prey Turn Predatory: Workplace Bullying as a Predictor of Counter Aggression/Bullying, Coping, and Wellbeing", *European Journal of Work and Organizational Psychology*, Vol. 15. No. 3, pp. 352–377.

Lehman, G. (2006) "The Palawa Voice", *The Companion to Tasmanian History*, Centre for Tasmanian Historical Studies, University of Tasmania, Hobart, viewed 27 March 2019, http://www.utas.edu.au/library/companion_to_tasmanian_history/P/Palawa%20Voice.htm

Liljeblad, J. & Verschuuren, B. (eds) (2019) *Indigenous Perspectives on Sacred Natural Sites Culture, Governance and Conservation*, Routledge, London.

Little Bear, L. (2000) "Jagged Worldviews Colliding", in M. Battiste (ed), *Reclaiming Indigenous Voice and Vision*, University of British Columbia Press, Vancouver, pp. 77–85.

Lonetree, A. (2012) *Decolonizing Museums: Representing Native America in National and Tribal Museums*, The University of North Carolina Press, Chapel Hill.

Luciano, D. & Chen, M.Y. (2015) "Has the Queer Ever Been Human?", *Journal of Lesbian and Gay Studies*, Vol. 21, No. 2–3, pp. iv–207.

Lynch, C. (2017) "The Role of Art in Decolonisation", *Artsource*, viewed 18 October 2020, http://www.artsource.net.au/Magazine/Articles/The-Role-of-Art-in-Decolonisation#_edn8

Madley, B. (2008) "From Terror to Genocide: Britain's Tasmanian Penal Colony and Australia's History Wars", *Journal of British Studies*, Vol. 47, No. 1, pp. 77–106.

Maher, P. (1999) "A Review of 'Traditional' Aboriginal Health Beliefs", *Australian Journal of Rural Health*, Vol. 7, pp. 229–236.

Mahuika, N. (2009) "Revitalizing Te Ika-a-Maui", *New Zealand Journal of History*, Vol. 43, No. 2, pp. 133–149.

Malagon, M.C., Huber, L.P. & Velez, V.N. (2009) "Our Experiences, Our Methods: Using Grounded Theory to Inform a Critical Race Theory Methodology", *Seattle Journal for Social Justice*, Vol. 8, Issue 1, Article 10.

Malcolm, L.W.G. (1920) "Short Notes on the Inhabitants of Cape Barren Island, Bass Strait, Tasmania", *Royal Anthropological Institute of Great Britain and Ireland*, Vol. 20, pp. 145–149.

Mallett, M. (2001) *My Past – Their Future: Stories from Cape Barren Island*, Blubber Head Press, Tasmania.

Malsbary, C. (2008) "Review: Decolonizing Methodologies: Research and Indigenous Peoples by Tuhiwai Smith", *InterActions: UCLA Journal of Education and Information Studies*, Vol. 4, Issue 2.

Manne, R. (2003) *Whitewash on Keith Windschuttle's Fabrication of Aboriginal History*, Schwartz Publishing, Melbourne.

Manokha, I. (2018) "Surveillance, Panopticism and Self-Discipline in the Digital Age", *Surveillance and Society*, Vol. 16, No. 2, pp. 219–237.

Maracle, L. (1996) *I am Woman: A Native Perspective on Sociology and Feminism*, Press Gang Publishers, Vancouver.

Marks, K. (2013) "Channelling Mannalargenna: Surviving, Belonging, Challenging, Enduring", in J. Schultz & N. Cica (eds), *Griffith Review*, No. 39, pp. 174–192.

Martin, K. (2003) "Ways of Knowing, Ways of Being and Ways of Doing: A Theoretical Framework and Methods for Indigenous Research and Indigenist Research", *Journal of Australian Studies*, Vol. 27, No. 76, pp. 203–214.

Martin, K. & Mirraboopa, B. (2003) "Ways of Knowing, Being and Doing: A Theoretical Framework and Methods for Indigenous and Indigenist Research", *Journal of Australian Studies*, Vol. 27, No. 76, pp. 203–214.

Marwick, E. (2012) "The Public Domain: Social Surveillance in Everyday Life", *Surveillance and Society*, Vol. 9, No. 4, pp. 378–393.

Matson-Green, V. (1994) "Pallawah Women: Their Historical Contribution to Our Survival, *yah taweh tiwah warraweh – mena pallawah trouwerner lowanna* (Greetings from the Ancestors – I am an Aboriginal Tasmanian Woman), Part II: Leaders Among Pallawah Women", in P. Brock (ed), *Women, Rites and Sites*, AIATSIS, Canberra, pp. 65–69.

Maxwell, R. (2018) "Yas Queen! Ladies Step It Up for Miss First Nation, Stay True to Yourself", *Koori Mail*, 31 October, pp. 30–31, viewed 28 October 2020, https://koorimail.com/

Maynard, F. (1985) "The Settlement of Cape Barren Island", *Aboriginal and Islander Health Worker Journal*, Vol. 9, No. 4, pp. 3–5.

McCormick, A., Fisher, K. & Brierley, G. (2015) "Quantitative Assessment of the Relationships among Ecological, Morphological and Aesthetic Values in a River Rehabilitation Initiative", *Journal of Environmental Management*, Vol. 153, No. 1, pp. 60–67.

McGrath, A. (2015) "Deep Histories in Time, or Crossing the Great Divide?", in J. McGrath & M. Jebb (eds), *Long History, Deep Time: Deepening the Histories of Place*, ANU Press and Aboriginal History, Canberra, ACT, pp. 1–32.

McGrath, A. & Jebb, M. (2015) *Long History, Deep Time: Deepening the Histories of Place*, ANU Press and Aboriginal History, Canberra, ACT.

McKemmish, S., Iacovino, L., Ketelaar, E., Castan, M. & Russell, L. (2011) "Resetting Relationships: Archives and Indigenous Human Rights in Australia", *Archives & Manuscripts*, Vol. 39, No. 1, pp. 107–144.

McLaughlin, J. & Whatman, S. (2011) "The Potential of Critical Race Theory in Decolonizing University Curricula", *Asia Pacific Journal of Education*, Vol. 31, No. 4, pp. 365–377.

McLaughlin, J. & Whatman, S. (2011) "The Potential of Critical Race Theory in Decolonizing University Curricula", *Asia Pacific Journal of Education*, Vol. 31, No. 4, pp. 365–377.

McQuire, A. (2020) "We Must Bear Witness to Black Deaths in Our Own Country", 31 May 2020, *Canberra Times*, viewed 18 October 2020, https://www.canberratimes.com.au/story/6775418/we-must-bear-witness-to-black-deaths-in-our-own-country/

Mead, H.M. & Grove, N. (2004) *Nga pepeha a nga tipuna: The Sayings of the Ancestors*, Victoria University Press, New Zealand.

Melville, A. (2006) "Mapping the Wilderness: Toponymic Constructions of Cradle Mountain/Lake St Clair National Park, Tasmania, Australia", *Cartographica*, Vol. 41, No. 3, pp. 229–246.

Memmott, P., Stacy, R., Chambers, C. & Keys, C. (2001) "Violence in Indigenous Communities: Full Report", Canberra: Attorney-General's Department Crime Prevention Branch, viewed 19 October 2019, https://webarchive.nla.gov.au/awa/20050719160636/http://www.ag.gov.au/agd/www/rwpattach.nsf/viewasattachmentPersonal/5210C36F7DE2A926CA256B4300022F10/$file/violenceindigenous.pdf

Memon, P. & Kirk, N. (2012) "Role of Indigenous Māori People in Collaborative Water Governance in Aotearoa/New Zealand", *Journal of Environmental Planning and Management*, Vol. 55, No. 7, pp. 941–959.

Memon, A. & Skelton, P. (2007) "Institutional Arrangements and Planning Practices to Allocate Freshwater Resources in New Zealand: A Way Forward", *New Zealand Journal of Environmental Law*, Vol. 11, pp. 241–277.

Mercredi, M. (2006) *Morningstar: A Warrior's Spirit*, Coteau Books, Regina, Saskatchewan.

Mertens, D.M., Cram, F. & Chilisa B. (eds) (2013) *Indigenous Pathways into Social Research Voices of a New Generation*, Routledge, London.

Mita, M. (1989) "Mereta Mita On. . ." *New Zealand Listener*, 14 October 1989, p. 30.

Mol, A. (2002) *The Body Multiple*, Duke University Press, NC.

Monaghan, J. (2013) "Settler Governmentality and Racializing Surveillance in Canada's North-West", *Canadian Journal of Sociology*, Vol. 38, No. 4, p. 487.

Monture-Angus, P. (1995) *Thunder in My Soul: A Mohawk Woman Speaks*, Fernwood Publishing, Halifax, Nova Scotia.

Moreton-Robinson, A. (2003) "I Still Call Australia Home: Indigenous Belonging and Place in a White Postcolonising Society", in S. Ahmed (ed), *Uprootings/Regroundings: Questions of Home and Migration*, Berg Publishing, Oxford, UK, pp. 23–40.

Moreton-Robinson, A. (2004) "Whiteness, Epistemology and Indigenous Representation", in A. Moreton-Robinson (ed), *Whitening Race: Essays in Social and Cultural Criticism*, Aboriginal Studies Press, Australia, pp. 75–88.

Moreton-Robinson, A. (2011) "The White Man's Burden", *Australian Feminist Studies*, Vol. 26, No. 70, pp. 413–431.

Moreton-Robinson, A. (2013) "Towards an Australian Indigenous Women's Standpoint Theory", *Australian Feminist Studies*, Vol. 28, No. 78, pp. 331–347.

Moreton-Robinson, A. (2015) *The White Possessive: Property, Power, and Indigenous Sovereignty*, University of Minnesota Press, Minneapolis.

Morris, L. (2017) "The Last Indigenous Tasmanian", *National Geographic*, viewed 6 April 2019, https://www.nationalgeographic.com.au/australia/the-last-indigenous-tasmanian.aspx

Mortimer-Sandilands, C. & Erickson, B. (2010) "Introduction: A Genealogy of Queer Ecologies", in C. Mortimer-Sandilands & B. Erickson (eds), *Queer Ecologies: Sex, Nature, Politics, Desire*, Indiana University Press, Bloomington, IN, pp. 1–50.

Moses, A.D. (2010) "Time, Indigeneity, and Peoplehood: The Postcolony in Australia", *Postcolonial Studies*, Vol. 13, No. 1, pp. 9–32.

Mould, S.A., Fryirs, K. & Howitt, R. (2018) "Practicing Sociogeomorphology: Relationships and Dialog in River Research and Management", *Society and Natural Resources*, Vol. 31, No. 1, pp. 106–120.

Moulton, K. (2018) "I Can Still Hear Them Calling. Echoes of My Ancestors", in K. Garcia-Anton (ed), *Sovereign Words: Indigenous Art, Curation and Criticism*, Office for Contemporary Art Norway, Valiz, Amsterdam, pp. 197–214.

Mühlhäuser, P. (2015) *Expert Report on the Distinctiveness of Norfolk Islander Ethnicity, Culture and the Norf'k Language (Norfolk Island – South Pacific)*, Professor Peter Mühlhäuser.

Mulder, R., Pouwelse, M., Lodewijkx, H. & Bownam, C. (2013) "Workplace Mobbing and Bystanders' Helping Behaviour Towards Victims: The Role of Gender, Perceived Responsibility and Anticipated Stigma by Association", *International Journal of Psychology*, Vol. 49, No. 4, pp. 304–312.

Muldoon, P. & Schaap, A. (2012) "Aboriginal Sovereignty and the Politics of Reconciliation: The Constituent Power of the Aboriginal Embassy in Australia", *Environment and Planning D: Society and Space*, Vol. 30, pp. 534–550.

Mungwini, P. (2013) "Surveillance and Cultural Panopticism: Situating Foucault in African Modernities", *South African Journal of Philosophy*, Vol. 31, No. 2, pp. 340–353.

Munro, K.L. (2020) "Why 'Blak' not Black?: Artist Destiny Deacon and the Origins of This Word", *NITV*, viewed 29 June 2019, https://www.sbs.com.au/nitv/article/2020/05/07/why-blak-not-black-artist-destiny-deacon-and-origins-word-1

Mustonen, T. (2013) "Rebirth of Indigenous Arctic Nations and Polar Resource Management: Critical Perspectives from Siberia and Sámi Areas of Finland", *Biodiversity*, Vol. 14, No.1, pp. 19–27.

Mustonen, T. (2015) "Communal Visual Histories to Detect Environmental Change in Northern Areas: Examples of Emerging North American and Eurasian Practices", *Ambio*, Vol. 44, pp. 766–777.

Mustonen, T. & Feodoroff, P. (2018) "Skolt Sámi and Atlantic Salmon Collaborative Management of Näätämö Watershed, Finland as a Case of Indigenous Evaluation and Knowledge in the Eurasian Arctic", in F. Cram, K.A. Tibbetts & J. LaFrance (eds), *Indigenous Evaluation. New Directions for Evaluation*, Vol. 159, pp. 107–119.

Mutu, M. (2018) "Behind the Smoke and Mirrors of the Treaty of Waitangi Claims Settlement Process in New Zealand: No Prospect for Justice and Reconciliation for Māori Without Constitutional Transformation", *Journal of Global Ethics*, Vol. 14, No. 2, pp. 208–221.

Mutu, M. (2019) "The Treaty Claims Settlement Process in New Zealand and Its Impact on Māori", *Land*, Vol. 8, p. 152 (online journal).

Nakata, M. (2007) *Disciplining the Savages: Savaging the Disciplines*, Aboriginal Studies Press, Canberra.

Nakata, N., Nakata, V., Keech, S. & Bolt, R. (2012) "Decolonial Goals and Pedagogies for Indigenous Studies", *Decolonization: Indigeneity, Education & Society*, Vol. 1, No. 1, pp. 120–140.

Namie, G. & Namie, R. (2009) *The Bully at Work: What You Can Do to Stop the Hurt and Reclaim Your Dignity on the Job*, Second Edition, Sourcebooks, Naperville.

National Indigenous Unit of the National Tertiary Education Union (NTEU) (2011) *I'm Not a Racist But. . .: Report on Cultural Respect, Racial Discrimination, Lateral Violence and Related Policy at Australia's Universities*, National Tertiary Education Union, Melbourne.

Ndlovu-Gatsheni, S. (2017) "Decolonising Research Methodology Must Include Undoing Its Dirty History", *The Conversation*, 27 September, viewed 13 March 2019, https://theconversation.com/decolonising-research-methodology-must-include-undoing-its-dirty-history-83912

Neidjie, B., Davis, S. & Fox, A. (1985) *Kakadu Man Bill Neidjie*, Mybrood P/L, Allan Fox & Associates, NSW.

Nettelbeck, A. & Smandych, R. (2010) "Policing Indigenous Peoples on Two Colonial Frontiers: Australia's Mounted Police and Canada's North-West Mounted Police", *Australian & New Zealand Journal of Criminology*, Vol. 43, No. 2, pp, 356–375.

New Zealand Government (2007) *Vision Mātauranga: Unlocking the Innovation Potential of Māori Knowledge, Resources and People*, Ministry of Research, Science and Technology, Wellington, New Zealand.

Nicholas, C.L. (2006) "Disciplinary-Interdisciplinary GLBTQ (Identity) Studies and Hecht's Layering Perspective", *Communication Quarterly*, Vol. 5, No. 3, pp. 305–330.

Nicholls, R. (2009) "Research and Indigenous Participation: Critical Reflexive Methods", *International Journal of Social Research Methodology*, Vol. 12, No. 2, pp. 117–126.

Nichols, V. (2009) "Frontispiece", in Tasmanian Museum and Art Gallery, *tayenebe Tasmanian Aboriginal Women's Fibre Work*, Tasmanian Museum and Art Gallery, Hobart.

Nichols, V. (2017) *Fibres, Sea People, Sharing Knowledge, The Orb*, Tasmanian Government Department of Education, viewed 18 January 2019, https://www.theorb.tas.gov.au/

Nietschmann, B.Q. (1992) *The Interdependence of Biological and Cultural Diversity*, Centre for World Indigenous Studies, Occasional Paper 21, Kenmore, WA.

NIWA. (2014) *Maniapoto Priorities for the Restoration of the Waipā River Catchment*, NIWA, Wellington.

Ormond-Parker, L. & Sloggett, R. (2012) "Local Archives and Community Collecting in the Digital Age", *Archival Science*, Vol. 12, No. 2, pp. 191–212.

Ortley, J. (2005) "Decolonizing Methodologies: Research and Indigenous Peoples (review)", *The American Indian Quarterly*, Vol. 29, No. 1&2, pp. 285–288.

O'Sullivan, D. (2017) *Indigeneity a Politics of Potential Australia, Fiji and New Zealand*, Policy Press, University of Bristol, UK.

Page, S. & Asmar, C. (2008) "Beneath the Teaching Iceberg: Exposing the Hidden Support Dimensions of Indigenous Academic Work", *The Australian Journal of Indigenous Education*, Vol. 37 (Supplement), pp. 109–117.

Paradies, Y. (2006) "A Systematic Review of Empirical Research on Self-Reported Racism and Health", *International Journal of Epidemiology*, Vol. 35, No. 4, pp. 888–901.

Paradies, Y. (2018) "Racism and Indigenous Health", in D. McQueen (ed), *Oxford Research Encyclopaedia of Global Public Health*, viewed 17 October 2019, https://oxfordre.com/publichealth/view/10.1093/acrefore/9780190632366.001.0001/acrefore-9780190632366-e-86

Paradies, Y. & Cunningham, J. (2009) "Experiences of Racism Among Urban Indigenous Australians: Findings from the DRUID Study", *Ethnic and Racial Studies*, Vol. 32, No. 3, pp. 548–576.

Parsons, M. & Nalau, J. (2016) "Historical Analogies as Tools in Understanding Transformation", *Global Environmental Change*, Vol. 38, pp. 82–96.

Parsons, M., Nalau, J., Fisher, K. & Brown, C. (2019) "Disrupting Path Dependency: Making Room for Indigenous Knowledge in River Management", *Global Environmental Change*, Vol. 56, pp. 95–113.

Paterson-Shallard, H., Fisher, K., Parsons, M. & Makey, L. (2020) "Holistic Approaches to River Restoration in Aotearoa New Zealand", *Environmental Science and Policy*, Vol. 106, pp. 250–259.

Paton, R. (2015) "The Mutability of Time and Space as a Means of Healing History in an Australian Aboriginal Community", in J. McGrath & M. Jebb (eds), *Long History, Deep Time: Deepening the Histories of Place*, ANU Press and Aboriginal History, Canberra, ACT, pp. 67–82.

Pechenkina, E., Kowal, E. & Paradies, Y. (2011) "Indigenous Australian Students' Participation Rates in Higher Education: Exploring the Role of Universities", *The Australian Journal of Indigenous Education*, Vol. 40, pp. 59–68.

Pecl, G.T., Araújo, M.B., Bell, J.D., Blanchard, J., Bonebrake, T.C. . . . Williams, S.E. (2017) "Biodiversity Redistribution Under Climate Change: Impacts on Ecosystems and Human Well-Being", *Science*, Vol. 355, Issue 6332, eaai9214, viewed 10 October 2020 https://science.sciencemag.org/content/355/6332/eaai9214

Peeters, B. (2004) "Tall Poppies and Egalitarianism in Australian Discourse: From Key Word to Cultural Value", *English World-Wide*, Vol. 25, No. 1, pp. 1–25.

Peeters, B. (2015) "Tall Poppies in the Land Down Under: An Applied Entholinguistic Approach", *International Journal of Language and Culture*, Vol. 2, No. 2, pp. 219–243.

Perry, J. (1979) "The Problem of the Essential Indexical", *Noûs*, Vol. 13, No. 3, pp. 3–21.

Perso, T.F. & Hayward, C. (2015) *Teaching Indigenous Students: Cultural Awareness and Classroom Strategies for Improving Learning Outcomes*, Allen & Unwin, Crows Nest.

Pete, S. (2016) "Commentary 100 Ways: Indigenizing & Decolonize Academic Programs", *Aboriginal Policy Studies*, Vol. 6, No. 1, pp. 81–89.

Petersen, D., Barber, M., Zelin, N. & Yarbrough, E. (2020) "Lesbian the L in LGBTQ² IAPA", in P. Levounis & E. Yarbrough (eds), *Pocket Guide to LGBTQ Mental Health Understanding the Spectrum of Gender and Sexuality*, American Psychiatric Association Publishing, Washington, DC, pp. 1–16.

Phillips, G. (2009) "Healing Identity in Contemporary Australia: What Is a Real/Traditional/Grassroots Aborigine?", *Australian Institute of Aboriginal and Torres Strait Islander Studies Seminar Series*, Canberra, 18 May 2009, viewed 9 May 2020, http://www.vimeo.com/moogaloop.swf?clip_id=9173079

Pihama, L., Greensill, H., Manuirirangi, H. & Simmond, N. (2019) *He Kare-ā-roto: a Selection of Whakataukī Related to Māori Emotions*, Te Kotahi Research Institute, Hamilton, Aotearoa/New Zealand, viewed 1 October 2019, https://issuu.com/tekotahi/docs/he_kare-aa-roto

Pihama, L., Reynolds, P., Smith, C., Reid, J., Smith L.T. & Te Nana, R. (2014) "Positioning Historical Trauma Theory Within Aotearoa New Zealand", *AlterNative: An International Journal of Indigenous Peoples*, Vol. 10, No. 3, pp. 248–262.

Pimbert, M.P. & Borrini-Feyerabend, G. (2019) *Nourishing Life – Territories of Life and Food Sovereignty*, Policy Brief of the ICCA Consortium No. 6., ICCA Consortium, Centre for Agroecology, Water and Resilience at Coventry University and CENESTA, Tehran.

Plomley, N.J.B. (ed) (1966) *Friendly Mission: The Tasmanian Journals and Papers of George Augustus Robinson, 1829–1834*, Tasmanian Historical Research Association, Hobart, Tasmania.

Plomley, N.J.B. (1976) *A Word-list of the Tasmanian Aboriginal Languages*, in association with the Government of Tasmania, Launceston, Tasmania.

Plomley, N.J.B. (1983) *The Baudin Expedition and the Tasmanian Aborigines 1802*, Blubber Head Press, Hobart.

Plomley, N.J.B. (1987) *Weep in Silence: A History of the Flinders Island Aboriginal Settlement*, Blubber Head Press, Hobart.

Plumwood, V. (1991) "Nature, Self, and Gender: Feminism, Environmental Philosophy, and the Critique of Rationalism", *Hypatia*, Vol. 6, No. 1, pp. 3–27.

Plumwood, V. (2003) "Decolonizing Relationships with Nature", in W. Adams & M. Mulligan (eds), *Decolonizing Nature Strategies for Conservation in a Post-Colonial Era*, Earthscan Publications, London, pp. 51–78.

Plumwood, V. (2006) "The Concept of a Cultural Landscape: Nature, Culture and Agency in the Land", *Ethics and the Environment*, Vol. 11, No. 2, pp. 115–150.

Plumwood, V. (2010) "Nature and the Active Voice", *Australian Humanities Review*, Issue 46, pp. 113–129.

Poll, M. (2015) "Provenance and Repatriation", *Medium*, viewed 18 October 2020, https://medium.com/@mattpoll2/provenance-and-repatriation-90397ffeb00a

Pukui, M.K. & Varez, D. (1983) *Ōlelo Noʻeau: Hawaiian Proverbs & Poetical Sayings*, Bishop Museum Press, Honolulu, Hawaiʻi.

Pulani Louis, R. (2007) "Can you Hear Me Now? Voices From the Margin: Using Indigenous Methodologies in Geographic Research", *Geographical Research*, Vol. 45, No. 2, pp. 130–139.

Purcell, L. (2002) *Black Chicks Talking*, Hodder, Sydney.

Rahaman, M.M. & Varis, O. (2005) "Integrated Water Resources Management: Evolution, Prospects and Future Challenges", *Sustainability: Science, Practice and Policy*, Vol. 1, No. 1, pp. 1–8.

Ratcliff, P. (1997) "Tasmanian Aboriginality: The Persistence of a Tasmanian Aboriginal Community into the 21st Century: A Non/Aboriginal Perspective", *Papers and Proceedings: Tasmanian Historical Research Association*, Vol. 44, No. 3, pp. 174–186.

Razack, S. (2015) *Dying from Improvement: Inquests and Inquiries into Indigenous Deaths in Custody*, University of Toronto Press, Toronto.

Reimerson, E. (2013) "Between Nature and Culture: Exploring Space for Indigenous Agency in the Convention on Biological Diversity", *Environmental Politics*, Vol. 22, No. 6, pp. 992–1009.

Reynolds, H. (1995) *Fate of a Free People*, Penguin Books, Melbourne.

Reynolds, H. (2006) *The Other Side of the Frontier: Aboriginal Resistance to the European Invasion of Australia*, University of New South Wales Press.

Reynolds, H. (2008) *Nowhere People*, Penguin, Camberwell, Victoria.

Reynolds, H. (2012) *A History of Tasmania*, Cambridge University Press.

Reynolds, P. (2019) "Bounty Hat", *The Encyclopedia of Crafts in Asia Pacific Region (APR) Traditional Handmade Products*, viewed 13 March 2019, https://encyclocraftsapr.com/bounty-hat/#

Richardson, J. & McCord, L.B. (2001) "Are Workplace Bullies Sabotaging Your Ability to Compete? Learn to Identify and Extinguish Problem Behavior", *Graziadio Business Review*, Vol. 4, No. 4, (online journal), viewed 17 October 2019, https://gbr.pepperdine.edu/2010/08/are-workplace-bullies-sabotaging-your-ability-to-compete/

Rigney, L. (1999) "Internationalization of an Indigenous Anticolonial Cultural Critique of Research Methodologies: A Guide to Indigenist Research Methodology and Its Principles", *Wicazo Sa Review*, Vol. 14, No. 2, pp. 109–121.

Rigney, L. (2001) "A First Perspective of Indigenous Australian Participation in Science: Framing Indigenous Research Towards Indigenous Australian Intellectual Sovereignty", *Kaurna Higher Education Journal*, Vol 7. pp. 1–13.

Rigney, L. (2006) "Indigenist Research and Aboriginal Australia", in J. Kunnie & N. Goduka (eds), *Indigenous Peoples' Wisdom and Power: Affirming Our Knowledge Through Narratives*, Ashgate, Aldershot, UK, pp. 32–48.

RiverOfLife, M., Poelina, A., Bagnall, D., & Lim, M. (2020) "Recognizing the Martuwarra's First Law Right to Life as a Living Ancestral Being", *Transnational Environmental Law*, Vol. 9, No. 3, pp. 541–568.

Roberts, S., Demarco, R. & Griffin, M. (2009) "The Effect of Oppressed Group Behaviours on the Culture of the Nursing Workplace: A Review of the Evidence and Interventions for Change", *Journal of Nursing Management*, No. 3, pp. 288–293.

Robertson, B., Demosthenous, C. & Demosthenous, H. (2005) "Stories from the Aboriginal Women of the Yarning Circle: When Cultures Collide", *Hecate Press*, The University of Queensland Australia, Brisbane, pp. 34–44.

Robinson, H. (2012) "Remembering Things Differently: Museums, Libraries and Archives as Memory Institutions and the Implications for Convergence", *Museum Management and Curatorship*, Vol. 27, No. 4, pp. 413–429.

Robinson, S. (1994) "The Aboriginal Embassy: An Account of the Protests of 1972", *Aboriginal History*, Vol. 18, No. 1, pp. 49–63.

Roithmayr, D. (1999) "Introduction to Critical Race Theory in Educational Research and Praxis", in L. Parker, D. Dehyle & S. Villenas (eds), *Race Is. . .Race Isn't: Critical Race Theory and Qualitative Studies in Education*, Westview, Boulder, CO, pp. 1–6.

Rose, D.B. (1996) *Nourishing Terrains: Australian Aboriginal Views of Landscape and Wilderness*, Australian Heritage Commission, Canberra, ACT.

Rose, D.B. (2000) *Dingo Makes Us Human*, Australian National University Press, Canberra.

Rose, D.B. (2004) *Reports from a Wild Country*, UNSW Press, Sydney, NSW.

Ross, D. (2017) "'Black Country, White Wilderness': Conservation, Colonialism and Conflict in Tasmania", *Journal for Undergraduate Ethnography*, Vol. 1, pp. 1–23.

Ross, L. (2009) "From the 'F' Word to Indigenous/Feminisms", *Wicaz Sa Review*, Vol. 24, No. 2, pp. 39–52.

Royal Australian College of General Practitioners [RACGP] (2014) *Abuse and Violence: Working with Our Patients in General Practice*, Fourth Edition, RACGP, Melbourne, viewed 17 October, https://www.racgp.org.au/clinical-resources/clinical-guidelines/key-racgp-guidelines/view-all-racgp-guidelines/white-book

Royal Commission into Aboriginal Deaths in Custody [RCIADIC] (1998) *Final Report*, Australian Government Publishing Services, Canberra, viewed 17 October 2019, http://www.austlii.edu.au/au/other/IndigLRes/rciadic/

Rumsey, A. (1994) "The Dreaming, Human Agency and Inscriptive Practice", *Oceania*, Vol. 65, No. 2, pp. 116–130.

Ruru, J. (2013) "Indigenous Restitution in Settling Water Claims: The Developing Cultural and Commercial Redress Opportunities in Aotearoa, New Zealand", *Washington International Law Journal*, Vol. 22, No. 2, pp. 311–352.

Ruru, J. (2018) "Listening to Papatūānuku: A Call to Reform Water Law", *Journal of the Royal Society of New Zealand*, Vol. 48, No. 2–3, pp. 215–224.

Russell, L. (2001) *Savage Imaginings: Historical and Contemporary Constructions of Australian Aboriginalities*, Australian Scholarly Publishing, Melbourne, Australia.

Russell, L. (2005) "Indigenous Knowledge and Archives: Accessing Hidden History and Understandings", *Australian Academic and Research Libraries*, Vol. 36, No. 2, pp. 161–171.

Ryan, L. (1996) *The Aboriginal Tasmanians*, Second Edition, Allen & Unwin, NSW.

Ryan, L. (2012) *Tasmanian Aborigines: A History Since 1803*, Allen & Unwin, NSW.

Said, E. (1978) *Orientalism*, Pantheon, New York.

Saito, N.T. (2005) "Race and Decolonization: Whiteness as Property in the American Settler Colonial Project", *Harvard Journal on Racial & Ethnic Justice*, Vol. 31, pp. 31–68.

Salmon, E. (2000) "Kincentric Ecology: Indigenous Perceptions of the Human-Nature Relationship", *Ecological Applications*, Vol. 10, No. 5, pp. 1327–1332.

Salmond, A. (2012) "Ontological Quarrels: Indigeneity, Exclusion and Citizenship in a Relational World", *Anthropological Theory*, Vol. 12, No. 2, pp. 115–141.

Salmond, A. (2014) "Tears of Rangi: Water, Power, and People in New Zealand", *HAU: Journal of Ethnographic Theory*, Vol. 4, No. 3, pp. 285–309.

Salmond, A., Tadaki, M. & Gregory, T. (2014) "Enacting New Freshwater Geographies: Te Awaroa and the Transformative Imagination", *New Zealand Geographer*, Vol. 70, No. 1, pp. 47–55.

Samson, B. (2001) "Irruptions of the Dreamings in Post-Colonial Australia", *Oceania*, Vol. 72, No. 1, pp. 1–32.

Sarra, C. (2006) "Armed for Success", *Griffith REVIEW*, Vol. 11, pp. 78–86, viewed 17 October 2019, https://griffithreview.com/edition-11-getting-smart/armed-for-success

Schnabel, L. (2014) "The Question of Subjectivity in Three Emerging Feminist Science Studies Frameworks: Feminist Postcolonial Science Studies, New Feminist Materialisms, and Queer Ecologies", *Women's Studies International Forum*, Vol. 44, pp. 10–16.

Schultz, T. (2018) "Mapping Indigenous Futures: Decolonising Techno-Colonising Designs", *Strategic Design Journal*, Vol. 11, No. 2, pp. 79–91.

Seamster, L. & Ray, V. (2018) "Against Teleology in the Study of Race: Toward the Abolition of the Progress Paradigm", *Sociological Theory*, Vol. 36, No. 4, pp, 315–342.

Sebag-Montefiore, C. (2016) "Jonathan Jones Unites Indigenous and Settler History in Massive Public Artwork in Sydney", 30 September, 2016, *The Guardian*, viewed 18 October 2020, https://www.theguardian.com/artanddesign/2016/sep/30/lost-in-the-flames-sydneys-garden-palace-resurrected-through-indigenous-eyes

Sedgwick, E.K. (1993) *Tendencies*, Duke University Press, Durham, NC.

Semple, J. (1993) *Bentham's Prison: A Study of the Panopticon Penitentiary*, Clarendon Press, Oxford.

Sentance, N. (2018) "My Ancestors Are in Our Memory Institutions, But Their Voices Are Missing", 6 March 2018, *The Guardian*, viewed on 18 October 2020, https://www.theguardian.com/commentisfree/2018/mar/06/my-ancestors-are-in-our-memory-institutions-but-their-voices-are-missing

Sentance, N. (2019) "Review: Nathan Sentence on Natalie Harkin's Disrupting the Colonial Archive", *Sydney Review of Books*, viewed 18 October 2020, https://sydneyreviewofbooks.com/natalie-harkin-archival-poetics/

Seymour, N. (2015) *Strange Natures Futurity, Empathy, and the Queer Ecological Imagination*, University of Illinois Press, Urbana, Chicago, and Springfield.

Shallcross, L. (2019) *What Is Workplace Mobbing?* Workplace Mobbing Australia, Albany Creek, viewed 17 October 2019, https://workplacemobbing.com.au/#workplace-mobbing

Shallcross, L., Sheehan, M. & Ramsay, S. (2008) "Workplace Mobbing: Experiences in the Public Sector", *International Journal of Organisational Behaviour*, Vol. 13, No. 2, pp. 56–70.

Sheehan, N.W. (2011) "Indigenous Knowledge and Respectful Design: An Evidence-Based Approach", *Design Issues*, Vol. 27, No. 4, pp. 68–80.

Sheridan, J. & Roronhiakewen "He Clears the Sky" Dan Longboat (2006) "The Haudenosaunee Imagination and the Ecology of the Sacred", *Space and Culture*, Vol. 9, pp. 365–381.

Sheridan, J. & Roronhiakewen "He Clears the Sky" Dan Longboat (2014) "Walking Back Into Creation: Environmental Apartheid and the Eternal-Initiating an Indigenous Mind Claim", *Space and Culture*, Vol. 17, pp. 308–324.

Sherwood, J. (2013) "Colonisation – It's Bad for Your Health: The Context of Aboriginal Health", *Contemporary Nurse*, Vol. 46, No. 1, pp. 28–40.

Shine, R. (2017) "Claiming Aboriginality: Have Tasmania's Indigenous Services Been 'Swamped with White People'?" *ABC News*, 1 July 2017, viewed 16 August 2019, https://www.abc.net.au/news/2017-07-01/tasmanias-aboriginality-criteria-relaxation-affecting-services/8670254

Shiva, V. (1995) "Democratising Biology: Reinventing Biology from a Feminist, Ecological and Third World Perspective", in L. Birke & R. Hubbard (eds), *Reinventing Biology*, University of Indiana Press, Bloomington, IN, pp. 50–74.

Simpson, A. (2014) *Mohawk Interruptus: Political Life Across the Borders of Settler States*, Duke University Press, London.

Sissons, J. (2005) *First Peoples: Indigenous Cultures and Their Futures*, Reaktion Book, London.

Smith, A. (1993) "For All Those Who Were Indian in a Former Life", in C. Adams (ed), *Ecofeminism and the Sacred*, Continuum, New York, pp. 168–171.

Smith, A. (1997) "Ecofeminism through an Anticolonial Framework", in K. Warren (ed), *Ecofeminism: Women, Culture, Nature*, Indiana University Press, Bloomington, pp. 21–37.

Smith, A. (2010) "Queer Theory and Native Studies the Heteronormativity of Settler Colonialism", *GLQ: A Journal of Lesbian and Gay Studies*, Duke University Press, Durham, NC, Vol. 16, No. 1–2, pp. 41–68.

Smith, C. (2013) "Becoming a Kaupapa Māori Researcher", in D.M. Mertens, F. Cram & B. Chilisa (eds), *Indigenous Pathways into Social Research Voices of a New Generation*, Routledge, London, UK, pp. 89–99.

Smith, B.R. (2005) "'We Got Our Own Management': Local Knowledge, Government and Development in Cape York Peninsula", *Australian Aboriginal Studies*, Vol. 2, pp. 4–15.

Smith, C. (2000) "How I Became a Queer Heterosexual", in C. Thomas (ed), *Straight with a Twist: Queer Theory and the Subject of Heterosexuality*, Urbana: University of Illinois Press, pp. 60–67.

Smith, L.T. (1999) *Decolonizing Methodologies: Research and Indigenous Peoples*, Zed Books, London.

Smith, L.T. (2004) "Twenty-five Indigenous Projects", in W.K. Carroll (ed), *Critical Strategies for Social Research*, Canadian Scholars' Press, Toronto, pp. 75–90.

Smith, L.T. (2005a) "Building a Research Agenda for Indigenous Epistemologies and Education", *Anthropology and Education Quarterly*, Vol. 36, Issue 1, pp. 93–95.

Smith, L.T. (2005b) "On Tricky Ground: Researching the Native in the Age of Uncertainty", in N.K. Denzin & Y.S. Lincoln (eds), *The Sage Handbook of Qualitative Research*, Sage Publications, pp. 85–107.

Smith, L.T. (2006) "Researching in the Margins: Issues for Māori Researchers a Discussion Paper", Alternative, Vol. 2, No. 1, pp. 4–27.

Smith, L.T. (2007) "The Native and the Neoliberal Down Under: Neoliberalism and 'Endangered Authenticities'", in M, De La Cadena & O. Starn (eds), *Indigenous Experience Today*, Berg, Oxford, pp. 333–354.

Smith, L.T. (2012) *Decolonizing Methodologies: Research and Indigenous Peoples*, Second Edition, Zed Books, London.

Smith, L.T. (2014) "Social Justice, Transformation and Indigenous Methodologies", in R.E. Rinehart, K.N. Barbour & C.C. Pope (eds), *Ethnographic Worldviews: Transformations and Social Justice*, Springer Science + Business Media, pp. 15–20.

Smith, L.T. (2015a) "Kaupapa Māori Research – Some Kaupapa Māori Principles", in L. Pihama & K. South (eds), *Kaupapa Rangahau A Reader: A Collection of Readings from the Kaupapa Maori Research Workshop Series Led*, Te Kotahi Research Institute, pp. 46–52.

Smith, L.T. (2015b) "Decolonizing Knowledge: Toward a Critical Indigenous Research Justice Praxis", in A.J. Jolivétte (ed), *Research Justice Methodologies for Social Change*, Policy Press, University of Bristol, Bristol, pp. 205–210.

Smith, L.T., Tuck, E. & Yang, W. (eds) (2019) *Indigenous Decolonizing Studies in Education Mapping the Long View*, Routledge, New York.

Smith, L.T., Maxwell, T.K., Puke, H. & Temara, P. (2016) "Indigenous Knowledge, Methodology and Mayhem: What is the Role of Methodology in Producing

Indigenous Insights? A Discussion from Mātauranga Māori", *Knowledge Cultures*, Vol. 4, No. 3, pp. 131–156.

Smith, R.R. (2003) "Queer Theory, Gay Movements, and Political Communication", *Journal of Homosexuality*, Vol. 45, No. 2–4, pp. 345–348.

Snipp, M. (2016) "What Does Data Sovereignty Imply: What Does It Look Like?" in T. Kukutai & J. Taylor (eds) *Indigenous Data Sovereignty: Towards an Agenda*, ANU Press, Canberra, pp. 39–56.

Sonn, C., Bishop, B., & Humphries, R. (2000) "Encounters With the Dominant Culture: Voices of Indigenous Students in Mainstream Higher Education", *Australian Psychologist*, Vol. 35, No. 2, pp. 128–135.

Spivak, G. (1988) "Can the Subaltern Speak?", in C. Nelson & L Grossberg (eds), *Marxism and Interpretation of Culture*, University of Illinois Press, Chicago, pp. 271–313.

Spivak, G. (1999) *A Critique of Postcolonial Reason: Toward a History of the Vanishing Present*, Harvard University Press, Cambridge.

St-Denis, N. & Walsh, C. (2016) "Reclaiming My Indigenous Identity and the Emerging Warrior: An Autoethnography", *Journal of Indigenous Social Development*, Vol. 5, No. 1, pp. 1–17.

Stanner, W. (1979) *White Man Got No Dreaming*, Australian National University Press, Canberra.

Stilwell, F. (2017) "Erik Paul: Australian Political Economy of Violence and Non-violence", *Journal of Australian Political Economy*, No. 79, p. 151.

Stone, S. (1991) "The Empire Strikes Back: a Posttranssexual Manifesto", in J. Epstein & K. Straub (eds), *Body Guards: The Cultural Politics of Gender Ambiguity*, Routledge, NY, pp. 280–304.

Storå, N. (1971) *Burial Customs of the Skolt Lapps*, Suomalainen Tiedeakatemia, Helsinki.

Strelein, L. & Tran, T. (2013) "Building Indigenous Governance from Native Title: Moving Away from 'Fitting in' to 'Creating a Decolonised Space'", *Review of Constitutional Studies*, Vol. 18, No. 1, pp. 9–47.

Stronach, M. & Adair, D. (2014) "Dadirri: Reflections on a Research Methodology Used to Build Trust Between a Non-Indigenous Researcher and Indigenous Participants", *Cosmopolitan Civil Societies: An Interdisciplinary Journal*, Vol. 6, No. 2, pp. 117–134.

Sturgeon, N. (2010) "Penguin Family Values: The Nature of Planetary Environmental Reproductive Justice", in C. Mortimer-Sandilands & B. Erickson (eds), *Queer Ecologies: Sex, Nature, Politics, Desire*, Indiana University Press, Bloomington, IN, pp. 102–133.

Sullivan, C. (2020) *Launching the "Preliminary Report to Community" Sharing the Stories of #lgbtiq+ #blaq youth @theNICE @westernsydenyu @westsyduics @blaq blah.org.au*, Twitter, viewed 15 March 2021, https://twitter.com/rin_sullivan/status/1325592317441445890

Sundberg, J. (2014) "Decolonizing Posthumanist Geographies", *Cultural Geographies*, Vol. 21, No. 1, pp. 33–47.

TAC (2013) "nina tunapri mina kani?" *palawa kani Dictionary*, palawa kani Language Program, Tasmanian Aboriginal Centre, Hobart, Tasmania.

Tadaki, M. & Sinner, J. (2014) "Measure, Model, Optimise: Understanding Reductionist Concepts of Value in Freshwater Governance", *Geoforum*, Vol. 51, pp. 140–151.

Tasmanian Government (2020) *Eligibility for Tasmanian Government Aboriginal and Torres Strait Islander Programs and Services*, Tasmanian Government, Department of Communities Tasmania, Hobart, Tasmania, viewed 18 October 2020, https://www. communites.tas.gov.au/csr/oaa/eligibility policy

Tatum, B.D. (1997) "Defining Racism: 'Can't We Talk?'", in B.D. Tatum (ed), *Why Are All the Black Kids Sitting Together in the Cafeteria? And Other Conversations About Race*, Basic Books, New York, pp. 3–17.

Taylor, R. (2012) "The National Confessional", *Meanjin*, Vol. 71, No. 3, pp. 22–36.

Taylor J. & Kukutai T. (2015) "Indigenous Data Sovereignty and Indicators: Reflections from Australia and Aotearoa New Zealand", paper presented at the *UNPFII Expert Group Meeting on The Way Forward: Indigenous Peoples and Agenda 2030*, United Nations Department of Economic and Social Affairs, New York, 22–23 October 2015, viewed 27 October 2020 https://www.researchgate.net/publication/309486068_Indigenous_data_sovereignty_and_indicators_reflections_from_Australia_and_Aotearoa_New_Zealand/link/5812d68708ae1f5510c2bb56/download

Te Aho, L. (2010) "Indigenous Challenges to Enhance Freshwater Governance and Management in Aotearoa New Zealand – The Waikato River Settlement", *The Journal of Water Law*, Vol. 20, No. 5, pp. 285–292.

Te Aho, L. (2019) "Te Mana o te Wai: An Indigenous Perspective on Rivers and River Management", *River Research and Applications*, Vol. 35, No. 10, pp. 1615–1621.

tebrakunna country & Lee, E. (2017) "Performing Colonisation: The Manufacture of Black Female Bodies in Tourism Research", *Annals of Tourism Research*, Vol. 66, pp. 95–104.

tebrakunna country & Lee, E. (2018) "Black Female Cultural Safety: What is Wellness for Us?", in B. Grimwood, H.M. Mair & K. Caton (eds), *Tourism and Wellness: Travel for the Good of All?*, Lexington Books, Anthropology of Tourism: Heritage, Mobility, and Society Series, Canada, pp. 1–20.

tebrakunna country & Lee, E. (2019) "'Reset the Relationship': Decolonising Government to Increase Indigenous Benefit", *Cultural Geographies*, Vol. 26, No. 4, pp. 415–434.

The Advocate (2017) "Aboriginal Identity Remains a Can of Worms", *The Advocate*, 14 November 2017, viewed 5 October 2019, https://www.theadvocate.com.au/story/5053214/aboriginal-identity-remains-a-can-of-worms/

Thorpe, K. (2019) "Speaking Back to Colonial Collections: Building Living Aboriginal Archives", *Artlink*, Vol. 39, No. 2, pp. 42–49.

Thorpe, K. & Galassi, M. (2014) "Rediscovering Indigenous Languages: The Role and Impact of Libraries and Archives in Cultural Revitalisation", *Australian Academic & Research Libraries*, Vol. 45, No. 2, pp. 81–100.

Thorner, S., Edmonds, F., Clarke, M. & Balla, P. (2018) "Maree's Backyard: Intercultural Collaborations for Indigenous Sovereignty in Melbourne", *Oceania*, Vol. 88, No. 3, pp. 269–291.

Tindale, N. (1939) "Harvard and Adelaide Universities Anthropological Expedition 1938 1939", Vol. 2, No. 2, pp. 759–1142.

Tindale, N. (1941) *Survey of the Half-Caste Problem in South Australia*, Royal Geographical Society, Adelaide.

Tipa, G. (2009) "Exploring Indigenous Understandings of River Dynamics and River Flows: A Case from New Zealand", *Environmental Communication: A Journal of Nature and Culture*, Vol. 3, No. 1, pp. 95–120.

Tipa, G., Harmsworth, G.R., Williams, E. & Kitson, J.C. (2016) "Integrating mātauranga Māori into Freshwater Management, Planning and Decision-making", in P.G. Jellyman, T. Davie, C.P. Pearson & J.S. Harding (eds), *Advances in New Zealand Freshwater Science*, New Zealand Hydrological Society.

TMAG (2009) *tayenebe Tasmanian Aboriginal Women's Fibre Work*, Tasmanian Museum and Art Gallery, Hobart.

Tohe, L. (2000, Autumn) "There Is No Word for Feminism in My Language", *Wicazo Sa Review*, Vol. 15, No. 2, pp. 103–110.

Tonkinson, R. (2011) "Landscape, Transformations, and Immutability in an Aboriginal Australian Culture", in P. Meusburger, M. Heffernan & E. Wunder (eds), *Cultural Memories*, Springer, London, pp. 329–345.

Torpey Hurst, J. (2015) "Lingering Inheritance", in J. McGrath & M. Jebb (eds), *Long History, Deep Time: Deepening the Histories of Place*, ANU Press and Aboriginal History, Canberra, ACT, pp. 133–151.

Toussaint, S. (2004) "Preface to New Edition", in P.M. Kaberry, *Aboriginal Woman Sacred and Profane*, Routledge, London, p. ix.

Trask, H-K. (1999) "'Lovely Hula Hands': Corporate Tourism and the Prostitution of Hawaiian Culture", in H-K. Trask (ed), *From a Native Daughter: Colonialism and Sovereignty in Hawai'i* (revised edition), University of Hawai'i Press, Honolulu, pp. 136–147.

Truth and Reconciliation Commission of Canada (TRC) (2015) *Final Report of the Truth and Reconciliation Commission of Canada: Summary: Honouring the Truth, Reconciling for the Future*, Truth and Reconciliation Commission of Canada, Winnipeg.

Tuck, E. (2013) "Commentary: Decolonizing Methodologies 15 Years Later", *AlterNative: An International Journal of Indigenous Peoples*, Vol. 9, Issue 4, pp. 365–372.

Tuck, E. & McKenzie, M. (2015) *Place in Research: Theory, Methodology, and Methods*, Routledge, London.

Tuck, E. & Yang, K.W. (2012) "Decolonization Is Not A Metaphor", *Decolonization: Indigeneity, Education & Society*, Vol. 1, No. 1, pp. 1–40.

Tur, S.U., Blanch, F.R. & Wilson, C. (2010) "Developing a Collaborative Approach to Standpoint in Indigenous Australian Research", *The Australian Journal of Indigenous Education*, Vol. 39, pp. 58–67.

Turnbull, P. (2017) *Science, Museums and Collecting the Indigenous Dead in Colonial Australia*, Palgrave Macmillan, New York.

Twale, D.J. & DeLuca, B.M. (2008) *Faculty Incivility: The Rise of the Academic Bully Culture and What to Do About It*, Jossey-Bass, San Francisco.

Unger, N.C. (2010) "From Jook Joints to Sisterspace: The Role of Nature in Lesbian Alternative Environments in the United States", in C. Mortimer-Sandilands & B. Erickson (eds), *Queer Ecologies: Sex, Nature, Politics, Desire*, Indiana University Press, Bloomington, IN, pp. 173–198.

United Nations (UNDRIP) (2007) *United Nations Declaration of the Rights of Indigenous Peoples*, viewed 18 October 2020, https://www.un.org/development/desa/indigenouspeoples/declaration-on-the-rights-of-indigenous-peoples.html

Universities Australia & Indigenous Higher Education Advisory Council (2011) "Guiding Principles for Developing Indigenous Cultural Competency in Australian Universities", Universities Australia, Canberra, http://www.universitiesaustralia.edu.au/lightbox/1313

VanderBerg, R. (2012) "Converging Libraries, Archives and Museums: Overcoming Distinctions, But For What Gain?", *Archives and Manuscripts*, Vol. 40, pp. 136–146.

Veracini, L. (2017) "Decolonizing Settler Colonialism: Kill the Settler in Him and Save the Man", *American Indian Culture and Research Journal*, Vol. 41, No. 1, pp. 1–18.

Veracini, L. (2018) "Where Does Colonialism Come From?", *Rethinking History: The Journal of Theory and Practice*, Vol. 22, No. 2, pp. 184–202.

Verschuuren, B. (2019) "Indigenous Perspectives in a Global Discourse on the Conservation of Sacred Heritage", in J. Liljeblad & B. Verschuuren (eds), *Indigenous Perspectives on Sacred Natural Sites Culture, Governance and Conservation*, Routledge, London, pp. 209–222.

wa Thiong'o, N. (1986) *Decolonising the Mind: The Politics of Language in African Literature*, James Currey, London.

Wahlquist, C. (2020) "Rio Tinto Blasts 46,000-year-old Aboriginal Site to Expand Iron Ore Mine", 26 May 2020, *The Guardian*, viewed 18 October 2020, https://www.theguardian.com/australia-news/2020/may/26/rio-tinto-blasts-46000-year-old-aboriginal-site-to-expand-iron-ore-mine

Waikato Regional Council. (2014) *Waipā Catchment Plan*, Waikato Regional Council, Hamilton.

Wall, K. & Baker, M. (2012) "Race and Education: Hidden Links Between Media and Indigenous Academic Self-Concept", *Journal of Student Engagement: Education Matters*, Vol. 2, No. 1, pp. 54–63.

Walter, M. (2005) "Using the 'Power of the Data' Within Indigenous Research Practice", *Australian Aboriginal Studies*, Vol. 2, pp. 27–34.

Walter, M. (2016) "Data Politics and Indigenous Representation in Australian Statistics", in T. Kuktai & J. Taylor (eds) *Indigenous Data Sovereignty: Toward an Agenda*, ANU Press, Canberra, Australia, pp. 79–98.

Walter, M. & Andersen, C. (2013) *Indigenous Statistics: A Quantitative Research Methodology*, Left Coast Press, CA.

Walter, M. & Russo Carroll, S. (2020) "Indigenous Data Sovereignty, Governance and the Link to Indigenous Policy", in M. Walter, T. Kukutai, S. Russo Carroll & D. Lonebear-Rodriguez (eds) *Indigenous Data Sovereignty and Policy*, Routledge, London, pp, 1–20.

Walter, M. & Suina, M. (2019) "Indigenous Data, Indigenous Methodologies and Indigenous Data Sovereignty", *International Journal of Social Research Methodology*, Vol. 22, Issue 3, pp. 223–243.

Walter, M., Lovett, R., Bodkin Andrews, G. & Lee, V. (2018) *Indigenous Data Sovereignty Briefing Paper 1*, Miaim nayri Wingara Data Sovereignty Group and the Australian Indigenous Governance Institute, viewed 29 October 2020, https://static1. squarespace.com/static/5b3043afb40b9d20411f3512/t/5b70e7742b6a28f3a0e14683/ 1534125946810/Indigenous+Data+Sovereignty+Summit+June+2018+Briefing+ Paper.pdf

Wane, N. & Chandler, D.J. (2002) "African Women, Cultural Knowledge, and Environmental Education with a Focus on Kenya's Indigenous Women", *Canadian Journal of Environmental Education*, Vol. 7, No. 1, pp. 86–98.

Warnock, C. & Baker-Galloway, M. (2015) *Focus on Resource Management Law*, LexisNexis NZ, Wellington.

Washuta, E. & Warburton, T. (eds) (2019) *Shapes of Native Nonfiction*, University of Washington Press, Seattle.

Waterman, S. (2018) "Indigeneity in the Methods: Indigenous Feminist Theory in Content Analysis", in R. Minthorn & H. Shotton (eds), *Reclaiming Indigenous Research*, First Edition, Rutgers University Press, New Brunswick, pp. 178–190.

Watson, I. (2005) "Settled and Unsettled Spaces: Are We Free to Roam?", *Australian Critical Race and Whiteness Studies Association Journal*, Vol. 1, pp. 40–52.

Watson, I. (2007a) "De-Colonisation and Aboriginal Peoples: Past and Future Strategies", *Australian Feminist Law Journal*, Vol. 26, No. 1, pp. 111–121.

Watson, I. (2007b) "Settled and Unsettled Spaces: Are We Free to Roam?", in A. Moreton-Robinson (ed), *Sovereign Subject: Indigenous Sovereignty Matters*, Allen & Unwin, Crows Nest, Sydney, pp. 15–32.

Watson, I. (2017) "Standing Our Ground and Telling the One True Story", in P. Dudgeon, J. Herbert, J. Milroy & D. Oxenham (eds), *Us Women, Our Ways, Our World*, Magabala Books Aboriginal Corporation, Broome, Western Australia, pp. 129–142.

Watson, K. (2005) "Queer Theory", *Group Analysis*, Vol. 98, No. 1, pp. 67–81.

Weber-Pillwax, C. (2004) "Indigenous Researchers and Indigenous Research Methods: Cultural Influences of Cultural Determinants of Research Methods", *Pimatisiwin: A Journal of Aboriginal and Indigenous Community Health*, Vol. 2, No. 1, pp. 77–79.

Weir, J. (2012) "Country, Native Title and Ecology", in J. Weir (ed), *Country, Native Title and Ecology*, Australian National University Press, Canberra, ACT, pp. 1–20.

Wells, H.G. (1898) *The War of the Worlds*, William Heinemann, London.

West, E.G. (2000) "An Alternative to Existing Australian Research and Teaching Models: the Japanangka Teaching and Research Paradigm, an Australian Aboriginal Model", PhD thesis, University of Tasmania.

West, J. (1852) *The History of Tasmania*, University of Cambridge Press, London.

West, V. (2017) *The First Tasmanians: Our Story* [Exhibition], Queen Victoria Museum and Art Gallery, Royal Park, Launceston, Tasmania, viewed 13 March 2019.

Westhues, K. (2003) "The Mobbings at Medaille College in 2002", *New York Academe*, Vol. 30, No. 1, pp. 8–10.

Wheen, N.R. & Hayward, J. (2012) "The Meaning of Treaty Settlements and the Evolution of the Treaty Settlement Process", in N.R. Wheen & J. Hayward (eds), *Treaty of Waitangi Settlements*, Bridget Williams Books, Wellington.

Wilcock, D., Brierley, G. & Howitt, R. (2013) "Ethnogeomorphology", *Progress in Physical Geography*, Vol. 37, No. 5, pp. 573–600.

Wilkinson, R. (2005) *The Impact of Inequality: How to Make Sick Societies Healthier*, Routledge, London.

Williams, D.V. (2011) *A Simple Nullity? The Wi Parata Case in New Zealand Law and History*, Auckland University Press, Auckland.

Williams, P. (2017) *New Zealand Landscape: Behind the Scene*, Elsevier, Amsterdam.

Wilson, C. (2001) "Decolonizing Methodologies: Research and Indigenous Peoples", *Social Policy Journal of New Zealand*, Vol. 17, pp. 214–217.

Wilson, E. (2008) *The Creation Story of Trowernna (Tasmania): A Tasmanian Aboriginal Dreamtime Story/Retold by Worawee Emma Wilson and Kaye McPherson*, Manuta Tunapee Puggaluggalia Publishers, Lindisfarne, Tasmania.

Wilson, E.O. (1984) *Biophilia*, the President and Fellows of Harvard College, Twelfth Printing, United States of America.

Wilson, K. (2005) "Ecofeminism and First Nations Peoples in Canada: Linking Culture, Gender and Nature", *Gender, Place & Culture A Journal of Feminist Geography*, Vol. 12, No. 3, pp. 333–355.

Wilson, S. (2008) *Research Is Ceremony Indigenous Research Methods*, Fernwood Publishing, Winnipeg, Nova Scotia.

Windschuttle, K. (2002) *The Fabrication of Aboriginal History. Volume One, Van Diemen's Land 1803–1847*, Macleay Press, Sydney.

Wohl, E., Lane, S.N. & Wilcox, A.C. (2015) "The Science and Practice of River Restoration", *Water Resources Research*, Vol. 51, pp. 5974–5997.

Wolfe, P. (2006) "Settler Colonialism and the Elimination of the Native", *Journal of Genocide Research*, Vol. 8, No. 4, pp. 387–409.

Woodley, E. (2002) *Local and Indigenous Knowledge as an Emergent Property of Complexity: A Case Study in the Solomon Islands*, PhD Thesis, The University of Guelph, Ontario, Canada.

Wriggs, D.W. (2007) "Queer Theory and its Future in Psychology: Exploring Issues of Race Privilege", *Social and Personality Psychology Compass*, Vol. 1, pp. 39–52.

Wright, S., Lloyd, K., Suchet-Pearson, S., Burarrwanga, L., Tofa, M. & Bawaka Country (2012) "Telling Stories in, Through and With Country: Engaging with Indigenous and More-Than-Human Methodologies at Bawaka, NE Australia", *Journal of Cultural Geography*, Vol. 29, No. 1, pp. 39–60.

Writer, J.H. (2008) "Unmasking, Exposing, and Confronting: Critical Race Theory, Tribal Critical Race Theory and Multicultural Education", *International Journal of Multicultural Education*, Vol. 10, No. 2, pp. 1–15.

Yep, G.A. & Elia, J.P. (2007) "Queering/Quaring Blackness in Noah's Arc", in T. Peele (ed), *Queer Popular Culture: Literature, Media, Film and Television*, Palgrave Macmillan, New York, pp. 27–40.

Yep, G.A., Lovaas, K.E. & Elia, J.P. (2003) "Introduction: Queering Communication: Starting the Conversation", *Journal of Homosexuality*, Vol. 45, No. 2–4, pp. 1–10.

Yosso, T., Smith, W., Ceja, M. & Solórzano, D. (2009) "Critical Race Theory, Racial Microaggressions, and Campus Racial Climate for Latina/O Undergraduates", *Harvard Educational Review*, Vol. 79, No. 4, 659–691.

Young, M.I. (2005) *Pimiatisiwin: Walking in a Good Way*, Pemmican Publications, Winnipeg, Manitoba.

Yunkaporta, T. (2009) *Aboriginal Pedagogies at the Cultural Interface*, PhD thesis, James Cook University.

Yunkaporta, T. (2019) *Sand Talk: How Indigenous Thinking Can Save the World*, Text Publishing, Melbourne, Australia.

Index